Indian Philosophical Systems

This scholarly work of Dr S.M.S. Chari's deals with the critical review of seventeen philosophical systems as presented in an important philosophical treatise of the thirteenth century titled *Paramata-bhaṅga* contributed by Vedānta Deśika, an illustrious successor to Rāmānuja, who is the chief exponent of Viśiṣṭādvaita Vedānta. The main objective of *Paramata-bhaṅga* is to establish that Viśiṣṭādvaita is a sound system of philosophy as compared to the several other Non-Vedic as well as Vedic schools and also Vedānta schools developed by Śaṅkara, Yādavaprakāśa, Bhāskara, and other exponents of post-Rāmānuja period. The original text written in Maṇipravāḷa (a mixture of Tamil and Sanskrit) language contains, besides a brief account of the fundamental doctrines of Viśiṣṭādvaita. The schools covered are Cārvāka, Buddhism, Jainism, Sāṅkhya, Yoga, Vaiśeṣika, Nyāya, Pūrvamīmāṁsā, Pāśupata, Śabdabrahma-vivartavāda, and Advaita Vedānta.

Among the extant philosophical classics, *Paramata-bhaṅga* is a unique work. Realizing the importance of the *Paramata-bhaṅga* for the comparative study of Indian philosophy, late Dr Chari tried to give a lucid exposition of this treatise in English. This volume, which is the first of its kind, would be invaluable for students of Indian philosophy in general and Viśiṣṭādvaita in particular.

Dr S.M. Srinivasa Chari was a distinguished scholar trained up by eminent traditional teachers. He did his PhD from the University of Madras. His other published works are: *Advaita and Viśiṣṭādvaita*: A study based on Vedānta Deśika's *Śatadūṣaṇī* with a Foreword by Dr S. Radhakrishnan; *Fundamentals of Viśiṣṭādvaita*: A study based on Vedānta Deśika's *Tattva-muktā-kalāpa; Vaiṣṇavism—Its Philosophy, Theology and Religious Discipline*; *The Philosophy and Theistic Mysticism of the Ālvārs*; *The Philosophy of the Vedāntasūtra*: A study based on the Evaluation of the commentaries of Śaṅkara, Rāmānuja, and Madhva; *The Philosophy of the Upaniṣads*: A study based on the Evaluation of the commentaries of Śaṅkara, Rāmānuja, and Madhva; *The Philosophy of the Bhagavadgītā*: A study based on the Evaluation of the commentaries of Śaṅkara, Rāmānuja, and Madhva; and *The Philosophy of Viśiṣṭādvaita Vedānta*: A study based on Vedānta Deśika's *Adhikaraṇa Sārāvalī*.

Indian Philosophical Systems

A Critical Review based on Vedānta Deśika's *Paramata-bhaṅga*

S.M.S. Chari

Munshiram Manoharlal Publishers Pvt. Ltd.

ISBN 978-81-215-1199-5
First published 2011

PRINTED IN INDIA
Published by Vikram Jain *for*
Munshiram Manoharlal Publishers Pvt. Ltd.
PO Box 5715, 54 Rani Jhansi Road, New Delhi 110 055, INDIA

www.mrmlbooks.com

To the memory of
my Ācārya
Śrī Goṣṭhīpuram Sowmyanārāyaṇācārya Swāmī
with profound respect and gratitude

Contents

Foreword (उपोद्घातम्)

श्रीभगवद्रामानुजमुनिभिः प्रवर्तितस्य विशिष्टाद्वैतदर्शनस्य पोषणार्थं रक्षणार्थं च कृतावतारैः निगमान्तमहादेशिकैः शताधिकानि ग्रन्थरत्नानि प्रणीतानि अध्ययनाध्यापनप्रणाल्या प्रचारमुपगतानि च प्रकाशन्ते इति विश्वविदितमेतत्। हयग्रीवकृपाकटाक्षवशात् प्राप्तं सर्वतन्त्रस्वातन्त्र्यं काव्यनाटकादिनिर्माणनैपुण्यं अप्रतिमप्रतिभा तर्ककौशलम् इत्यादिकं तेषां ग्रन्थेषु स्पष्टं प्रकटं भवति। स्वमतसंरक्षणार्थं मतान्तरपरिशीलनं स्वमतानुसारिणां विश्वासदार्ढ्याच अवश्यकर्तव्यमिति प्राक्तनग्रन्थपरिशीलिनां स्पष्टम्। तस्मात् भगवद्रामानुजसिद्धान्तरक्षणाय मतान्तरखण्डनं तत्त्वमुक्ताकलापन्यायसिद्धाञ्जनादिग्रन्थेषु आचार्यवर्यैः तत्र तत्र सुष्ठु विहितम्। तथापि इदं परतया तत्तन्मानुवादपूर्वकं परिशीलनं कर्तव्यमिति अभिप्रायेण परमतभङ्गाभिधानं ग्रन्थमन्वग्रहीषुः आचार्यवर्याः।

अयं च ग्रन्थः संस्कृतपदमिश्रया द्रविडभाषया मणिप्रवालनामिकया संदृब्धः अतिप्रौढः गम्भीरार्थश्च शास्त्रेषु चिरपरिचयवतां विदुषामपि दुरूहः। तथापि तत्तन्मतस्वरूपं तत्तन्मतपोषकयुक्तिप्रदर्शनपूर्वकं सम्यगनूद्य तद्दूषणं प्रमाणयुक्तिभ्यां ग्रन्थेऽत्र कृतमिति इतरग्रन्थापेक्षयात्र विशेषः। माधवाचार्यादिकृतसर्वदर्शनादि ग्रन्थेष्वदृश्याः तत्तन्मतपोषकतया आचार्यैः प्रोक्ताः अनेका युक्तयोऽत्र दृश्यन्ते तेषां समाधानार्थं प्रदर्शिताः प्रतियुक्तयोऽपि आचार्यप्रदर्शिताः अत्र अवलोक्यन्ते।

अनेन नूतनेन ग्रन्थेन दार्शनिका नितरामुपकृता भवन्ति। अत्र नास्तिकदर्शनानि त्रीणि आस्तिकदर्शनानि षट् भर्तृहरिप्रभृतिभिः प्रवर्तितं वैयाकरणदर्शनं निरीश्वरमीमांसादर्शनं, तत्काले स्थितानि शाङ्करभास्करयादवप्रकाशमतानि च परिशीलितानि। माध्वमतं आचार्यसमीपप्राक्कालेऽवतीर्णमपि विष्णुपारम्यप्रपञ्चसत्यत्वादिस्वीकारत् स्वसन्निकृष्टमतत्वेन स्वीकृत्य तद्दूषणं न कृतमाचार्यैः। पाञ्चरात्रप्रामाण्यं च तदप्रामाण्ययुक्त्या भासखण्डनपूर्वकं स्थापितमिति स्थितिः। आदौ चिदचिदीश्वरतत्त्वानि अधिकारत्रयेण प्रतिपाद्य तदनन्तरं बहुभिः अधिकारैः मतान्तराणि अनुवादपूर्वकं खण्डितानि।

अस्य परमतभङ्गनाम्नः ग्रन्थरत्नस्य एतावत्पर्यन्तम् आङ्ग्लभाषायां न केनापि विमर्शपूर्वकम् अध्ययनम् (critical study) कृतम्। तत्तु न सामान्यं कार्यम्।

शास्त्रेषु विशिष्य दर्शनेषु पाण्डित्यं भाषान्तरनैपुण्यं धारयालेखनसामर्थ्यं चावश्यकम्। इदं महत्तरं कार्यं दार्शनिकप्रवरैः एस्.एम्. श्रीनिवासाचार्यैः निर्व्यूढमिति महान् सन्तोष उपजायते। एते हि संस्कृते दर्शने च एम्.ए. उपाधिधारिणः पी.एच्.डी. उपाधिधारिणः शास्त्रोक्तरीत्या गुरुकुलवासेन प्रख्यातानामाचार्यश्रेष्ठानां गोष्ठीपुरं स्वामीति प्रसिद्धानां सौम्यनारायणाचार्याणां सकाशात् अधिगतश्रीभाष्यादिग्रन्थाः उपनिषत्प्रस्थाने सूत्रप्रस्थाने गीताप्रस्थाने च विशिष्टाद्वैतमेव अभिप्रेतमिति—तथा आल्वार् प्रबन्धेषु, रहस्यग्रन्थेषु च तत् अभिप्रेतमिति निरूपणपरान् ग्रन्थान् विलिख्य प्रकाशितवन्तः। एवं तत्त्वमुक्ताकलापस्य अधिकरणसारावल्याश्च विशिष्टमध्ययनं एतैः प्रकाशितम्।

अधुना परमतभङ्गस्य विशिष्टमध्ययनं प्रकाश्यते। इतः परं लेखनार्थमवशिष्टं किमपि नास्ति। आङ्ग्लभाषायां विशिष्टाद्वैतदर्शनस्थापकतया बहुप्रकाराः ग्रन्थाः अन्यैः न कैरपि कृता इति मन्ये।

प्रायो नवतिवयस्का अपीमे अनवरतं ग्रन्थपरामर्शे व्यापृता इति महतः प्रमोदस्य स्थानमेतत्।

स्वकीयं जीवनं भगवद्रामानुजदर्शनमतयोः पोषणार्थं व्ययितमिति जानन्तः सर्वेऽपि श्रीवैष्णवाः सन्तुष्टा भवेयुः अभिनन्देयुश्चैतान् आचार्यानिति प्रार्थये।

महामहोपाध्यायः
एन्.एस्. रामानुजताताचार्यः
(N.S. RAMANUJA TATACHARYA)

Preface

VEDĀNTA DEŚIKA, an illustrious successor to Rāmānuja, wrote two important philosophical treatises titled *Tattva-muktā-kalāpa* and *Adhikaraṇa-sārāvalī*, devoted primarily to establish that Viśiṣṭādvaita Vedānta is a sound system of philosophy. He also contributed another important philosophical work under the title *Paramata-bhaṅga* in which he presents a critical review of the main tenets of sixteen schools of thought covering the non-Vedic schools such as Cārvāka, Buddhism, Jainism and also Vedic schools such as Nyāya, Vaiśeṣika, Sāṅkhya, Yoga, Pāśupata, Pūrvamīmāṁsā, Vaiyākaraṇa, Bhāskara, Advaita, and Viśiṣṭādvaita. The main purpose of this work is to show how Viśiṣṭādvaita Vedānta expounded by Śrī Rāmānuja on the unquestionable authority of the Upaniṣads and the *Vedāntasūtra* of Bādarāyaṇa is the soundest system of philosophy as compared to all other Indian philosophical schools of thought, including Advaita Vedānta of Śaṅkara as well as other Vedānta schools which were in vogue prior to Rāmānuja and those which were developed later. This is a unique classic since in one compendium Vedānta Deśika gives a brief exposition of the main tenets of all the Indian philosophical systems including Vedānta and highlights their merits as well as defects.

In two of my earlier publications, I have dealt with *Tattva-muktā-kalāpa* and *Adhikaraṇa-sārāvalī* and justified the claim of Vedānta Deśika that Viśiṣṭādvaita Darśana is a sound system both on philosophical and logical grounds. I have now taken up the study of *Paramata-bhaṅga* to demonstrate through a critical review of all other schools of thought including the Vedānta schools, how Viśiṣṭādvaita can be regarded as the soundest philosophical system.

The original text is written in Maṇipravāḷa, which is Tamil language intermixed with Sanskrit words in a terse style, not easily comprehensible. The statements expressing the prima facie views of the exponents of the concerned schools of thought and also the criticisms against them are brief and cryptic, but significant with deeper implications. In order to make it accessible to the modern scholars interested in the comparative and critical study of Indian philosophy, I have attempted to present it in English.

In order to enhance the value of this treatise, I have drawn material from the source books of the different Darśanas and also included the details of the criticisms furnished in other works of Deśika such as *Tattva-muktā-kalāpa, Sarvārtha-siddhi, Nyāya-siddhāñjana, Nyāya-pariśuddhi, Seśvara-mīmāṁsā,* and *Śatadūṣaṇī.*

In dealing with the Vedānta schools, Vedānta Deśika mentions in the *Paramata-bhaṅga* only those of Śaṅkara, Bhāskara, Yādavaprakāśa, and Vaiyākaraṇa. The later schools of Vedānta such as Madhva's Dvaita, Bhedābheda of Nimbārka, Śuddhādvaita of Vallabha, Acintya-bhedābheda of Caitanya school, and other Śaivite schools of Vedānta are left out since most of these were developed in post-Deśika period. However, in order to claim that Viśiṣṭādvaita is a sounder system of Vedānta, it is considered desirable to present also, a comparative and critical analysis of the main doctrines of these later schools. I have therefore extended the scope of my treatise to include the consideration of all schools of Vedānta.

It is for the first time that such an attempt is made to present in English and in one volume, a critique of all schools of thought along with Viśiṣṭādvaita. It is hoped that this book would be invaluable for a comparative study of Indian philosophy in general and a fuller understanding of Viśiṣṭādvaita. I should pay my respects to revered Ācārya, the late, Śrī Goṣṭhīpuram Sowmyanārāyaṇācārya Swāmī who imported to me the knowledge of Vedānta. I also wish to pay my respects to His Holiness Śivan Śatakapa Nārāyaṇa, Yatīndra Mahādeśikan, the present pontiff of Aholia Mutt and also to His Holiness Śrī Abhinava Vāgīśa Brahmatantra Parakala Swamy, the present pontiff of

Parakala Mutt, for inspiring me with blessings to undertake this work. I also express my grateful thanks to the three eminent traditional scholars Mm. N.S. Ramanuja Tatacharya, Mm. K.S. Varadacharya, and Mm. V. Srivatsaṅkacharya who have helped me in understanding the crucial texts in the *Paramata-bhaṅga.* In the last I am again very grateful to Mm. N.S. Ramanuja Tatacharya for evincing keen interest in my work and for graciously writing the Foreword.

S.M. SRINIVASA CHARI

Bangalore
February 7, 2007

Abbreviations

AV	*Advaita and Viśiṣṭādvaita—A Study based on Śatadūṣaṇī*
BG	*Bhagavadgītā*
Bṛ. Up.	*Bṛhadāraṇyaka Upaniṣad*
Ch. Up.	*Chāndogya Upaniṣad*
FVV	*Fundamentals of Viśiṣṭādvaita*
Īśa. Up.	*Īśāvāsyopaniṣad*
Ka. Up.	*Kaṭha Upaniṣad*
Kai. Up.	*Kaivalya Upaniṣad*
Māṇḍ. Up.	*Māṇḍūkya Upaniṣad*
Mbh.	*Mahābhārata*
Muṇḍ. Up.	*Muṇḍakopaniṣad*
NS	*Nyāya-siddhāñjana*
OIP	*Outlines of Indian Philosophy*
PMB	*Paramata-bhaṅga*
RB	*Rāmānujabhāṣya on VS*
RTS	*Rahasya-trayasāra*
ŚB	*Śaṅkarabhāṣya on VS*
SD	*Śatadūṣaṇī*
Śvet. Up.	*Śvetāśvatara Upaniṣad*
Tait. Āra.	*Taittirīya Āraṇyaka*
Tait. Up.	*Taittirīya Upaniṣad*
TMK	*Tattva-muktākalāpa*
VS	*Vedāntasūtra*
YS	*Pātañjala Yogasūtra*

PART I
Fundamental Doctrines of Viśiṣṭādvaita

1

The Doctrine of *Jīva* (*Cit-tattva*)

After briefly explaining the fundamental metaphysical categories of Viśiṣṭādvaita, Vedānta Deśika takes up for detailed examination the doctrine of *jīva* first, following the order in which the three *tattvas* are mentioned in the *Śvetāśvatara Upaniṣad*. Regarding the specific nature of *jīva*, it is defined as that entity which is sentient in character (*cetana*), which is wholly and always supported (*ādheya*), and controlled by a Higher Being (*vidheya*), and which exists for the benefit of the Supreme Being (*śeṣa*). Besides, it should be *aṇu* or monadic in nature. In other words, *jīva* is that sentient being which is dependent for its existence on the Supreme Being, which is wholly and always controlled by Him and which exists for the benefit of *Paramātman* and it is also *aṇu* by nature. Alternatively, *jīva* is defined as that spiritual entity which is self-manifest as "I" (*ahaṁ pratyaya*) and which is qualified by the characteristics of *ādheyatva, vidheyatva, śeṣatva,* and *aṇutva.* Each of these terms defining the nature of *jīva* is full of metaphysical significance. The term *cetana* means that which possesses knowledge as a *dharma* or attribute. It is therefore a sentient being or spiritual entity unlike non-sentient material entity. The other terms, viz., *ādheyatva, vidheyatva,* and *śeṣatva* would substantiate that the *jīva* is the *śarīra* or body of *Īśvara* in a metaphysical sense and organic or inherent relationship between the *jīva* and *Īśvara* similar to the physical body of the *jīva.*

An objection may be raised against this theory. In our ordinary experience, we only know that the *jīva* is the supporter of the physical body but we do not comprehend that the *jīva* is also the body of *Īśvara.* Is it then appropriate to regard *jīva* as a body of *Īśvara*, which fact is not comprehensible to us? Though, prime facie, this objection is relevant, it is to be admitted, contends Vedānta Désika, on the basis of the Scriptural texts which state that *jīva* is the *śarīra* of *Īśvara*. The *Antaryāmī Brāhmaṇa* clearly states that the *jīva* is the *śarīra* of *Paramātman* who by virtue of His immanence is its Inner Controller.[1]

It may also be questioned whether it would be appropriate to regard *vidheyatva* or being subjected to the control of *Īśvara* as the nature of *jīvātman*, because it is found that *jīva* is capable of functioning on its own in all activities, both religious and non-religious, and in view of it, it is free to do what it likes and not obligated to obey the commands of a Higher Being. In reply to this, Vedānta Deśika explains that *Īśvara* has endowed *jīva* with knowledge and capacity and also proper guidance to act in the right direction through the aid of sacred texts. Therefore, it is not inappropriate to attribute the characteristic of *vidheyatva* to *jīva*. For one who is dependent upon the body, mind, sense organs, past *karma*, and other factors for engaging himself in activities, the need to follow the dictates of the *śāstra* or sacred texts in performing the prescribed deeds and avoidance of what is prohibited (*vidheyatva*), is fully justified.

When *jīva* as a sentient being should be able to act on its own, according to its desires, would it be appropriate to regard it as *para-śeṣa-bhūta*, that is, dependent in all matters on the Higher Being? This objection is ruled out on the ground that a person such as a servant, though he serves his master for selfish purposes such as for wages, he is still considered subordinate (*śeṣa*) insofar as he gives pleasure to his master in serving him loyally. In view of this, Rāmānuja defines *śeṣatva* as the desire on the part of the subordinate to cause delight to the one who is the Higher Being. Thus it is stated: *paragatā atiśaya ādhāna icchayā upādeyatvameva yasya svarūpaṁ.*[2] Such a character constitutes the *svarūpa* of *jīva*, that is, *jīva* by its very nature is always subordinate or dependent on the Lord. When the sole motive of the servant is to please his master, the minor selfish purposes for which he may work do not affect his *śeṣatva*. The attribution of *śeṣatva* to *jīva* is also justified on the basis of the principle laid down by the Mīmāṁsā, according to which the person who performs the *yāga* purely for selfish purposes such as attaining *svarga,* etc. is regarded as *śeṣa* of the *karma.*

A more serious objection is raised against the concept of *śarīratva* employed in respect of *jīva* as *śarīra* of *Īśvara.* When *jīvātman* is not a mere conglomeration of the various physical and mental organs but also the *śarīra* or owner of the physical body, how can such a *jīva* be regarded as the *śarīra* of *Īśvara (śarīrin)*? This is justified if we properly understand the true meaning of the term *śarīra.* As Rāmānuja explains, the word *śarīra* is not to be taken in the ordinary sense as a physical body. The definition offered by Naiyāyikas for *śarīra*[3] is found to be logically defective, since such a description is not applicable to the physical elements and other entities which are described in the *Antaryāmī Brāhmaṇa* as *śarīra* of *Paramātman.* A correct definition of *śarīrā,* which is applicable to all entities, both sentient and non-sentient, is offered by Rāmānuja. Thus it is defined: *yasya cetanasya yaddravyam sarvātmanā svārthe niyantuṁ dhārayituṁ ca śakyam tat tatśeṣataikasvarūpam tat tasya śarīram.* That is, in respect of a sentient being—either *Paramātman* or *jīvātman,* whatever entity wholly and always controlled, sustained and that which exists for the purpose of its controller, that entity is to be regarded as *śarīra* or body, in the technical sense.[4] The two entities should be inseparably related, as long as they endure. The physical body is inseparably related to the *jīva.* The body is sustained and controlled by *jīva.* The body exists for the purpose of *jīva.* Thus *jīva* is a *śarīrī* or the owner of the physical body, which is its *śarīra.* On the basis of the same logic, the relationship between *Paramātman* and *jīvātman* and so also other entities in the universe are regarded as *śarīra* of *Paramātman.* In view of this explanation, it is but appropriate to regard *jīva* as the *śarīra* of *Paramātman.*

The admission of *aṇutva* for *jīva* is also questioned by the Naiyāyikas who regard *jīva* as *vibhu* or all-pervasive. There are a few arguments in support of this theory. First, wherever the body moves, it is found that it experiences both pleasure and pain. In order to account for it, the admission of movement of *jīvātman* to all places, would amount to unnecessary additional explanation (*gaurava*). If some fortunes arise in distant places far away from the *jīva*, the *jīva* cannot experience it unless it is present there. Besides yogis, *muktas*, *nitya-jīvas* living in the transcendental world, are capable of assuming at the same time several bodies. The *Gītā* also describes *jīva* as eternal and also as omnipresent (*nityaḥ sarvagataḥ sthāṇuḥ*). Taking all these facts into consideration, it would be more appropriate to admit *vibhutva* for *jīva* as in the case of *Paramātman*. The Scriptural statement speaking of *jīva* as *aṇu* is to be interpreted in a different way, according to the critics.

The argument is untenable, contends Vedānta Deśika. It is warranted from our experience that whenever the body experiences pleasure and pain, it experiences them as associated with *jīvātman*, which also moves along with the body. It is superfluous to postulate for this purpose, the *vibhutva* of *jīva*, which is not warranted by Scripture. Fortunes or misfortunes can arise in distant places, out of the will of God and it is not necessary that *jīva* should be present there. In the case of the yogis, the same one *jīva* residing in the heart of the body can activate out of his yogic power, all other bodies created by him. The Upaniṣads which speak of the exit of the *jīva* from the body (*utkrānti*), and its movement to higher realms do not allow for admission of *vibhutva* since what is *vibhu* cannot have a movement. Hence, the *sarvagatatva* for *jīvātman* is to be interpreted appropriately, in the sense that it is capable of entering into all bodies (*aṇupraveśa*). The Upaniṣads categorically state that *jīva* is *aṇu*.[5]

The Jainas believe that *jīvātman* is of the dimension of the physical body possessed by *jīva*. The argument in support of this theory is that the judgment "I am fat" and the experience of pain in the leg and the pleasure arising in the head prove the fact that *jīva* is pervasive in all parts of the body.

This is untenable, contends Vedānta Deśika. The judgment "I am fat" is a case of delusion. The experience of pain in the leg by the *jīva* can easily be explained on the basis of the fact that the attributive knowledge of *jīva* which pervades all over the body, experiences the pain and not by the *jīva* directly. If this explanation is not admitted, it would amount to the admission of *jīva* breaking up into several parts in respect of the yogis who can assume different bodies. The description of *jīva* as *ananta* or infinite in the state of *mukti* is to be understood in the sense that the attributive knowledge of *jīva* (*dharma-bhūta-jñāna*) becomes infinite in its range since it becomes totally free from *karma* which had eclipsed the *jñāna* in the state of bondage. Otherwise, it would conflict with the Śrutis declaring *jīva* as *nirvikāra*. The pervasion of *jīva* throughout the body is to be taken in the sense that it pervades through its *jñāna* which is its essential attribute and not by its *svarūpa* since it is monadic in nature, as warranted by the Śruti.

The Sāṅkhyas and so also the Advaitins hold the theory that *jīva* is essentially of the nature of *jñāna* (*jñāna-svarūpa*) and hence its pervasion (*vyāpti*) means pervasion of the very *svarūpa*. This is not a sound theory because it contradicts the judgment *ahaṁ jānāmi* or "I know." Here the notion "I" stands for the *jīvātman* and knowledge (of the object) is the attributive knowledge of the self. It is well-established by *pramāṇas* that the notion "I" (*aham-artha*) is *jīvātman*. The Scriptural and Smṛti texts also affirm that *jīvātman* is both of the nature of knowledge and also possesses knowledge as its *dharma* (*jñāna-guṇaka*).[6] The stray Scriptural statements which state that *jīvātman* is only of the nature of knowledge (*prajñā-ghana eva*) is to be understood that *ātman* is wholly constituted of consciousness and that it has no element of *jaḍatva* or invertness. This is comparable to the illustration of *saindhava-ghana* or the lump of salt cited by the *Bṛhadāraṇyaka Upaniṣad* which implies that it is wholly of the nature of salt and does not contain in it any non-salt particle (*jaḍāṁśu-vyudāsādi para*).

According to the Vīśiṣṭadvaita, the entity denoted by "I" (*ahamartha*) is the true self. It is not to be confused with the *ahaṅkāra* or ego which is caused by the delusion of the physical body as the self. Nor is it the product of *mahat-tattva*, the evolute of *prakṛti*. The *antaḥkaraṇa* which is the internal sense organ, which is inert or *jaḍa* like any physical product, cannot be regarded as the true self, which is of the nature of pure consciousness. Viśiṣṭādvaita Vedānta draws a distinction between *pratyak* and *parāk*. What is self-revealed, that is, self-manifest, is *pratyak*, whereas what manifests itself for others is *parāk*. The *jīvātman* reveals itself for itself, whereas *dharma-bhūta-*

jñāna reveals objects to the self, but it itself does not know the objects revealed to the self. *Dharma-bhūta-jñāna* is also self-luminous because at the time it reveals the objects to the self, it does not require another knowledge to prove its functioning. The Advaitins contend that if knowledge is revealed by some other knowledge, it ceases to be knowledge. This is untenable because it cannot be proved by inferential argument adopted by the Advaitins in support of it.[7] The Scriptural texts also do not support this theory.

The *jīva* is eternal (*nitya*) as stated in the Upaniṣads. The birth and death of *jīva,* the presence and absence of *jñāna* for *jīva,* the Scriptural statements that *jīva* is created by *Īśvara* and the statement that *puruṣa* dissolves itself in *Paramātman* should not be construed to mean that *jīvas* are not eternal (*anitya*). Death and birth of *jīva* imply the association and dissociation of a *jīva* with the body. The presence or absence of knowledge is to be understood as the various modifications of *dharma-bhūta-jñāna* to which it is subject and this does not affect the *svarūpa* of *jīva* which is only its *āśraya. Jīvātman* does not undergo any transformation in the same way as a lump of clay. It is therefore appropriate to regard it as *nirvikāra.* The changes which take place in the body, do not affect the *jīva,* which is its *āśraya.* Hence, *jīva* is eternal in nature. In view of it, the theories that *jīva* lasts as long as the body lasts, that it endures upto the state of dissolution (*āpraḷaya-sthāyī*), that it endures upto the state of total liberation, etc., are all untenable. That body itself is the self, as Cārvākas maintain, is also a wrong theory, as will be discussed in the chapter on Cārvāka system.

There are three types of *jīvas:* (1) those who are caught up in the cycle of births and deaths (*anuvṛtta saṁsārī*); (2) those who are liberated from bondage (*nivṛtta saṁsārī*; and (3) those who never had any bondage (*saṁsāra-atyanta-abhāvavān*). These three categories are named as *baddha, mukta,* and *nitya* in Viśiṣṭādvatia. The intrinsic nature of all these *jīvas* is the same (*svarūpam ekaprakāram*). If there are differences among the *baddha jīvas,* it is all due to the influence of the past *karma* of the respective individual souls. The types of the bodies assumed by the *jīvas* make the distinction between human beings, celestial beings, and lower forms of living beings. But as far as their intrinsic nature is concerned, they are the same. In the case of *nityas* and *muktas,* they are differentiated on the basis of the activities they assume out of their own desire in accordance with the will of the *Paramātman.*

The plurality of the *jīvas* (*jīva-nānātva*) is to be admitted. For those who do not admit the difference between the *ātmans,* it would lead to the position that the pleasure and pain experienced by one individual should also be experienced by others. But this is not the case. If it is argued that the differences in respect of the experiences of individuals are due to the differences in the bodies, then the different bodies assumed by some yogis and Saubhari, the Purāṇic person, would have to be different. But it is not so. In the same way, the differences that exist in respect of the sense organs would not offer a solution. The differences that exist among the *antaḥkaraṇas* or internal sense organs of different individuals, would not offer a solution since they cease to exist with the dissolution of *prakṛti* and its products at the end of the epoch (*kalpānte*).

After the *jīvas* are totally liberated from *karma* or bondage and attain *mukti,* there is no return to the mundane existence from that state. As the *jīvas* are totally free from bondage, there cannot be any difference in their experience of the bliss of Brahman (*ānanda-tāratamya*), as conceived by Madhvas. The admission of *ānanda-tāratamya,* according to Vedānta Deśika, is not warranted by the valid *pramāṇas* (*pramāṇa-upapatti-viruddha*). The *mokṣa* proper, is the experience of the bliss of Brahman in its fullest form with all the glory of Brahman as stated by the *Taittirīya Upaniṣad* (*so' snute sarvān kāmān bahmaṇā saha*). The theory of Vaiśeṣikas that in the state of *mukti, jīva* is like a piece of stone without any experience of joy, is also opposed to Scriptural texts.

According to the Sāṅkhyas, the *jīvātman* who is termed as *puruṣa,* is neither the doer (*kartā*) nor the enjoyer (*bhoktā*) and he does not become either bound or liberated, nor passes through births and deaths. In view of it, there cannot be any differentiation of *jīvas* as *baddhas, mukta,* and *nityas.* Hence, all are *muktas.* This theory is unsound since it is opposed to the Sacred texts which teach about the attainment of heavenly bliss (*svarga*) and *mokṣa* and the means to be adopted to attain the same.

Kartṛtva cannot be denied for the *jīva*, as otherwise, the dictates of the Sacred texts to perform certain meritorious deeds and abstaining from evil acts would be rendered meaningless. The *Vedāntasūtra* clearly states: *kartā śāstrārthavattvāt.*[8]

There are some objections against the acceptance of the category of *jīvas* as *muktas*. The basis for this view is that *jīvas* after liberation from bondage, become one with *Īśvara*, as in the case of the rivers entering into the sea become merged in it. This theory is unsound because it directly conflicts with the Scriptural texts which speak of *sāmya* or equality between *jīva* and Brahman after liberation.[9] So also states the *Gītā*: *mama sādharmyaṁ āgatāḥ.*[10] This equality or similarity is not in every way but only in respect of certain characteristics. The lump of poison and the piece of gold weighed together and found equal in weight, is not equal in every respect, such as value. The *Kaṭha Upaniṣad* offers an illustration of the water in the cup when poured into the pure water in the jug, becomes the same as that of the jug (*yathodakaṁ śuddhe śuddhamāsiktam tādṛgeva bhavati*).[11] In this case, the water in the cup becomes mixed with the water in the jug. It does not imply identity (*aikya*) in respect of *svarūpa*, but *saṁśleṣa* (becoming united). In the same way, the illustration of the rivers entering the ocean does not convey the idea that they become lost in the ocean but they exist in it as indistinguishable. The fact that the quantity of water in the jug increases with the addition of water from the cup supports the fact that the cup-water is not lost in the jug-water. Similarly, the water sprinkled (poured) over the molten iron rod is not lost in it, but is present in an imperceptible manner. All these illustrations convey the sense of difference and not identity between *jīvātman* and Brahman.

The statement of the *Sūtrakāra*: "*jagad-vyāpāra varjam*" in respect of *muktātmā* is intended to convey the idea that the liberated *jīvas* do not possess the distinguishing characteristics of Brahman. It may be argued that the *mukta jīva* has acquired the capacity to perform cosmic functions, but it does not perform the same. This would amount to the admission that *muktātmā* is the cause of the universe and that it is immanent as *Antaryāmī* everywhere. Then the *jīva* will have to be regarded as *sarva-śarīrī* or Inner controller of all. But such view would be opposed to the Scriptural texts. Hence it is to be admitted that whatever capacity or power the *muktātman* gains in the state of *mokṣa,* is only to the limited extent of performing services to the Lord in accordance with His will.

In the state of *mukti,* whatever the *muktātmā* wills to do and also accomplishes, is in accordance with the will of the Lord. Though he is a free individual, not being conditioned by *karma* (*akarma-vaśyaḥ*), he does not desire for anything other than what is pleasing to the Lord. Whatever he desires to do, it will be fulfilled by the will of *Paramātman* without any obstruction. In view of this, the *satya-saṅkalpatva* of the *muktātmā* is not affected.

The new status attained by the *muktātmā* in the form of everlasting experience of bliss of *Paramātman* is due to the removal of the obstruction (*pratibandhaka-nivṛtti*) in the form of *karma,* and also the will of God, similar to the manifestation of the luster of the diamond after the removal of the dirt eclipsing it. In the case of *nitya-jīvas,* those who have never had bondage, their experience of the bliss of *Paramātman* is due to the *nityecchā,* that is, permanent will of the Lord.

REFERENCES

1. See *Br. Up.*, V.7.22 (Mādhyandina version). *Ya ātmani tiṣṭhan ātmanaḥ antaraḥ, yaṁ ātmā na veda, yasya ātmā śarīram, yo ātmānam antaro yamayati sa ta (tava) ātmā antaryāmī amṛtaḥ.*
2. See *Vedārtha-saṅgraha.*
3. See *infra*, chap. 22, p. 219.
4. For fuller implication of the definition, see *FVV*, chap. 1, pp.49–50.
5. See *Muṇḍ. Up.*, III.1.9, *eṣo aṇurātmā cetasā veditavyaḥ.*
6. *Br. Up.*, VI.3.30, *na hi vijñātuḥ vijñāteḥ viparilopo vidyate.*
7. For detailed criticism of Advaita theory of *anubhūti*, see *SD*, *vāda* 20. Also see *Advaita and Viśiṣṭādvaita*, pp.49–50.
8. *VS*, II.3.33.
9. See *Muṇḍ. Up.*, III.1.30, *nirañjanaḥ paramam samyam upaiti.*
10. *BG*, XIV.2.
11. *Ka. Up.*, II.1.14.

2

The Doctrine of Cosmic Matter (*Acit-tattva*)

THE *ŚVETĀŚVATARA UPANIṢAD* which mentions the three fundamental metaphysical principles describes the *acit tattva* as *bhogya* as contrasted to the *bhoktā* or *jīvātman* and *preritārā* or the controller because it has neither the capacity to experience (*bhoktṛtva*) nor the capacity to control (*prerakatva*). It is only the object of experience (*bhogya*). *Acit*, also termed as *acetana*, is defined as that which is devoid of *jñātrva*. The term *jñātṛ* means that which is the subject of knowledge. *Jñātṛtva* implies either that which reveals to itself, like *jīvasvarūpa* or that which manifests itself as "I" (*ahaṁtva*). In the absence of these important functions or characteristics, the theory which upholds that mere *jñāna-svarūpa* is *pratyak* or that which manifests to itself and also the theory that non-sentient entities such as *ahaṅkāra* is *jīvātman*, are untenable as these are opposed to all *pramāṇas*. However, in Viśiṣṭādvaita, Vedānta, the *dharma-bhūta-jñāna* or the knowledge which is an attribute of the self is also regarded as *acetana*, even though it is of the nature of knowledge. It is categorized as *jñāna* because it is not the subject of knowledge, unlike *jīvātman*. It only reveals the object to the self but it does not know the object. It is also regarded as a *dravya* because it is subject to modifications or *avasthās* of *jñāna*.

Viśiṣṭādvaita acknowledges three kinds of *acit dravyas*. These are: (1) *prakṛti*, characterized by the three *guṇas—sattva, rajas,* and *tamas*; (2) *kāla* or time; and (3) *Śuddha-sattva* or transcendental spiritual realm which is of the nature of pure *sattva*. These are categorized as *acetanas* because these do not possess knowledge, unlike *cit* or *jīvātman*. The common characteristic between *prakṛti* and *kāla* is the absence of the quality of *śuddha-sattva.* The common characteristic of *prakṛti* and *śuddha-sattva* is the possession of the quality of *sattva.* What is common to both *kāla* and *śuddha-sattva* is the absence of the qualities of *rajas* and *tamas.* Similalry, the common features between *kāla* and *jīvātman* is the observe of the three *guṇas—sattva, rajas,* and *tamas.*

Prakṛti, also named as *triguṇa,* is a *dravya* or substance which is the *āśraya* or locus for the three *guṇas,* viz., *sattva, rajas,* and *tamas.* The *prakṛti* in the form of body affects the knowledge of the *baddha jīva* by causing in it contraction and expansion and thereby prevents it from obtaining the true knowledge of *Paramātman* (*bhagavat-svarūpa-tirodhāna*).

The Advaitins maintain that the true nature of the undifferentiated Brahman, which is only pure consciousness, is eclipsed by *ajñāna.* This is not a sound theory because it amounts to the destruction of the very *svarūpa* of Brahman. The Sāṅkhyas maintain that the three *guṇas* are *dravyas* or substances and not qualities (*guṇas*) and when these are in equilibrium (*sāmyāvasthā*), it is known as *mūla-prakṛti* or primordial cosmic matter. This view would conflict with the teaching of the *Gītā,* which clearly states that *sattva, rajas,* and *tamas* are *guṇas* of *prakṛti.* The theories which maintain that *dharma* and *dharmī* are identical, and the relation between them is one of difference and non-difference, stand opposed to our experience. Though *sattva, rajas,* and *tamas* could also be regarded as *dravyas,* in certain contexts, it would be more appropriate to admit them as *guṇas* with reference to the *prakṛti.*

The Vaiśeṣikas do not accept these three *guṇas* since these are not evident to perception. The Sāṅkhyas, on the contrary, accept it on the basis of inference. Both these views are also opposed to the Scriptural texts (*āgamabādha*). Similarly, there is no Scriptural proof for the theory of some Advaitins that the three forms of Brahman—*sattva, rajas,* and *tamas* represent the reflections of *sat, cit,* and *ānanda* in the *māyā.* The description of *sattva, rajas,* and *tamas* as red, white, and black, etc. in the *Chāndogya Upaniṣad* is to be taken in a figurative sense.

Sattva, rajas, and *tamas* are the *guṇas* of *prakṛti.* These are admitted on the basis of the influences they exert on the individuals. *Sattva* is the quality which causes illumination (*prakāśa*), lightness (*lāghava*), and happiness (*sukha*). It enhances the knowledge and happiness in individuals. In case of some individuals, the *sattva-guṇa* is inherent at the time of birth due to the grace of God in accordance with their extraordinary merit of previous life and makes then develop interest in pursuing the means of attaining *mokṣa.* There are numerous Purāṇic episodes which reveal how certain individuals, due to the grace of God, are enabled to develop spiritual interest due to their past *puṇya-karma.*

The quality of *rajas* causes passion, attachment to things, movement, etc. and induces individuals in activities. It also makes persons indulge in prohibited and undesirable acts and thereby causes bondage.

Tamas is the cause of ignorance, lethargy, and sleepiness. It hinders the progress in our endeavours. All these details are provided in the *Bhagavadgītā* (XVII).

These three *guṇas* are present in an individual in varying proportion, just as *vāta, pitta, kapha* (the chemical elements) in one's body and the qualities such as colour, taste, and odour in a substance. They are subject to fluctuations due to different places (*pradeśa-bheda*) and different times (*kāla-bheda*) which cause either their manifestations or suppressions due to the mutual influence of the *guṇas.* These variations of *guṇas* in an individual influence the mental and physical activities. The division of human beings into four classes as Brāhmaṇas, Kṣatriyas, Vaiśyas, and Sūdras as mentioned in the *Gītā* are due to the presence or absence of these inherent qualities of *sattva, rajas,* and *tamas* in different proportion. The classification of the Purāṇas into *sāttvika, rājasika,* and *tāmasika* mentioned in the *Padmapurāṇa* is also ascribed to the influence of the *guṇas* on the mental traits of their authors.

The statements in the *Śvetāśvatara Upaniṣad* that *kāla, svabhāva, niyati, yadṛcchā, prakṛti,* and *puruṣa* are the cause of cosmic creation, represents the prima facie view (*pūrvapakṣa*). All these are rejected in the latter part of the Upaniṣad and it is affirmed that *Īśvara* with the association of *prakṛti,* is the cause of the Universe.

Prakṛti by nature is eternal but it is also constantly changing (*nitya satata-vikriyā*). But both during the state of dissolution and prior to creation, the *guṇas* remain in a state of equilibrium, similar to the ocean remaining calm without any waves. At the time of creation, disturbance of the *guṇas* takes place in respect of a small part of *prakṛti* as in the case of waves arising in a part of the huge ocean. It is only that portion of *prakṛti* that undergoes modification. On the basis of such an explanation, we speak of the difference between *samaṣṭi* or the creation of the aggregate universe and *vyaṣṭi* or the creation of the variegated universe. In other words there is no total transformation of the *triguṇātmaka prakṛti*, but only a small part of it undergoes modification, while the rest of it remains undisturbed.

In describing the order of dissolution of *prakṛti*, *Subāla Upaniṣad* states: "*avyaktam akṣare līyate, akṣaram tamasi līyate, tamaḥ ekī bhavati pare deve*" (*avyakta* is dissolved in *akṣara*, *akṣara* becomes *tamas*, *tamas* becomes united in *Para devatā*). This would imply that prior to *avyakta* (unmanifest *prakṛti*), there are two states, viz., *akṣara* and *tamas*. What are these two states? The term *akṣara* normally denotes the aggregate of all *jīvas*, viz., *Caturmukha Brahmā* in whom all *jīvas* rest prior to creation (*kṣetrajña samaṣṭi*). But the *samaṣṭi-puruṣa* cannot be placed between *avyakta* and *tamas*. Hence *akṣara* in this context is to be taken as *prakṛti* or non-sentient cosmic matter associated with *jīva-samaṣṭi* (*puruṣa*). *Tamas* which becomes united with *Paradevatā*, therefore, stands for the *sūkṣmāvasthā* of both *prakṛti* and *samaṣṭi-puruṣa*. There is no other principle higher than *tamas*, since it finally becomes united with *Paramātman*.

The theory of Yādavaprakāśa that *prakṛti* and *puruṣa* are the very manifestations of Brahman is not tenable because both *puruṣa* and *prakṛti* are *anādi*, as stated in the *Gītā*[1] and hence they cannot originate from Brahman. It would also militate against the Scriptural texts speaking of Brahman as *nirvikāra*.

Sṛṣṭi or creation of a *tattva* is to be understood in the sense that Brahman as associated with *cit* and *acit* in their subtle forms, assumes a different state, that is, Brahman as associated with *cit* and *acit* in their manifest forms. The same view is expressed by sage Manu in the following statement: *āsīd-idam tamo bhūtam...so abhidhyāya śarīrāt svāt sisṛkṣuḥ vividhāḥ prajāḥ* [All this (the universe) was in the beginning (prior to creation) *tamas* (unmanifest); He (*Paramātman*) by His will created all the living beings].

The concept of *māyā* applied to *tamas* only signifies that it possesses the power of creating variegated objects (*vicitra-sṛṣṭi-upakaraṇa*). It does not mean the illusory principle as conceived by the Advaitin. If it is taken as the illusory principle, then it would conflict with the statement: *deva māyeva nirmitā* (it was created as *deva māyā*).

Mahat is the next important evolute arising from the part of *prakṛti* in which the *guṇas* are in a state of fluctuation. It is called *mahān* or *mahat-tattva* because it is the most important evolute which is greater than all the subsequent evolutes. Some Sāṅkhyas designate *mahān* as *buddhi* (*mahān vai buddhilakṣaṇaḥ*), because in the functioning of *manas*, *mahat-tattva* is of great help for the act of determination or *adhyavasāya*. For those who ascribe to *buddhi* the capacity to know (*jñātṛtva*), it would amount to the denial of the sentient *jīvātman* as a separate entity. Even *mahat-tattva* is also characterized by the three *guṇas: sattva, rajas,* and *tamas* which exist in it in varying proportion. This *mahat-tattva* and all its other evolutes are different for each individual, after the variegated creation takes place.

The evolute which originates from *mahat* is known as *ahaṅkāra*. It is so called because it causes the experience that the body itself is *ātman*. This *ahaṅkāra-tattva* is different from the entity denoted by the notion of "I" which is regarded as *jīvātman* by the Viśiṣṭādvaitin. But the Sāṅkhyas and the Advaitins regard the evolute named *ahaṅkāra* itself as the *ahamartha* or the notion of "I." But this view would be opposed to the *pramāṇas* which clearly reveal the distinction between what is *ātmā* and what is not *ātmā*. Thus, the Upaniṣadic text describing *jīva* and matter as *bhoktā* and *bhogya* draw a clear distinction between *jīvātman* and the non-sentient cosmic matter. The statement which speaks of the rejection of *ahaṅkāra* as an undesirable trait, do not refer to the negation of the *ātma-tattva*, but on the contrary, it advocates to give up the delusion of body as self or the self-conceited feeling of oneself as great.

The *ahaṅkāra-tattva,* like *mahat,* is of three kinds due to the fluctuation of the three *guṇas.* These are *sāttvika ahaṅkāra, rājasa ahaṅkāra,* and *tāmasa ahaṅkāra. Sāttvika ahaṅkāra* is the cause of the *indriyas* or the sense organs. *Tāmasa ahaṅkāra* is the cause of the five *tanmātras* or subtle elements. *Rājasa ahaṅkāra* acts as a generating force for both. It also acts as the instrumental cause for the evolution of the *indriyas* and *tanmātras.*

From the *sāttvika ahaṅkāra* originate all the eleven *indriyas* including *manas* or mind. The view of *Hiraṇyagarbha* (founder of yoga) that the *indriyas* are the different forms of *ahaṅkāra* does not conform to the Scriptural texts teaching the origin of *indriyas* from *ahaṅkāra.* The Śaiva sect which maintains that the five *karmendriyas* room the products of *rājasa ahaṅkāra* is also opposed to the Scriptural and Smṛti texts. It is also not correct to say that *karmendriyas* come into existence along with the concerned physical bodies at the time of creation, because it stands opposed to the Scriptural text which says that all eleven *indriyas* originate from *ahaṅkāra* at the time of creation. The mention of six *indriyas* only, including *manas,* as originating from *prakṛti,* by the *Gītā* is only illustrative of all eleven *indriyas* (*upalakṣaṇaparam*).

Manas is the *indriya* which serves as an accessory for the functioning of the five sense organs and it is directly instrumental for causing desire and memory. It is also helpful in causing knowledge and a desire to act while *karmendriyas* are functioning. The theory of Sāṅkhyas which categorizes separately the five *jñānendriyas* and five *karmendriyas* and mentions that *manas* is useful for both, is not sound.

If *manas* is regarded as a *karmendriya* because it is either directly or indirectly useful for the activities of the *karmendriyas,* then even ear (*śrotra*) and other sense organs are to be admitted as *karmendriyas. Manas* itself is sometimes named as *buddhi, ahaṅkāra* and *citta* on the basis of its threefold functions, viz., determination, attachment to an entity, and thinking. This does not amount to the denial of the existence of *mahat-tattva* and *ahaṅkāra,* the two evolutes. The implication of this view is that when an individual performs these three functions, the same *manas* is named differently as *buddhi, ahaṅkāra,* and *citta*. In view of this, the theory of the Sāṅkhyas that sense organs are thirteen in number and that *antaḥkaraṇa* or internal organ is of three kinds, stands refuted. *Adhyavasāya* (determination), *kāma* (desire), *saṅkalpa* (will), etc. are actually the various modifications or states (*avasthās*) of *dharma-bhūta-jñāna* of the *jīva* during the state of bondage. But these are regarded as functions of mind insofar as these modifications arise due to the influence of the various sense organs. In the *Gītā* verse, *manas* is also included in the category of *indriyas* (*indriyāṇi daśaikaṁ ca*). This is justified since *manas*, like the other *indriyas* are the products of *sāttvika ahaṅkāra*.

All the *indriyas*, as pointed out in the *Vedāntasūtra*,[2] are monadic in character (*aṇuvaśca*). As *indriyas* are the modified products of the *ahaṅkāra* (*vikāridravya*), they can assume different dimensions such as big or small in accordance with the dimensions of the respective bodies of the living beings. Some Buddhists admit three types of *indriyas* classified as masculine, feminine, and *jīvendriya* due to different types of functions of the bodies. But this theory is rejected by Vedānta Deśika as imaginary and irrelevant.

The theory that *manas* is *nitya* and also *vibhu* as held by some Vaiśeṣikas, stands opposed to the teaching of the Scriptural texts which categorically state that all the eleven *indriyas* including *manas* are the products of *sāttvika ahaṅkāra*. Similarly, there are other theories about *manas* held by Bhāṭṭa Mīmāṁsakas and some Buddhists, but all these are untenable.

How the *indriyas* which are located in the body are able to grasp or come into contact with objects outside them? This is a question which has engaged all schools of thought and different explanations are offered by them.[3] Without going into the critical examination of these theories Vedānta Deśika states in a general way that the functioning of the *indriyas* with reference to their contact with different kinds of external objects are to be explained in accordance with the nature of the objects and our experience. In the case of the comprehension by the visual organ of subtle objects hidden in crystals, clear water, mirror, etc., the subtle rays radiating from the eyes come into contact with them. If they cannot grasp them, it is due to the hindrance which prevents the entry of the rays of light into it. In the case of the organ comprehending the odour in the flower which exists far from the organ, the odour itself which travels from the flower through the media of air (*vāyu*), reaches the organ.

The followers of the Bhedābheda-vāda maintain the view that from *ahaṅkāra tattva* combined with the five physical elements, originate the five sense organs as well as the respective *karmendriyas* and only *manas* emanates from *ahaṅkāra*. The Vaiśeṣikas, on the other hand, do not accept the five *karmendriyas*. If the *karmendriyas* are rejected, then on the same ground, we could as well reject the *jñānendriyas*.

The mention of lesser number of *indriyas* in some of the Scriptural texts is not intended to deny the existence of other *indriyas*. These have a different purport. The statement that *ākāśa* is to be included in the *indriyas* and that *indriyas* are to be included among the *tanmātras*, are to be taken in the sense of *saṁsarga*, that is, as being united in them. Otherwise, all these statements would be opposed to the Scriptural teaching which points out that *indriyas* are the products of *sāttvika ahaṅkāra* and that they are all modified effects of the causal substance, viz., *ahaṅkāra tattva*.

All the eleven *indriyas* are different, similar to the five elements, and exist in the individuals separately and as such they are countless. As stated by Manu,[4] these *indriyas* in their subtle form, are implanted by *Īśvara* in the subtle bodies of all the living beings.

The Sāṅkhyas who also admit the existence of *liṅga-śarīra*, the subtle body, believe that it endures upto the end of an epoch (*ākalpa-sthāyī*) and it comprises the five subtle elements (*tanmātra*) and eleven subtle *indriyas* and *buddhi* (*mahat-tattva*). When *jīva* transmigrates through the cycle of births and deaths, these too go along with it. According to Ānandānubhava, an Advaitin who has written a commentary on *Nyāya-ratna Dīpāvalī* and *Iṣṭasiddhi*, the *liṅga-śarīra* comprises nineteen parts—eleven *indriyas*, five *tanmātras*, and the rest three are *mahat*, *ahaṅkāra*, and *prakṛti*.

The term *bhūtas* or physical elements are the substances (*dravyas*) which serve as the basis (*āśraya*) for the *guṇas* such as sound, colour, etc., which are objects of the sense organs. These are classified as gross (*sthūla*) and subtle (*sūkṣma*).

The subtle ones are named as *tanmātras* and the gross ones are called *bhūtas*. This difference between *tanmātra* and *bhūta* is drawn on the basis of the variation of the *guṇas* possessed by them as in the example of sugarcane juice and sugar candy. The variation of *guṇas* in the *tanmātras* is not perceptible to us. Even in respect of the gross physical elements, which are perceptible, we cannot know the variation of *sattva, rajas,* and *tamas,* which exist in them in different proportion.

There are various theories regarding the order in which the *tanmātras* evolve, and also how the *pañca-bhūtas* evolve from the *tanmātras.* Vedānta Désika critically examines them and sets out the correct theory on the basis of the Scriptural and Smṛti texts. The important deviation from that of the Sāṅkhyas is, all the five *tanmātras* according to the Sāṅkhyas evolve together out of the *tāmasa ahaṅkāra,* whereas for Viśiṣṭādvaita, only *śabda-tanmātra* comes out of *tāmasa ahaṅkāra.* From *śabda-tanmātra* arises *ākāśa* or the gross space. From *ākāśa* comes *sparśa-tanmātra* which in turn causes *vāyu.* From *vāyu* comes *rūpa-tanmātra.* From this comes *tejas* which produces (*rasa*) *tanmātra. Rasa-tanmātra* causes *jala.* From *jala* comes *gandha-tanmātra.* From this evolves *pṛthivī.* (See p. 21, for the order of evolution of the *tanmātras* and *bhūtas* as stated in *Tattva-muktākalāpa.*)

Each element is characterized by a specific quality. *Ākāśa* possesses the quality of sound only. Air possesses the qualities of sound and touch. *Tejas* or fire possesses three *guṇas,* viz., sound, touch, and colour. Water is characterized by sound, touch, colour, and taste. *Pṛthivī* possesses all the five *guṇas*—sound, touch, colour, taste, and odour. Since the *bhūtas* evolve one after another in a successive order starting from *ākāśa,* qualities inherent in the respective elements are transmitted to the next one. Even the Vaiśeṣikas accept the successive increase of the *guṇas* in the *bhūtas.* According to the theory of *Pañcīkaraṇa* or the admixture of all five elements in a certain proportion, it is possible to admit the presence of different *guṇas* in the five *bhūtas.* Though all *guṇas* are present in the *bhūtas* in different proportion, each *bhūta* is named separately as *pṛthivī, ap, tejas,* etc., because of the predominance of a particular element and lesser and lesser quantity of the other elements. For instance *pṛthivī* is so called because of the predominance of the half of *pṛthivī* element and one-eighth quantity of *jala, agni, vāyu,* and *ākāśa* respectively.

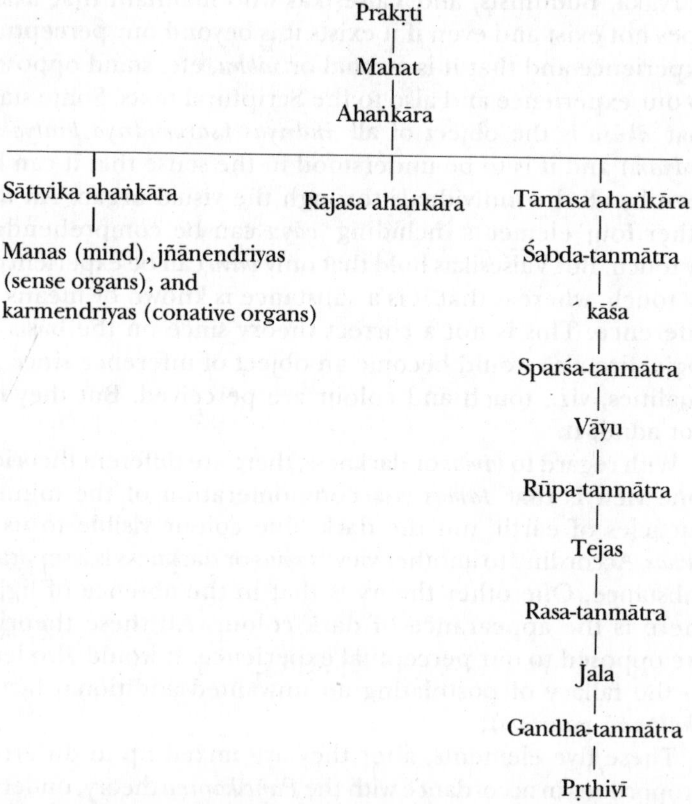

The *tṛvitkaraṇa* or admixture of the three elements referred to in the *Chāndogya Upaniṣad* is illustrative of the *Pañcīkaraṇa* theory taught in other parts of the Sacred texts. The presence of the *guṇas* of one element in the other elements such as blueness in *ākāśa,* odour and coldness in *vāyu,* whiteness and blackness in fire, colour and different tastes in water, hotness, etc., in *pṛthivī* are caused on account of the admixture of different elements by the process of *Pañcīkaraṇa.* This is to be admitted on the authority of the Scriptural texts.

Regarding *ākāśa* or Ether which is the first evolute emanating from *śabda-tanmātra,* it is described as that which provides space for other objects (*avakāśa-pradānam*). It is also defined as that which does not cause obstruction for tactile objects. It is therefore to be taken as a separate *tattva.* The theories of Cārvāka, Buddhists, and Vaiśeṣikas who maintain that *ākāśa* does not exist and even if it exists it is beyond our perceptual experience and that it is eternal or *vibhu,* etc. stand opposed to our experience and also to the Scriptural texts. Some state that *ākāśa* is the object of all *indriyas* (*sarvendriya pratyakṣa vedyam*) and it is to be understood in the sense that it can be seen by all the individuals through the visual organ. All the other four elements including *vāyu* can be comprehended by touch. But Vaiśeṣikas hold that only *vāyu* can be experienced by touch, whereas that it is a substance is known by means of inference. This is not a correct theory since on the basis of logic, fire also would become an object of inference since its qualities, viz., touch and colour are perceived. But they do not admit it.

With regard to *tamas* or darkness, there are different theories. One view is that *tamas* is a conglomeration of the minute particles of earth and the dark blue colour visible to us is *tamas.* According to another view, *tamas* or darkness is a separate substance. One other theory is that in the absence of light, there is the appearance of dark colour. All these theories are opposed to our perceptual experience. It would also lead to the fallacy of postulating an unwanted additional factor (*kalpanā gaurava*).

These five elements, after they are mixed up in different proportions in accordance with the *Pañcīkaraṇa* theory, undergo various modifications and serve human beings as either objects of enjoyment or means of enjoyment or as places of experience (*bhogasthāna*). The Jaina theory which admits a primordial cosmic substance named as *pudgala,* which evolves itself into five elements, sounds good but it suffers from the defect of not accounting an orderly process of evolution at specified points of time as in the case of *prakṛti* and its evolution. Moreover, it is opposed to the Scriptural texts.

The bodies which are intended for experience of pleasure and pain are of four types in accordance with the four kinds of living beings: *Devas* or celestial beings, human beings, animals, and inanimate objects (*sthāvaras*). In some Purāṇas, the last category is divided into two groups as *narakāntaka* and *sthāvarāntaka*. But both these states are included in the *sthāvara* category. The argument that there are no souls in *sthāvaras* to experience anything is also untenable because in that case one can argue that even in the lower form of living beings, there are no souls other than the bodies. Thus, all entities upto the five physical elements are regarded as *triguṇa-dravya*, since they are modifications of the same *prakṛti*. This is explained on the analogy of the palm-leaf and the ornament made out of it by rolling the same as the earring (*patra-tāṭaṅka nyāya*).

It is stated that the cosmic universe and several other realms called *aṇḍaja* are created by *Īśvara* through the evolution of *prakṛti* similar to the ocean giving rise to several waves, as part of the Divine Sport. In this connection, a question is raised: whether these come into existence simultaneously, at one time (*yugapat*) or in succession at different times (*krama sṛṣṭi*). If it be the latter, it cannot be said that the cosmic universe is the same as *prakṛti* in its manifested form. Hence it is to be admitted that the cosmic universe and all other *aṇḍaja* are created at the same time through the evolution of *prakṛti*. This view conforms to the teachings of the Scriptural and Smṛti texts.

The Nirīśvara Mīmāṁsakas maintain the view that the creation and also the dissolution of the universe and other *aṇḍaja* (realms) should not take place at the same time as there would be a break for the continuity or the Vedic tradition from a beginningless time and hence there is no need to postulate the evolution and dissolution of *prakṛti* which is not accessible to perceptual experience. This is not a correct theory as it falls outside the Vedic teachings. Allied to the Mīmāṁsakas, the Seśvara Sāṅkhyas enumerate twenty-five *tattvas* by adding *jīva* (*puruṣa*) to the twenty-four principles. But this view stands negated by several other statements which reckon twenty-six *tattvas* by adding *Īśvara* to the twenty-five principles. But in the *Mahābhārata* (in Śāntiparva), *Īśvara* is regarded as the twenty-fifth *tattva*. The implication of it is that though *jīva* and *Paramātman* are two separate entities, they are one in the sense that *Paramātman* is immanent in *jīva* and as being inseparably related to *jīva*, it is counted as the twenty-fifth principle. The relevant verse in the *Mahābhārata* reads: *anyaśca rājan, sa paraḥ tacca anyaḥ pañcaviṁśakaḥ; tatsthattvāt anupaśyanti hy-eka eveti sādhavaḥ.* It means: "The twenty-fifth *tattva* (*jīvātmā*) is different; *Paramātman* is also different. Nevertheless, since He (*Paramātman*) is immanent in the *jīva*, the two as inseparably related, constitute one *tattva.*" The *Vedāntasūtra* reading as "*avasthiteḥ iti kāśakṛtsnaḥ*" also signifies the same truth. Even the Scriptural text (*Mantrikopaniṣad*) says that *Īśvara* can be regarded either as the twenty-fifth or twenty-sixth *tattva* (*tam ṣaḍviṁśakam ityāhuḥ*). By adding to *prakṛti* the *tamas,* which is a different state of *prakṛti,* the total number of *tattvas* can be counted as twenty-seven. Some reckon twenty-seven *tattvas* by adding the *Antaryāmin* as a separate entity but this is not appropriate since *Antaryāmin* is not distinct from *Paramātman.* Some argue that there are only six *tattvas* on the basis of the *Taittirīya* passage dealing with the causation of the universe (*ātmā, ākāśa, vāyu, agni, āpaḥ,* and *pṛthivī*). But this is opposed to several other Scriptural texts. If in some texts mention is made of a smaller number of *tattvas,* while in others a larger number is enumerated, we have to take both into consideration to determine the total number of *tattvas.* There is not much difference when we make two statements, viz., (a) from milk comes cream and from cream comes curd, and (b) from milk we get curd. Similarly, when the Upaniṣads describe the total number of *tattvas* in two different ways, there should be no difference in the purport. If such an explanation is not accepted, then in the passage of *Chāndogya Upaniṣad* dealing with *sad-vidyā* in which mention is made only of *sat* or Brahman, *tejas, pa,* and *pṛthivi,* we have to say that there are only four *tattvas.* This is not a correct theory since, in other passages dealing with the creation of the universe, other *tattvas* are enumerated. The *Śaivāgamas* speak of thirty-six *tattvas* by adding several other *tattvas,* but it is not accepted by other orthodox schools. Hence this view is to be overlooked, according to Vedānta Deśika.

Vaiśeṣikas admit *dik* or directions as east, west, etc. as a separate metaphysical category. According to them it is *nitya* or eternal and *vibhu* or all-pervasive. But this cannot be regarded as a separate *tattva* since there is no mention of it in the enumeration of the *tattvas*. If there are some statements saying that *dik* is created (*diśaḥ srotrāt*), it is to be taken in the same sense as the creation of heaven, *antarikṣa,* etc. Hence it cannot be treated as a part of the *tattvas* evolved out of *prakṛti*. Some maintain the view that *dik* is recognized on the basis of the division of *ākāśa* with reference to the movement of the sun from one direction to another. Others (Sāṅkhyas) believe that the *ahaṅkāra-tattva* itself evolves into the form of *dik*. Even if these theories are accepted, still there is need for some other limiting adjuncts (*upādhi*) by means of which directions have to be recognized.

THE THEORY OF KĀLA

So far, the discussion of *prakṛti*, which is one of the three types of *acit-tattva* in Viśiṣṭādvaita, is discussed comprehensively by critically analyzing all other views related to it. Now we come to the discussion of *kāla* or time which is the second important *acit-tattva*. It is the substance (*dravya*) which is characterized by the notion of moments (*kṣaṇa*), hours, days, months, years, etc. and the notion of past, present, and future and also older and younger, etc. It is *nitya* or eternal and infinite but it undergoes modifications as moments, days, months, years, etc. Some believe that *kāla*, though it is eternal, is regarded as divisible into moments, minutes, etc. on the basis of the limiting adjuncts (*upādhi*). Others maintain that *kāla* and its divisions are created by *Īśvara* and hence it is like *prakṛti,* subject to modifications and the moments, minutes, hours, days, etc. are modified forms of *kāla*.

The view of the Cārvākas that *kāla* does not exist as separate entity is untenable because *kāla* is perceptible and its existence is proved by other *pramāṇas*. On the basis of the statement that there is nothing in the universe as eternal (*nityam hi nāsti jagati*), it may be argued that *kāla* also has a beginning and an end. But this would be opposed to the Smṛti text which states that *kāla* is *anādi* and *ananta* (infinite). Besides, it cannot be said that there is a time when *kāla* did not exist as it would be regarded as self-contradiction.

Some hold the view the *kāla* in the transcendental spiritual realm (*nitya vibhūti*) is eternal, whereas it is non-eternal in the physical world. This is not a correct theory. There cannot be two kinds of *kāla* as there is no *pramāṇa* in support of it. We cannot say that the same *kāla* can be both *nitya* and *anitya* as conceived by Jainas since it would amount to self-contradiction. Nor can it be explained by taking resort to the nature of two separate kinds of realms (*vibhūti-bheda*). The only way it can be resolved is to admit that in the cosmic universe we have the changes in terms of day and night whereas in the transcendental world the Supreme Being exists eternally shining like an early morning Sun (*anapāya prabhānvita nitya-udita āditya*). In other words, *nitya vibhūti* is all the time like daylight, without any shadow of night whereas it is not so in respect of the cosmic universe.

Even in the abode of *Īśvara*, the individual souls perform a variety of services at different times and occasions and this presupposes the operation of *kāla*, as otherwise it is not possible to explain the sequence of services as earlier and later. There are also statements which say that, in the higher realm, time does not operate (*na kālaḥ tatra vai prabhuḥ*). The *kāla* which is characterized with moments, minutes, hours, etc., causes modifications in that realm. The eternal Abode is divine, ageless, free from destruction, and unsurpassable. How do we explain all these statements if *kāla* is not accepted? Vedānta Deśika points out that the implication of all such statements is that the individuals, their activities, and the operation of the events, etc., though not conditioned by time, are controlled by the will of God (*Para saṅkalpa viśeṣa*). Hence it cannot be said that *kāla* does not exist in the transcendental realm.

Kāla is admitted as *vibhu* or all-pervasive. If this be so, how does it co-exist with *Īśvara* who is also *vibhu*? Only two spatial objects can co-exist but two *vibhu dravyas* cannot come together (*anyonya saṁyoga*). This objection is replied to by explaining on the basis of the theory adopted by the Naiyāyikas for whom *Īśvara*, though He does not possess *indriyas*, can have direct knowledge of all things. If this is acceptable, in the same way it is possible to admit that two *vibhu-dravyas* can somehow come together. *Īśvara* is considered as *vyāpaka* or one who pervades everything, whereas all other entities are *vyāpya* or that which is pervaded by Him. This is plausible on the basis of the relation of *niyantā* and *niyāmya* that exists between the two. The statement in the *Taittirīya Nārāyaṇa Upaniṣad* states that *Nārāyaṇa* (Brahman) exists by pervading both within and without (*antarbahiśca vyāpya nārāyaṇaḥ*). This statement is applicable only in respect of entities which have both inner and outer space. This is not applicable to entities such as *kāla* which is *vibhu* and devoid of outer space.

THE THEORY OF *ŚUDDHA-SATTVA*

Śuddha-sattva is the third important *acetana-tattva* admitted by Viśiṣṭādvaita Vedānta. It is defined as a *dravya* or substance which is characterized by pure unalloyed *sattva* (as different from *sattva* which is one of the three *guṇas* of *prakṛti*) and also free from *rajas* and *tamas* (two other qualities of *prakṛti*). This *sattva*, unlike the ordinary *sattva*, does not bind a person with knowledge, pleasure, etc. It constitutes the very Divine body of the Supreme Being, His *guṇas*, His abode, etc. The *Paramapada* or the divine Abode which is attained by the individuals after they are totally liberated from bondage caused by *karma* through the observance of *upāsanā*, is constituted of *śuddha-sattva* material. In the Vaiṣṇava theology, *śuddha-sattva* is often equated with *Paramapada*, though it is classified as a *dravya* characterized by unalloyed *sattva*. This Abode of *Paramātman* is described as immeasurable (*aparicchedya*). It exists beyond the *tamas* or the cosmic universe as stated in the Scriptural texts (*tamasaḥ parastāt*). Though it is a transcendental spiritual realm and eternal, how can we regard the products that exist there in the form of castles, towers, lakes, trees, etc. as eternal since such objects are normally subject to changes like decay? It is possible to explain that these are *nitya* only in a restricted sense, viz., that they endure for a long time (*sthirakāla-sthāyī*), in the same way as we explain the description of the *devas* as immortal (*amṛta*), *vāyu* and *antarikṣa* as *amṛta*. But this is not the correct explanation because these entities in the *Paramapada* are devoid of origin and destruction as in the case of the spiritual realm. Besides, the Smṛti texts describe that the Spiritual realm is *sanātana* or everlasting and *nitya-siddha* or ever-existing. Hence it is not appropriate to offer a different explanation on the basis of inferential argument as against strong Scriptural evidence. Therefore, whatever is stated by Scriptural texts as *nitya*, is to be accepted as such.

References

1. See *BG*, XIII.19: *Prakṛtim puruṣam caiva viddhi anādi ubhau api.*
2. *VS*, II.4.6.
3. See *FVV*, chap.10, pp. 327–28.
4. *teṣāṁ tu avayavān sūkṣmān ṣaṇṇamapi amitae dasām, sanniveśya ātmāmātrāstu sarvabhūtāni nirmame.*

3

The Doctrine of Brahman (*Para-tattva*)

THIS IS THE third fundamental doctrine of Viśiṣṭādvaita Vedānta. In presenting this doctrine, Vedānta Deśika confines his attention to answering all possible objections and counter theories of other schools of thought including Advaita regarding the essential nature of Brahman. Brahman is the ultimate Reality. It is immanent as the Inner controller of all beings, both *cetana* and *acetana*, as stated in the *Antaryāmī Brāhmaṇa*. At the same time, it is also a transcendental being, not being affected by the defects inherent in the *cetanas* and *acetanas*. Though *Īśvara* is beyond the comprehension of perceptual experience, being a supersensuous entity (*atīndriya*), He is to be known only by means of *śāstras* or Sacred texts. The existence of such a Supreme Being and also his *svarūpa* (essential nature), *guṇas* (attributes), and *vibhūti* (glory) cannot be defined. As stated in the second aphorism of the *Vedānta-sūtra* (*Janmādyasya yataḥ*) on the basis of the *Taittirīya Upaniṣad*, Brahman is the sole cause of the universe (*nikhila jagadeka kāraṇa*), that is, it is the cause of creation, sustenance, and dissolution of the universe. *Īśvara* is the Universal Self (*sarva-śarīrī*). He is the supporter (*ādhāra*) of all entities in the universe but He Himself does not need another supporter higher than Him. As stated in the Upaniṣad, He is self-existent and does not depend on anything else other than Himself (*sve-mahimni pratiṣtha*). *Īśvara* is also the worthy object of mediation for the aspirants to *mokṣa* (*manukṣopāsya*). He himself is the bestower of *mokṣa* (*mokṣa-prada*) and He Himself is the Supreme Goal to be attained (*muktaprāpya*). All these points constitute the distinguishing characteristics of *Īśvara* (*Īśvara-lakṣaṇa*) and these have to be necessarily admitted in order to uphold a perfect theory of the ultimate Reality.

According to Viśiṣṭādvaita, *Īśvara* is both *upādāna-kāraṇa* (material cause) and *nimitta kāraṇa* (instrumental cause) of the universe. As stated in the Upaniṣad, He wills to become the manifold universe (*bahusyāṁ prajāyeya*). As he creates the universe out of his will (*saṅkalpa*), He becomes the instrumental cause, that is, *Īśvara* as associated with the *saṅkalpa* (*saṅkalpa viśiṣṭa*) is the *nimitta kāraṇa*. He is the *upādāna kāraṇa* or material cause as associated with *cit* and *acit* in its unmanifest form (*sūkṣma cid-acid-viśiṣṭa*).

An objection is raised against the theory that *Īśvara* is the Creator of the universe. According to the Upaniṣadic statement, He is only a witness (*sākṣī*), unattached being, that is indifferent and devoid of all functions (*sākṣī cetā kevalo nirguṇaśca*).[1] If according to this statement, *Īśvara* is devoid of *kartṛtva* or the capacity to do any activities, how can He be regarded as the creator of the universe? Vedānta Deśika answers this objection by clarifying the implication of the concepts of *kartṛtva, udāsīnatva,* and *prerakatva* in respect of *Īśvara.*

Īśvara is the *kartā* since He alone creates the universe out of his *saṅkalpa* without depending on anybody else. He is the *preraka* since He prompts the individuals to perform acts by grating them the requisite knowledge and desire to perform an act. In respect of non-sentient entities also, He plays the role of *preraka* insofar as He causes the series of modifications in them and to this extent He is regarded as *kartā* or the one who causes the changes. The term *niyantṛtva* implies these two roles in respect of sentient and non-sentient activities. Besides, He is also regarded as *praśāsitāra* or Ruler in respect of sentient beings through His dictates laid down in the *śāstra.*

The *jīva* is also *kartā* but this *kartṛtva* is dependent upon *Īśvara* (*parāyatta*). Since he is not a *sarvajña* or omniscient, he needs knowledge to understand what is right or wrong. Since he is also not an omnipotent being, he is to be dependent upon the help and guidance of the Supreme Being. The contention that *jīva,* being solely dependent upon *Īśvara,* cannot be subject to the dictates of *śāstra,* is untenable. If the *jīva* needs a body, sense organ, past *karma,* suitable time, and other factors for doing these activities, there should be no objection to his being dependent on the guidance of *Īśvara* through the *śāstras*. Though God has the power to stop a person from doing an evil deed, He does not do so and approves his action (*anumantā*) in order to allow him to reap the benefits of the past *karma*. Whenever and act cannot be accomplished by his own effort, God plays an accessory role (*sahakāri*) by providing support to him.

In the matter of creating different types of individuals and also providing them the requisite guidance in doing what is good or bad, God does not play the role of being the primary cause (*pradhāna kāraṇa*) but it is got done in accordance with the past *karma* of the individuals and to this extent he is indifferent (*udāsīna*). Since God acts in accordance with the *karma* of *jīvas* in giving them the benefits, He escapes the criticism of being partial and cruel (*vaiṣamya nairghaṇya doṣa*).

An objection may be raised against the admission of *Īśvara* for the purpose of creation of the universe. What is the purpose of creating the universe by God? If he created the universe either to enjoy the joy of creation of the universe (*līlārasa*) or to protect the living beings (*jīva-rakṣaṇa*), would it not then conflict with the theory of God as *avāpta-samasta-kāma*, that is, all his desires are already fulfilled and there would be no need to achieve special benefits? Hence it would not be necessary to admit the existence of *Īśvara*. Alternatively, if *Īśvara* is accepted, it would suffice to postulate that He is only *nimitta kāraṇa* or instrumental cause of the universe, in the same way as *kāla* or the need of a specific time for creation.

This is not a sound argument, contends Vedānta Deśika. *Īśvara* is regarded as *avāpta-samasta-kāma* in the sense that as one who is of the nature of *ānanda* par excellence is capable of achieving anything desired by Him and He could create the universe as and when needed and also offer protection to the created individuals.

We may admit *Īśvara* for the purpose of the creation of the universe and its protection but would it be justifiable to regard Him as the *upādāna kāraṇa* or material cause? In our ordinary experience, we find, as in the example of the clay and the pot produced out of it, clay serves as the material, while the potter is instrumental for its production. Some of the Scriptural and Smṛti texts also conveys his idea that *Īśvara* is only the *nimitta kāraṇa* for the creation of the universe, while primordial cosmic matter *prakṛti* is the material cause. If this view is not accepted, it would amount to the modification of Brahman as the universe. In view of it, the Seśvara Sāṅkhya (Yoga), Pāśupata Vaiśeṣika, and other schools (Madhva's Dvaita) only uphold the theory of *Īśvara* as *nimitta kāraṇa.*

Viśiṣṭādvaita refutes this theory on the authority of the Scriptural and Smṛti texts. As stated by Bādarāyaṇa in the *Vedāntasūtra,* the *pratijña* or the general statement, viz., that by the knowledge of causal substance, all the products made out of it become known and the illustration of clay and pot in support of it, as stated in the *Chāndogya Upaniṣad*[2] in connection with the causation of the universe by Brahman, would stand explained if only Brahman is admitted as *upādāna kāraṇa.*[3] The Upaniṣad states that Brahman itself desired to become a manifold universe (*bahubhavana saṅkalpa*). It provides a few illustrations in support of it. Besides, it explicitly states that Brahman made itself as the universe (*tadātmānam svayamkuruta*).[4] We also find several instances in our common experience in which both *upādāna kāraṇa* and *nimitta kāraṇa* as different and also as non-distinct. Both in respect of sentient and non-sentient entities, whenever they undergo changes on their own, they serve as *upādāna* and also *nimitta* for the changes taking place.

It is pointed out by Vedānta Deśika that being the material cause of the universe would not be subject to transformation. Nor the defects found in the universe would be applicable to Brahman. This is explained by Rāmānuja on the analogy of the changes occuring in the physical body of an individual such as childhod, youth, old age, etc., which do not affect the Self within. Brahman does not actually undergo any transformation, as in the case of the clay assuming a new form and name as pot (*nāmāntara bhajanārha vikāra*), by being the *upādāna kāraṇa. Upādānatva* is of two kinds. An object is conceived as *upādāna kāraṇa,* when that itself modifies into a different state, as in the instance of the clay and the pot. An entity is also regarded as *upādāna kāraṇa,* when it serves as the basis for the *avasthās* or different states it undergoes.

The analogy of a boy growing as a youth, old man, etc., is of this type. In this case the individual self associated with the physical body, is the material cause by virtue of its being the *āśraya* or serving as substrate for the changes taking place in the body. In the first instance. there is total transformation of the clay (*svarūpa vikāra*) but it is not so in the second instance. Brahman is *ajaḍa dravya,* spiritual substance, since it is capable of assuming different states. Prior to the creation of the universe, Brahman is associated with *cit* and *acit* in their subtle forms. In the state after creation, it becomes Brahman as associated with *cit* and *acit* in their manifest forms. The changes take place in respect of *prakṛti* which is its *śarīra.* It becomes *upādāna kāraṇa* for the universe by its being the *ādhāra* or basis of *prakṛti.*

On the basis of this explanation, it is stated that Brahman being the *upādāna kāraṇa* of the universe, its *svarūpa* as *nirvikāra* is not affected. This is also supported by the Smṛti texts. The statement "*so abhidhyāya śarīrāt svāt*" which means: "*Paramātman* brings forth from its body, the universe" and the illustration cited by the *Muṇḍaka Upaniṣad* of the spider weaving out its web from its own body (saliva) convey this idea that Brahman itself is the *upādāna kāraṇa* of the universe.

When the Scriptural texts state that *Īśvara* is without a physical body (*aśarīra*), we have to regard him as *aśarīrin.* Even if we have to accept a body for Him, it will be like taking on a body like Indra assuming a body for ruling the universe. *Īśvara* can assume a transitory body temporarily out of His *saṅkalpa.* With the exception of these cases, would it be appropriate to admit that *cit* and *acit* are His *śarīra* in a primary sense? Hence it is contended that an explanation be offered for the material causality of Brahman on the basis of the soul and body relation, is to be taken in figurative sense (*upacāra*).

In reply to this objection, Vedānta Deśika points out that the texts which affirm the *guṇas,* spiritual body, birth, *karma* etc., and also those which negate the same, are to be understood on the basis of the principle adopted for reconciling the conflict between *saguṇa* and *nirguṇa śrutis.* What is intended in such texts negating the body, etc. for *Īśvara* is that *Īśvara* is devoid of a body caused by the *karma* (*karmāyatta śarīra*). He is devoid of finite knowledge which would be dependent on the mind and sense organs (*kāraṇāyatta jñāna*). Hence there should be no conflict between the two statements affirming a body and also negating a body. On the strength of the Scriptural texts which affirm that *Īśvara* is *akarma-vaśya* or not subject to *karma*, that He exists eternally at all time without anyone equal to or superior to Him and that He is *Sarveśvara*, the theories that uphold a series of Rulers as *Īśvara* or that the *muktātmā* is *Īśvara* stand untenable. If we accede to the view that *Īśvara* assumes transitory bodies, we can as well admit that He possesses an eternal and, spiritual body on the strength of the Scriptural texts.

It is to be noted that in Viśiṣṭādvaita Vedānta, *Īśvara* or Brahman as a *viśiṣṭa-tattva*, that is, as related inseparably to *cit* and *acit*, serves as the material cause of the universe. Mere *viśeṣya* or the pure undifferentiated Being as conceived by Advaita cannot be the cause of the universe. Even the Advaitin admits that Brahman as associated with the *māyā* (*Upahita Brahma*) is the material cause. The *acit* of *prakṛti* which actually evolves as the manifold universe, is the *śarīra* of Brahman in the technical sense, viz., that the former is always and wholly sustained and also controlled by the latter. Hence Brahman undergoes modification not directly, but through the media of *prakṛti*, which is its *śarīra*. As *prakṛti* is different from Brahman, the changes that take place in *prakṛti* do not affect Brahman which is its *āśraya*.

As it is well-established by scriptural texts that *Brahma-svarūpa* is not subject to any change or modification, it cannot be said, on the analogy of the piece of wood in the salt mine, that Brahman, in spite of its association with the cosmic universe, is affected in any way. Similarly, Brahman who is the Ruler of all, is also not subject to the dictates of the sacred texts, unlike the *jīvas*. Though He functions through the body which is assumed out of His *saṅkalpa*, He is untouched by the afflictions as in the casę of *jīvas*. As He is *Satyasaṅkalpa* or one whose desires are fulfilled without any obstruction, there is no scope for *Īśvara* to experience any affliction due to the non-fulfilment of his effort. There are a few stray statements in the Purāṇas which mention that even God is also struck with grief (*bhṛśam bhavati duḥkhitaḥ*) and on the basis of such statements, the view is advanced by some that God is only putting up an appearence of grief in order to delight His devotees and deceive His enemies. It would be a self-contradiction to speak of grief, state of ignorance, etc. for God who is an Omniscient Being during His incarnations. Even though God is connected either directly or indirectly with the objects considered to be defilements. He is not affected in any way by undesirable things and He Himself is capable of warding off the evils of others. Hence He is regarded as *amalin* or absolutely pure and devoid of all defilements (*heya-pratyanīka*). This rules out the possibility of God being touched by human afflictions or the defects inherent in the non-sentient entities.

How bondage and liberation is caused by *Īśvara*? God who is the primary cause of the universe also created the variety of living beings associated with variegated bodies, sense organs, and intellect, for serving His own purpose (*sva-sevārtham*), that is, with the good intention to become re-united with Him. Nevertheless, the individuals concerned misuse the opportunities provided to them and go in a wrong direction and get caught up in the cycle of birth and death. Nevertheless, the all-compassionate God who is keen to uplift them from the ocean of bondage always looks forwards for an effort by the individual concerned in the form of ardent request for protection as an excuse for redeeming him from bondage and granting him *mokṣa* or liberation from bondage and enjoyment of everlasting bliss of *Paramātman* from which state there is no return to mundane existence.

The theories which uphold *mokṣa* is granted to an individual by the unconditional *kṛpa* (*nirhetuka-kṛpa*) of God and His unchecked freedom, are unsound because that would result in the liberation of all souls (*sarva mukti*) at all times or alternatively partiality (arbitrariness) and cruelty on the part of God. The unchecked freedom of God is useful for the creation of the universe as and when desired by God without any obstruction. Similarly, the unconditional compassion is useful for an easy accessibility to God for seeking protection (*vaśikaraṇa saukarya*).

According to Yādavaprakāśa, Brahman, which is pure *Sat*, (*Sanmātra*) comprises three parts: *Īśvara*, *cit*, and *acit*. *Īśvara* is thus a part of Brahman. According to the Advaitin, Brahman associated with *māyā* (*māyopahita Brahma*) is *Īsvara*. He is conceived as of three forms, *viśva*, *tejasa*, and *prajñā*. Yādavaprakāśa also conceives three forms of Brahman as *prāṇamaya*, *manomaya*, and *vāṅmaya*. According to these theories, the question of Brahman granting *mokṣa* to *jīva*, as accepted by Viśiṣṭādvaita, is considered not relevant.

Vedānta Deśika refutes these theories as they are not supported by any valid *pramāṇa*. Similarly, the theory of Yādavaprakāśa which believes that *Īśvara*, *cit*, and *acit* are the parts of Brahman and they originate from Brahman and also dissolve in Brahman is also opposed to the Scriptural texts. Then what is the implication of *Śvetāśvatara* statement: "*Brahma trividham*?" Vedānta Deśika replies that his concept is to be interpreted in the sense that the *upāsanā* on Brahman is of three types: Brahman in its own form, Brahman as related to *cit*, and Brahman as related to *acit*.

How about the Upaniṣadic texts which equate Brahman and *jagat* and also Brahman and *jīva*? In all these instances, the equation as non-different is to be understood in the sense that Brahman is immanent in all as *Antaryāmin* and hence Brahman is the entire *jagat*, on the authority of *Antaryāmī Brāhmaṇa* which speaks of body-soul relation between Brahman and *jīva* as well as Brahman and non-sentient entities.

This interpretation is also supported by the *Gītā* verse:

Sarvagatvāt anantasya sa eva aham avasthitaḥ.

Since *Paramātman* is everywhere including one's self, it is relevant to say that "I am He." In the Scriptural texts which emphatically speak of difference between *jīva* and *Paramātman*, which cannot be interpreted in any other way except to accept difference between the two, there is absolute difference in respect of *svarūpa* of *cit*, *acit*, and *Īśvara*.

In view of it we have to admit that these texts speak of non-difference or unity (*aikya*) in the sense of *viśiṣṭaikya* or oneness as *viśiṣṭa-tattva*. Hence the theories of Advaitin which regard difference between these ontological entities as illusory caused by *avidyā* and that of Bhedābhedavādin for whom it is one of difference-cum-non-difference, are unsound.

It is seen that Brahman as associated with *cit* and *acit* which are real entities and undergoes modification as the universe (*pariṇāma*). This theory which is known as *viśiṣṭa-Brahma pariṇāmavāda,* is well-established by the Scriptural texts. As against this, there are several other theories of *Brahma-pariṇāma.* These are briefly mentioned by Vedānta Deśika and summarily rejected as untenable. These are:

1. *Aniyata-svarūpa pariṇāmavāda* held by Brahmadatta according to which Brahman is *vibhu,* and only some part of it undergoes direct transformation as *cit, acit,* and *Īśvara.*
2. *Pratiniyatāṁśatraya pariṇāmavāda,* held by Yādavaprakāśa, according to which Brahman is threefold in nature comprising *Īśvara, cit,* and *acit* and its respective parts undergo modification into *jīva, Īśvara,* and *acit.*
3. *Svarūpa-ekadeśa nityopādhi pariṇāmavāda* held by Bhāskara, according to which the very Brahman undergoes modification as *cit, acit,* and *Īśvara* due to *upādhi* (*avidyā*), which is real unlike an Advaita.
4. Theory of Sāṅkhya, according to which *prakṛti* itself evolves into the manifest universe.
5. The theory of Mādhyamika Buddhists, according to which everything is *śūnya* or undeterminable and there is no such thing as *pariṇāma.*
6. The theory of Vaibhāṣika and Sautrāntika, according to which everything is momentary (*kṣaṇika*).

All these theories are untenable as they are opposed to valid *pramāṇas.*

In order to rule out that Brahman as both *upādāna* and *nimitta kāraṇa* of the universe would be subject to change, non-sentience, affliction, etc. by becoming *jagat,* the Upaniṣad defines that Brahman is *satya, jñāna, ananta* as well as *ānanda.* These are the distinguishing characteristics of Brahman that do not denote the *svarūpa* or only the essential nature of Brahman, as the Advaitin contends. The view maintained by Advaitins that these Upaniṣadic texts emphasize that Brahman is an undifferentiated being (*nirviśeṣa*) or devoid of all attributes, conflicts not only with the earlier and later statements of the same passage but also with other Scriptural texts.

The fuller implications of the term *ananta* or "infinite," need to be understood. It implies absence of three kinds of limitation in respect of Brahman: (1) limitation by time, (2) limitation by space, and (3) limitation caused by another entity (*trividha-pariccheda*). Brahman is not conditioned by space, as is indicated in this statement "*yathā sarvagato viṣṇuḥ.*" It means *Paramātman* is present in all places and not limited to any particular area only. He is also not conditioned by time. He exists eternally at all times as associated with the spiritual body, as stated in the Smṛti text "*Śrīvatsavakṣā nityaśrīḥ ajayya śāśvato dhruvaḥ.*"

Brahman is also not conditioned by any other entity in this universe, because He is equated with the entire universe (*jagacca saḥ*). The *Chāndogya Upaniṣad* says: "*Sarvaṁ khalu idaṁ brahma.*" The Smṛti text says that "The entire universe is His body" (*jagat sarvam śarīram te*). Besides, there is nothing in this universe which is either equal to Him or even greater than him in respect of his *guṇas* (attributes), *vibhūti* (glory), and *vyāpāras* or cosmic functions. Hence, He is not limited by any other thing in this universe (*vastu pariccheda rāhitya*). *Īśvara* is regarded as *sarva-vyāpī*, that is, all-pervasive.

The *Taittirīya Upaniṣad* states that Nārāyaṇa pervades both within and also outside. How can He pervade in *jīvātman*, which being a *niravaya* entity, does not have space within it for pervasion? Similarly, in the case of *vibhudravya*, there is no space for the purpose of pervasion.

Vedānta Deśika explains that the proper implication of *antarvyāpti* in respect of *niravaya* entity is that wherever such an entity exists, it cannot be said that *Īśvara* is not present. Such entities which are *aṇu* or *vibhu*, are associated with the *svarūpa* of *Īśvara* (*sambandha mātrameva tayoḥ bhavet*).

The implication of the *kāla pariccheda rāhitva* needs to be understood. It is not in the sense of saying that God is *nitya*, that is, He exists all the time. This type of *nityatva* is common to other *dravyas* such as *prakṛti*, *kāla*, etc., insofar as their *svarūpa* is *nitya*, according to Viśiṣṭādvaita. It is not also in the sense of *dharma-bhūta jñana* being *nitya*, because this *nityatva* is also common to the *nitya jīvas*. Hence absence of *kāla-pariccheda* with reference to God is to be understood as an exclusive characteristic of *Īśvara* only.

Vastu pariccheda-rāhitva is also interpreted by some (Advaitins) in the sense of non-existence of a second entity (*vastvantarābhāva*) or absolute one entity without a second entity. But such an interpretation stands opposed to our perceptual experience and also Scriptural texts.

The concept of *amalatva* in respect of *Īśvara* is to be understood in the sense that defects normally found in the sentient and non-sentient entities are not applicable to *Īśvara*. It can also be interpreted to mean that *Īśvara* is capable of warding off the evils of the devotees who seek His protection.

Brahman and its essential nature as determined by the numerous Upaniṣadic texts, is also endowed with transcendental spiritual body and numerous auspicious attributes. This can be experienced only by those who attain Him through the means of either continuous meditation (*upāsanā*) in the prescribed manner or through the pathway of total surrender of oneself to Him as the sole protector and goal.

Among the several attributes, the six principal *guṇas*, viz., *jñāna*, *bala*, *aiśvarya*, *vīrya*, *śakti*, and *tejas*, as stated in the *Bhāgavata-śāstra*, are important as these are present at all times. Many other secondary qualities arising out of these manifest when need arises. All these details are provided in *Pāñcarātra Saṁhitās*. Just as *Paramātma-svarūpa* is *nitya*, so also is His *vigraha*. That such a Brahman who is endowed with a spiritual body, *guṇas*, etc., who is the cause of the universe and *Sarveśvara* is a personal God in the name of Nārāyaṇa. This fact is determined on the basis of the Upaniṣadic texts dealing with the causation of the universe (*kāraṇa-vākya*), the Smṛti text, Itihāsa, Purāṇas, and Dharmaśāstras. In view of this conclusion, the theories which speak of the other celestial deities such as Brahmā, Rudra, etc. as the Supreme Being are untenable. That Nārāyaṇa alone is the Supreme Goal to be attained is well-established in the *adhikaraṇa* dealing with the *Vedāntasūtra*: *"param ataḥ setūnmāna saṁbandha bheda vyapadeśebhyaḥ."*[5]

One other *adhikaraṇa* named Liṅgabhūyastvādhikaraṇa[6] also establishes that Nārāyaṇa as the Supreme Deity, is the object all *upāsanās* (*Sarvaparavidyā vedya*). The Sāttvika Purāṇas reveal beyond doubt that Nārāyaṇa is the Supreme Being.

The Tāmasa and Rājasa Purāṇas are not to be relied on to determine this fact. The *upāsanā* on other deities is not of any use for attaining *mokṣa*, since these deities do not possess the power to confer *mokṣa*. Only Viṣṇu or Nārāyaṇa is *mokṣaprada*, as is evident from the Śāstras.

The Supreme Being incarnates Himself in five forms: *para*, *vyūha*, *vibhava*, *arcā*, and *antaryāmī*. All these are different manifestations of the same one Being. All the five forms of *Paramātman* serve as the objects of meditation (*śubhāśraya*). Of these, the *arcā* or the manifestation of God in the form of image is accorded greater importance in Vaiṣṇavism because they are easily accessible for offering direct worship. In the state of *mukti*, God exists in His fullest form manifesting His full glory.

References

1. See *Śvet.Up.*,VI.11.
2. *Ch.Up.*, VI.1.2–6.
3. *VS*, I.IV: *prakṛtiśca pratijñādraṣṭānta anuparodhāt.*
4. *Tait.Up.*, II.7.1.
5. *VS*, III.2.30.
6. See ibid., III.3.43.

PART II

Critical Review of Other Schools

IN THE PRECEDING CHAPTERS, a brief account of the three fundamental doctrines of Viśiṣṭādvaita related to *cit*, *acit* and *Īśvara* have been presented comprehensively by answering all possible objections and refuting the counter theories against them. The objective of this presentation is to prove how the philosophical theories advanced by Rāmānuja are not only free from defects, both logical and philosophical, but also that they fully conform to the teachings of the Upaniṣads as well as Bādarāyaṇa's *Vedāntasūtras*. With this background, Vedānta Deśika attempts to review critically all the important philosophical schools of thought that were prevalent at his time—both the non-Vedic schools which do not accept the authority of the Vedas such as Cārvāka, Buddhism and Jainism, but also the Vedic schools which accept the authority of the Vedas such as Sāṅkhya, Yoga, Vaiśeṣika, Nyāya, Pūrva-mīmāṁsā, and also other Vedānta schools.

The main purpose of this critical review as explained earlier, is to show how the main tenets of these schools, as compared to Viśiṣṭādvaita, are philosophically untenable and that their teachings are also opposed to the Scriptural and Smṛti texts. Some of the schools, particularly the Cārvāka, Buddhists and Jainas who do not accept the Vedas as the source of authority in respect of Spiritual matters are not supported by the commonly accepted valid *pramāṇas* such as *pratyakṣa*, *anumāna*, and *śabda* or Revealed Scripture. Even among the *āstika* schools, most of them with the exception of the Vedānta schools, are opposed to the Upaniṣadic teachings in respect of the major theories advanced by them. Though the school of Advaita is developed on the basis of the Upaniṣads, it also suffers from logical inconsistencies and stands opposed to the Upaniṣadic texts and the *Vedāntasūtras* in respect of the main tenets such as the doctrine of *māyā*, the concept of *nirguṇa-brahman* and non-difference between *jīva* and Brahman as is evident from the critical review of this school. In a separate chapter named *Samudāyadoṣādhikāra*, Vedānta Deśika first mentions a few general criticisms which are applicable to all schools of thought. He then takes up each school separately for a detailed criticism of the main tenets of these schools and exposes their defects.

As stated earlier, the justification for undertaking a critical review is not merely for the purpose of defending one's own system, which is a common practice of the exponents of all systems. More importantly, as explained in the *Gītā* verse,[1] persons who are not knowledgeable with the correct philosophical teachings imparted by a qualified teacher (*ajñaḥ*), those who have not developed proper faith in what is taught (*aśrad-dhadhānāḥ*) and those who entertain doubts (*saṁśayātmā*), cannot hope to make any progress in the spiritual pursuits. In order to avoid such a situation, earnest students of Vedānta seeking spiritual progress are required to be guided in order to prevent them from being entrapped by the wrong theories of other schools which are not well-founded on the authority of the Scriptural texts as well as proper tradition (*sat-saṁpradāya*). It is also necessary to refute the systems which do not acknowledge the authority of the Vedas and also those who accept it but misinterpret the same to suit their pre-conceived theories.

There are four kinds of defects from which all these systems generally suffer. These are: (1) Adoption of logical arguments which do not fulfil the requisite logical canons (*aṅgarahita tarka*) in order to establish one's theory. (2) Even in respect of inferential arguments, the *hetu* or probans adopted stands opposed to *pratyakṣa*, which is the basis for *anumāna* or inference (*upajīvya*). (3) Formulation of theories which are directly opposed to the teachings of the Vedas which is free from defects (*nirdoṣa*) because it has come down to us in succession from a beginningless time in the same form. (4) Acceptance as the source of authority, the statements or teachings of human beings, who are likely to be subject to delusion and also have the intention of deceiving people. These points have been brought out while dealing with the criticism of the respective schools.

Regarding the supreme authoritativeness of the Veda, the first question to be considered is whether it is *nitya* or eternal as the Vedāntins and Mīmāṁsakas claim. The words and the sentences formed out of it are known to be non-permanent. How can Veda which is only a composition of sentences be claimed as eternal? In reply to this objection, it is pointed out that the *nityatva* of the Veda is to be understood in the sense that at all times, the Vedic statements are recited generation after generation in the same order without any change from time immemorial. Even if the persons who recite them and the letters (*varṇa*) which constitute the words and sentences may perish at the end of an epoch with the dissolution of the cosmic universe, yet the eternal and omniscient God, the cretor of the universe, has the memory of the Vedas and He teaches the Vedas to *Caturmukha-brahmā* soon after the creation of the universe in the same form and order. The latter imparts the same to the sages who in turn teach it to others in the same order. In this sense the eternal character of the Vedas is maintained. In the commentary on the *Pūrvamīmāṁsāsūtra*, Śabaraswāmī (the commentator on Jaimini's *sūtras*) has advanced the theory of *varṇa-nityatva*, that is, the letters are of eternal character. But according to the Vedānta Deśika, this theory is advanced by him in order to meet the criticisms of the Buddhists who deny the authority of the Vedas and hence it is not to be taken as his accepted view.

There are other arguments which question the *nityatva* of the Vedas. Vedānta Deśika examines them critically and rejects them as untenable. One of the arguments is that the Vedas, as they are available to us, are the compositions of particular human beings like any other literary work and hence they cannot be claimed to be *nitya.* In the Vedas we come across passages which are ascribed to persons such as Yājñavalkya, Viśvāmitra, Vaśiṣṭha, etc. But this arguments is untenable, contends Vedānta Deśika. The important point to be noted in defence of *Veda-nityatva* is that it is *apauruṣeya*, that is, it is not ascribed to any author. Even God, according to Vedānta, is not its author, but He is only a spokesperson of what already exists. We do not have any evidence to prove that it was written by someone at any particular point of time. The Smṛti text says that it is *anādinidhāna*, beginningless and eternal. It is self-valid or self-established (*svataḥ pramāṇa*). Such a claim cannot be made by the exponents of the *nāstika* schools. Their Āgamas or sacred texts which are adopted as the source of authority are the compositions of some individuals and they cannot therefore be *nitya* and also free from defects.

After making these general criticisms against the other schools of thought, Vedānta Deśika takes up for a detailed critical review, each school separately. The criticisms are confined to the main tenets of these schools which are found defective and which are also at variance with those of Viśiṣṭādvaita Vedānta. The following is the order in which these schools come up for examination.

1. Cārvāka
2. Buddhism—Mādhyamika, Yogācāra, Sautrāntika, and Vaibhāṣika
3. Advaita Vedānta
4. Jainism
5. Bhedābheda Vedānta of Bhāskara and Yādavaprakāśa
6. Śabda-brahma-Vivartavāda of Vaiyākaraṇa
7. Vaiśeṣika
8. Nyāya
9. Nirīśvara-mīmāṁsā
10. Nirīśvara-sāṅkhya
11. Yoga
12. Pāśupata
13. Pāñcarātra

The justification for adopting this order by overlooking the chronological order of these schools, we shall however take up the examination of these schools divided into three groups in the following order.

I. *Non-Vedic schools*

1. Cārvāka
2. Buddhism—Mādhyamika, Yogācāra, Sautrāntika, and Vaibhāṣika

3. Jainism

II. *Vedic schools*
1. Vaiśeṣika
2. Nyāya
3. Nirīśvara-mīmāṁsā
4. Sāṅkhya
5. Yoga
6. Pāśupata
7. Pāñcarātra

III. *Vedānta schools*
1. Śabda-brahma-Vivartavāda of Vaiyākaraṇa
2. Advaita of Śaṅkara
3. Dvaita Vedānta of Madhva
4. Bhedābheda-vedānta of Bhāskara and Yādava
5. Svābhāvika-bhedābheda Vedānta of Nimbārka
6. Acintya-bhedābheda Vedānta of Caitanya
7. Śuddhādvaita of Vallabha
8. Śivādvaita schools
9. Navya-viśiṣṭādvaita of Swamya-Narāyaṇa

The later schools of Vedānta are not covered in the *Paramata-bhaṅga,* so this is the reason for following this order and a summary on Vedānta schools.

VEDĀNTA SCHOOLS

Vedānta which is an important system of Philosophy is developed primarily on the basis of the Upaniṣads and *Brahmasūtras* of sage Bādarāyaṇa. But within this single system of philosophy several schools of thought, each one designated with different name, have come up based on the same source of authority, viz., the Upaniṣad, *Brahmasūtra,* and the *Bhagavadgītā,* due to the different interpretations offered by their exponents on the nature of the Ultimate Reality (Brahman) and also its relation to the individual self (*jīvātman*) and the universe (*jagat*). Among the extant schools, the principal ones are the Advaita Vedānta of Śaṅkara (AD 788), the Viśiṣṭādvaita Vedānta of Rāmānuja (AD 1017) and Dvaita Vedānta of Madhva (AD

1238). Earlier than Śaṅkara, there were a few schools of thought ascribed to Bhartṛhari, Bhartṛprapañca and Brahmadatta, as is evident from the references made to them in the works of Śaṅkara, Yāmuna (a predecessor to Rāmānuja), Rāmānuja and Vedānta Deśika.

Bādarāyaṇa also mentions the names of ancient *ācāryas* such as Ātreya, Aśmarathya, Bādari, Auḍulomi, Jaimini, Kāśakṛtsna, and Kārṣṇājini, in the *Brahmasūtras.* But it is not kown whether any of these sages had written commentaries on the *Vedāntasūtras.* Rāmānuja refers to sage Bodhāyana who is stated to be the earliest exponent of the Vedānta and who had also written an elabrorate *vṛtti* or glossary on the *Vedāntasūtras* as is evident from the statements quoted in his *Śrībhāṣya,* the commentary on the *Vedāntasūtras.* Śaṅkara also mentions in his works Upāvarṣa and Vṛttikāra as the ancient commentators on *Vedāntasūtra.* But it is established by Sudarśanasūrī in his glossary on *Śrībhāṣya* that Upāvarṣa and Vṛttikāra are the same person as Bodhāyana. Rāmānuja also refers to a few *pūrvācāryas* such as Ṭaṅka, Dramiḍa, Guhadeva, and Bhāruci. We do not have any works contributed by these exponents. Some details about the views expressed by Bhartṛhari, a grammarian (*vaiyākaraṇa*) on the theory of Śabda-brahma-vivartavāda is available in *Vākyapadīya.* Similarly some material about Bhartṛprapañca, referred to by Śaṅkara in his commentary on *Bṛhadāraṇyaka Upaniṣad* and Surésvara's *vārttika* is available. He is known to have held the theory Brahma-pariṇāmavāda and Bhedābheda relationship between Brahman and the *jīvas* as well as Brahman and the *jagat.* Brahmadatta, another Vedāntin, who is stated to have written a commentary on the *Vedāntasūtras* and who lived later than Bhṛtṛprapañca, also maintained Brahma-pariṇāmavāda and also the origin of the *jīvas* as is evident from references made to these views by Vedānta Deśika.[2] The two doctrines Brahma-vivartavāda and Brahma-pariṇāmavāda of Bhartṛhari and Bhartṛprapañca, respectively, seem to have influenced Śaṅkara's Brahma-vivartavāda and the Bhedābhedavāda of Bhāskara and Yādavaprakāśa.

Later than Śaṅkara and earlier than Rāmānuja, two schools of Vedānta emerged which are named Bhedābhedavāda, developed by Bhāskara and Yādavaprakāśa. Both have written a commentary on the *Brahmasūtras.* The *Bhāskarabhāṣya* is available, whereas Yādavaprakāśa's commentary is lost. But extracts of it have been quoted by Rāmānuja and Sudarśanasūri, the commentator on the *Śrībhāṣya* as well as Vedānta Deśika. These two schools are regarded as distinct on the basis of different interpretations offered on the nature of relationship between Brahman and *jīva* as well as Brahman and *jagat.* Bhāskara maintains that Brahman and *jīvas* as well as *jagat* is caused by the limiting adjuncts (*upādhi*) in the form of *avidyā* which is a real ontological principle, unlike in Advaita, whereas for Yādavaprakāśa difference is also *svābhāvika.* The disctinction between these two schools is drawn on the basis of the fact that Yādavaprakāśa's school is characterized as Svābhāvika-bhedābhedavāda, whereas Bhāskara school is regarded as Aupādhika-bhedābhedavāda.

A few other schools of Vedānta were developed later than Rāmānuja and Madhva by Nimbārka, followers of Caitanya and Vallabha by adopting a modified form of Bhedābheda. The school of Vedānta advanced by Nimbārka is characterized as Svābhāvika-bhedābhedavāda, whereas the one developed by Caitanya school is known by the name of Acintya-bhedābhedavāda. The Vedānta developed by Vallabhācārya, who follows mostly Madhva, calls his Vedānta as Śuddhādvaita, but it also admits the Bhedābheda relation between Brahman and *jīvas.*

In the *Paramata-bhaṅga,* Vedānta Deśika takes up for critical examination, the Vaiyākaraṇa school of Śabdabrahma-vivartavāda, the Advaita Vedānta of Śaṅkara and the Bhedābhedavāda school of Bhāskara and Yādavaprakāśa.

Regarding Viśiṣṭādvaita Vedānta, he has presented the three fundamental doctrines, viz., *cit* (*jīvātman*), *acit* (cosmic universe), and *Īśvara* at the very commencement of the *Paramata-bhaṅga* since it is not intended for criticism as in the case of other schools of Vedānta. As explained earlier, its objective is to show how these doctrines are philosophically sound by way of answering all possible objections against them.

Vedānta Deśika does not mention Dvaita Vedānta separately nor does he refer to Nimbārka's Bhedābhedavāda, the Acintyabhedavāda of Caitanya, Vallabha's Suddhādvaitavāda and Śivādvaita of Śaiva schools which were developed in the post-Deśika period. But he indicates in a general way, that criticisms pointed out against Bhedābheda of Bhāskara and Yādava would also be applicable to these schools. Regarding Dvaita Vedānta, though it is not included for critical review separately, a few criticisms are expressed gainst some doctrines in the *Paramata-bhaṅga.* As it occupies an important place among the three major schools of Vedānta, it is taken up for examination soon after Advaita. In order to complete the critical review of all Vedānta Schools, we have included in the present book a brief outline of the criticisms against all the later schools of Vedānta including Dvaita insofar as their main doctrines are concerned.

References

1. *BG,* IV.40: *ajñaḥ aśraddhadhānāśca saṁśayātmā vinaśyati.*
2. See *TMK,* II.16.

4
Cārvāka School

THIS APPEARS to be the oldest school of thought in the history of Indian philosophy developed in the post-Vedic period, as is evident from the fact that it is criticized by all the other schools including Buddhism. Though there are some stray references to the views of the Cārvākas in the Upaniṣads, it was developed as a system (Darśana) only in the post-Vedic period. Though its founder is stated to be Bṛhaspati, the guru of celestial deities, who taught it to the demons (*asuras*) to delude them since they did not believe the Vedic way of life leading to a spiritual goal, is it not accepted by other schools and even condemned as an unsound philosophy.

We do not have any literature on this system. Even the *Bṛhaspatisūtras* are lost. However, there are a few stray reference to the *sūtras* and also the theories of the Cārvāka in the treatises of other schools of thought, while refuting their views. From these references, we have reconstructed the Cārvāka philosophy to some extent.

In the *Paramata-bhaṅga,* Vedānta Deśika states in fairly good details, the views of the Cārvākas gathered from various sources. They are called Lokāyatikas or the one whose teachings are widely spread all over the world (*lokeṣu āyatam* or *vistṛtam*). The chapter devoted to the criticism of this school is named "Lokāyatika-bhaṅgādhikāra."[1]

According to Cārvāka, *pratyakṣa* or perception is the only *pramāṇa* or source of knowledge. Though *anumāna* or inference may be found to be a valid source of knowledge in a few cases, such as the inferential knowledge of fire on the yonder hill on the basis of the invariable concomitance between fire and smoke on the hill, as in the instance of the smoke coming from the chimney of the kitchen, it cannot be taken as a valid *pramāṇa* in all cases. Even if it is to be admitted as a *pramāṇa*, it is possible to regard such stray instances of inferential knowledge as part of *pratyakṣa*. *Śabda* or verbal testimony, which is the third source of knowledge, is also not accepted by Cārvāka. But we have several instances such as chanting of *mantras* and the wearing of the *yantra* or talisman, which confer good results by warding off evils and certain diseases. But these cases could also be explained according to the Cārvākas on the basis of our perceptual experience, as in the instances of the magnet having the capacity to attract the iron and the special stones radiating light when sun or moon shines over them. On the basis of these instances, *śabda* cannot be regarded as a *pramāṇa*. Even if *anumāna* is taken as a *pramāṇa*, as is commonly accepted by all, it cannot reveal what is supersensuous (*atīndriya*) such as *Īśvara*, *jīva*, etc.

THE PHILOSOPHY OF THE *CĀRVĀKA*

Coming to their philosophy, Vedānta Deśika quotes the following *sūtra* of Bṛhaspati which refers to the central doctrine of the *Cārvāka*: "*atha lokāyatam, pṛthivyāpas-tejo vāyur iti tattvam; tebhyaś caitanyam kiṇvādibhyo madaśaktivat.*" It means: "Now commences Lokāyatamata; the *tattvas* are earth, water, fire, and air; from the combination of these four arises consciousness, as in the example of the intoxicating quality (in the liquor) arising from the mixture of certain ingredients." Another illustration offered in support of this theory is the red colour produced by chewing together betel leaf, areca nut, and lime. A section of the Cārvākas also admits *ākaśa* or ether as a separate *tattva*, besides the four elements.

This school has gained some importance and wider popularity on account of several reasons. It emphasizes the value of the two human goals, viz., acquisition of wealth and enjoyment of sensual pleasures, which are generally desired by all and also attainable by human effort. It conforms to the *Kāmaśāstra* of Vātsyāyana which teaches the ways and means of enjoying sensual pleasures and *steyaśāstra*, dealing with the methods to be adopted for earning money by fraudulent means. As these teachings fall within the scope of our experience, there is no room to question their validity. In view of these facts, the advocacy of the enjoyment of pleasure as long as one lives (*yāvajjīvam sukhaṁ jīvet*) as the primary goal of life has great appeal to all persons. It is therefore considered by the Cārvākas a waste of time, money, and energy to engage oneself in all sorts of rigorous, religious observances by torturing one's body on the false assumption that there is some unknown higher spiritual goal to be attained.

Apart from the body, vital breath, digestive fire (*jaṭharāgni*), *indriyas,* and the heart, there does not exists a separate principle known as *ātman.* Nor is there any truth in the belief that after death one assumes another body. If it were true, one should fear for hell (*naraka*) and also refrain from causing injury to others. Since there is neither heaven nor hell, which are false assumptions, an individual should enjoy himself in the pleasure of young women (*taruṇī*), delicious food, good clothes, perfumes, etc., which constitute the heaven (*svarga*) which is evident to our experience (*pratyakṣa svarga*). Instead or aspiring for such pleasures, it is foolish to endeavour for something which is unknown to us by observing all kinds of rigorous penances in the form of fasting, etc.

According to the *Cārvāka,* the body itself is *ātman.* This fact is evident to us, he argues, as in the case of the experience that "I am fat," "I am lean." The fatness or leanness is the *dharma* of the body and hence the experience of one's self as "I am fat" arises. If this is negated then in the judgment "*agni* is *uṣṇa*" (fire is hot) *uṣṇatva* seen in the fire could also be negated. In the case of the experience "it is my body" (*mama śarīra*) which implies the difference between the body and one's self denoted by the word *mama,* it is argued that such statements are to be understood in the same way as the expression "the body of the wooden doll" (*śilāputraka śarīra*) or "head of *rāhu*" (*rāhośsirah*). That is, in the expression "the body of wooden doll, though doll and body are different, it means only one entity. In the same way, Rāhu, the mythological person himself represents the head. The expression, *rāhośsirah* (Rāhu's head) gives the impression of difference between the two but in actuality, it is not different. In the same way, the judgment *mamaśarīra* is to be understood in the sense that the body itself is the self.

An objection may be raised: Would it be appropriate to regard what is non-sentient (*acetana*) as the self or sentient being? To this objection, Cārvāka replies that since other than the four physical elements, viz., *pṛthivī*, *ap*, *tejas*, and *vāyu*, there is no other entity, it is to be admitted that body itself is the self. The Cārvākas further argue that by a special combination of these four elements in the body a new product named *caitanya* or conciseness is generated. There are several instances to prove the possibility of a new product by a special combination of two or more objects. The common illustration, as stated earlier, the intoxicating liquor which is produced by the concoction of certain ingredients. Poison is produced by the combination of different products. So also the herbal liquid known as *rasāyana* in Āyurveda is brought forth by the mixture of certain herbal products. In all these instances, the generation of a new product is admitted. Another instance which is perceptually known is the production of red colour by the combination of white lime and yellow turmeric powder. The water which does not possess the quality of hardness is found to be hard when the same falls on the ground from the water-bearing clouds as hail stones. The green mango on the tree assumes red and yellow colour and also sweetness over a period of time. The combination of the threads of different colours produces a piece of cloth of variegated colour. All these changes take place in a natural way because of the natural qualities inherent in the respective objects. In the same way, it is possible to account for the variation in the experience of pleasure and pain in one's body and the varied activities for attaining what is desired by the avoidance of what is not desirable.

Even without the admission of *caitanya* or *jñāna* as a separate *guṇa*, it is possible to explain the activities of an individual on the basis of the sense organs which serve as accessory cause, as in the example of the movements or functioning of dolls controlled by a person through the operation of the strings tied to them. Alternatively, it could be explained on the basis of the functioning of the body in a natural way such as inhalation and exhalation, the movement of the eyelids, similar to the blooming of the lotus flower with the petals spread out. Just as a cut piece of a plant or branch of a tree, when replanted, re-grows on its own accord, there is no need to postulate the presence of a *jīva* as possessing *jñāna*. Those who argue that the assumption of different types and grades of body are due to the previous *puṇya* and *pāpa* of an individual cannot explain how among the different levels or grades of living beings such as plants, animals, and human beings, one grade is higher than the other. The *jīva* of a plant does not assume the body of animals, nor the *jīvas* of animals assume the bodies of human beings. Hence, there cannot be any such things as *puṇya* or *pāpa*. In absence of *puṇya* or *pāpa*, which are claimed to cause bondage, there cannot be *mokṣa* or total liberation of an individual from bondage. The cessation or dissolution of body itself is *mokṣa*. The statements speaking of the highest bliss as *mokṣa*, are mere verbal expressions. Even the different Buddhist schools which uphold the theory *sarvaśūnyatva*, *kṣaṇikatva*, or momentary nature of objects, denial of independent existence of external objects, do not accept a permanent entity as *ātmā* with the *dharma* of *jñātṛtva* or capacity to know. Hence it is wiser to enjoy oneself in the pleasure that arises one's own effort or on its own accord.

The Cārvākas also claim that their system of philosophy is also supported by the Upaniṣads, unlike the Buddhist theories. In one of the passages of the *Chāndogya Upaniṣad*,[2] it is stated that Prajāpati, the chief of the celestial deities, taught this philosophy to Virocana, the chief of the demons along with Indra, that the body itself seen as reflected in the water is *ātmā*. Virocana accepted it as truth and he being convinced with this, taught the same in turn to his associates. This teaching is therefore claimed as the Upaniṣad of the *asuras* (demons) on the authority of the Vedas. As this philosophy was promulgated by no less a person than Bṛhaspati, the *guru* of the celestial deities, it enjoys the distinction of being the religion of the *devaguru*. Even a few orthodox sages upheld this theory, as is evident from the dialogue of the sage Jābāli in the assembly by Rāma as narrated in the *Rāmāyaṇa*.[3] In the *Mahābhārata* also there is a reference by name to Lokāyatikas who are stated to be present along with the exponents of other schools[4] in an assembly held in the hermitage of sage Kaṇva. All those persons who crave for wealth and sensual pleasure as the goal of life, unmindful *dharma,* are the followers of Cārvāka philosophy. Apart from showing respect to a superior person such as a king who may be regarded as God, there is no need to offer worship in the form of religious deeds to an unknown God. Thus, the *Cārvāka* philosophy is established on the basis of *pratyakṣa pramāṇa* and logical arguments (*tarka*) and should also be acceptable to other schools. Hence, it is claimed as a sound philosophy.

Criticism of the *Cārvāka* Theories

The first and foremost criticism of the Cārvāka school is directed to the non-acceptance of the valid *pramāṇas* other than *pratyakṣa.* In order to establish sound theories of any school of thought, it is necessary to admit valid *pramāṇas* in support of them (*mānādhīnomeyasiddhi*). Knowledge arises not only on the basis of *pratyakṣa* but also *anumāna* (inference) and *āgama* (verbal testimony). The knowledge derived from inference and verbal testimony is not invalid, since it is not contradicted by any other *pramāṇa.* Besides, such knowledge obtained through *anumāna* and *āgama* is not of doubtful character. If *pratyakṣa* is admitted as a valid source of knowledge, *anumāna* and *āgama* are also to be accepted as valid sources of knowledge. Otherwise, it is possible to deny the validity of even perception. It may be argued that only a few theories proved by *anumāna* and *āgama* appear to be valid, whereas what is revealed by perception is always found to be valid. But this argument, Vedānta Deśika contends, is equally applicable to perceptual knowledge. The cognition of a snake in the rope, which is perceptual, is not valid as it is negated by another cognition that it is not a snake.

Even the Cārvākas, who deny the validity of *anumāna* as a source of knowledge, do acknowledge the fact that hunger is overcome by eating the food and on that basis seek the food when one is hungry. Similarly, verbal testimony is also accorded some validity. Thus, for instance, a person who has come to know through a reliable person that wealth is hidden in the ground at a distant place, endeavours to obtain it by special effort and is even prepared to spend money to unearth it. If one does not trust the words of the person who tells the availability of wealth, he would not make any effort to secure it. It is generally seen that persons who accept with faith the statements of reliable individuals, follows their teachings. It is also found that astrology which predicts the future events which are not seen or known, is accepted as beneficial. Similarly, the *mantra-śāstra* is found useful to ward off evils which are yet to occur at a later period. In the same way, one has to believe the statements of the Sacred texts which speak of the attainment of bliss or *mokṣa* in a higher realm. If a higher realm exists and if one believes in it and follows the prescribed *sādhana*, he is sure to be benefited. Even if such a realm does not exist, the pursuit of religious way of life does not cause any harm to him.

Vedānta Deśika further contends that it is not correct to regard *anumāna* and *āgama* as part of *pratyakṣa*, as Cārvāka maintains, because knowledge also arises during the non-functioning of the external sense organs on the basis of the memory of a past event or the memory of objects seen in the past. Mind is a common accessory cause (instrument) for all types of knowledge and hence what is remembered through the mind cannot be considered as perception proper.

The Cārvākas claim that *Nītiśāstra* and *Kāmaśāstra* which teach the ways and means of acquisition of wealth and the satiation of sensual pleasures respectively support the *Cārvāka* philosophy which upholds pleasures as the goal of life. This is far from the truth. *Nītiśāstra* does not permit the acquisition of wealth as opposed to *dharma*. Similarly, the money acquired by using force is permitted only in the case of the Kṣatriyas for the purpose of giving it away in charity to the pious persons (*sādhus*). Similarly, the teachings of *Kāmaśāstra* regarding the various ways of indulging in sensual pleasures are permitted within the limit of the *Dharmaśāstra*.

The Cārvākas criticize the rigid orthodox way of life in accordance with one's *varṇa* or caste and *āśramas* or stages of life as laid down by the Sacred texts by condemning the very caste system as Brāhmaṇas, etc. on the ground that among the human beings the distinction in the form of Brāhmaṇas, etc., is not perceptible. Vedānta Deśika refutes this view because the caste system has been in vogue from time immemorial. As explained in the *Gītā*, it is created by God on the basis of the *guṇas—sattva, rajas,* and *tamas* inherent in the body.[5] Even if it is totally wiped out due to the admixture of different races and castes, it will be recreated as and when the next evolution of the universe takes place.

It cannot be said that the Vedic orthodox way of life which demands rigorous religious observances are mere conventional customs created by some orthodox people for selfish purposes, because it has come down to us from time immemorial, through generation after generation. What is well-established by unbroken tradition cannot be questioned.

The Physical Body is not *Ātman*

After criticizing the theory of *pratyakṣa* as the only source of *pramāṇa* and the non-admission of *anumāna* and *āgama* as *pramāṇa*, Vedānta Deśika refutes the main doctrine of Cārvāka that the physical body is the *ātman* or individual self. The judgment "This is my body" clearly conveys the idea that the body constituted of the combination of five physical elements consisting of legs, arms, etc. is distinct from the notion "I" (self). The physical components are perceptible to the eyes and other sense organs. In the absence of the functioning of the sense organs, the body is not seen. The *ātman* is always of unchanging nature unlike the physical body, and it experiences pleasure and pain all over the body. It manifests itself as "I" (*ahaṁ*) and that itself is not seen by the sense organs. An individual who has controlled his mind after fully arresting the functions of all the sense organs is able to visualize the *ātman* during the state of *samādhi* or trance. If one does not directly see this difference between the self and the body and gets the experience, that "I am fat" (*sthūlo' haṁ*), it is due to the fact that the body and the soul are so inseparably related, like the heated iron rod appearing as red, that the *dharma* or characteristic of the body is super-imposed on the self just as the redness which is the property of fire is imposed on the iron rod. Just as the cognition of the flame of a lamp is the same (*jvālaikya*) stands sublated by the inferential argument that it is constantly changing being dependent on the supply of oil and the burning of the wick, in the same way the judgment "it is my body" stands sublated when it is realized that body and self are two separate entities with distinct characters. In the judgment *mama ātmān* or "my body," "myself" denoting *ātmā* refers to the nature *ātman,* whereas body refers to a different entity as in the example "my house." House is not the self and it is different from the self. In the same way, body is not the self. The example of the wooden doll is not comparable to the judgment "my *śarīra.*" The doll is lifeless, whereas body related to the soul is not so.

Ākāśa as the Fifth Element cannot be Denied

The theory that apart from the four physical elements, viz., *pṛthivī, ap, tejas,* and *vāyu,* there is no other *tattva* or reality is most unsound, for the reason that on the basis of other *pramāṇas* other *tattvas* such as *ākāśa* are proven to exist. In the matter of non-sensuous and spiritual entities such as self, which are beyond the scope of the sense perception, we have to admit them since they are capable of being known by other *pramāṇas.* Though they are not visually perceived, their existence cannot be questioned since they could be comprehended by other sources of knowledge. If these are not admitted purely on the limited basis that they are not directly perceived, then even the four physical elements admitted by the Cārvākas as *tattvas,* could be denied by adopting the logic of Mādhyamikas for whom no real entity exists. If on the basis of mere non-perception of an object without acknowledging the principle of what is capable of knowing (*yogya*) and what is not capable of being apprehended (*ayogya*), the existence of non-perceptible object is denied, it would amount to a ridiculous theory. As Udayana, the author of *Nyāyakusumāñjali* jokingly points out, it would be similar to a Cārvāka who has gone out of his house on an errand, and who does not see on the way his wife and children and other possessions, starts weeping by beating the chest that they are dead or lost (*gṛhādbahir-gataḥ cārvākaḥ soras-tadam śokavikalo vikrośet*).

Consciousness is not Generated by The Combination of the Physical Elements

The *Cārvāka* maintains the theory that *caitanya* or consciousness is a new principle which emerges out of the combination of the four physical elements of which the body is constituted, similar to the emergence of the intoxicating equality out of the admixture of certain ingredients. This is also untenable. The question is raised, whether this consciousness is present in each of the four elements or only in the combination of the four (*samudāya*). If it is present in each part of the body, then each part should possess *caitanya* or consciousness. If it is so, it would amount to saying that there are several *jīvas* in the same body. In that case, conflict among the different *jīvas* would be inevitable as in the case of the several rulers ruling the same kingdom and consequently there would be no unity of purpose and action. Further, if *jīva* exists in each part of the body, with the removal of any one of the limbs, its experience cannot be re-colleted by another as there is no transmission of the experience from one limb to the other.

In order to overcome the above difficulty, it may be argued that consciousness (*jīva*) is present in the aggregate of the parts. This view is also untenable. If *caitanya* is not found in the parts, it would not be present in the aggregate of the parts. A quality which does not exist in the parts cannot be present in the aggregate of the parts. Besides the physical body being an aggregate of several limbs is non-sentient in character, like a pot and as such it cannot possess *caitanya*. The illustration of the emergence of the intoxicating element out of the mingling of certain ingredients does not serve the purpose of supporting the *Cārvāka* theory. The element that produces the intoxicating quality is present in the ingredients in a potential form and it therefore causes the emergence of a new property. In the case of the physical body, there is no evidence to show that consciousness is present in each of the physical parts of body.[6]

In all the other instances cited by the Cārvākas in support of their theory such as the hardness of the water falling from the clouds in the form of hail stones, the transformation of the green colour of mango into red and yellow, the *rasāyana*

(Ayurvedic herbal liquid) made out of the boiling of the different herbal juices, the cloth of variegated colour woven from the threads of different colour, these changes which take place are evident to our experience and these arise out of the natural process of change from that which already exists in a potential and different form. These do not support the theory that a new product emerges out of the combination of the parts or ingredients. On the basis of these instances, it cannot be said that by the combination of the different parts of the body, a new product such as *caitanya* or *jīva* arises.

The Cārvākas who do not admit the causal relationship between cause and effect cannot uphold the theory that *caitanya* is caused by the combination of the limbs of the physical body constituted of four elements. That is, those who do not accept the principle that every effect must have a cause, cannot prove that *caitanya* emerges from the combination of the four elements. The illustration cited by Cārvāka, viz., the sharpness or crookedness of thorns in support of the production of an effect without a cause does not prove this theory (*ahetuka utpatti*). Even in such instances, some causal factor is involved. If that is not perceptible, it is to be assumed that some unforeseen factor influences the growth of sharpness or crookedness in the thorns.

The Cārvākas do not admit the theory of causality. By adopting a dialectic[7] they contend that it is difficult to determine the nature of *kāraṇa* or what is accepted as a causal factor. The arguments advanced by them to refute the commonly accepted relation between cause and effect untenable, when these are subjected to logical analysis. In view of it, the thesis maintained by Cārvāka, viz., that *caitanya* is caused by the combination of four elements, involves self-contradiction and stands opposed to one's own activities for achieving the same goal or purpose.

It may be argued that it is possible to explain all mental functions by the instruments of knowledge such as mind and sense organs (*caitanya sāmagrī*) and that there is no need to admit *caitanya* or a sentient principle as *jīva* separately. But this view stands opposed to our experience. Our experience is the form, "I know this object." This experience implies a subject, an object and that act of knowing the object. Just as the object such as the pot seen cannot be denied, the knowing by the subject also cannot be denied. It is not possible to explain the mental activities by the mere instruments of *jñāna* without the presence of *caitanya* which activates them. Even in the cases of the wooden dolls, which are found to prattle words, it is not without the influence of a sentient being. Such activities by non-sentient entities can be accounted for either through the power of their being possessed by spirits or through the will of God who is the Supreme Deity to be worshipped by all and also the bestower of the boons. All activities need to be initiated and regulated by an intelligent being (*caitanya-mūla*). The illustrations of the blooming of the petals of the lotus flower and the exhalation and inhalations of living beings do not substantiate the *Cārvāka* theory of spontaneous activity without the control of a sentient being. Even in these instances, it is also controlled by *Paramātman*. If a branch of a tree which is cut and replanted grows, it is due to the fact that another *jīva* abides in it. Since *jīvas* are infinite in number, it is always possible that if one *jīva* leaves the body, another *jīva* becomes associated with it.

The gradations of *jīvas* due to the assumption of different types of bodies from the lowest form such as plants, trees, germs, insects, reptiles, animals, human beings, celestial beings etc., is due to the variations in respect of the sins and merits accumulated from the series of several previous births. Such an explanation cannot be offered by those who subscribe to the theory that body itself is self, because with the physical death, continuation of life is inconceivable. When it is established that *jīvātman* is an eternal, spiritual principle and, distinct from bodily experiences pleasure and pain in accordance with one's *puṇya* and *pāpa*, the mere enjoyment of sensual pleasure in one's lifetime as the goal of life as conceived by Cārvāka, is not sustainable. Nor the cessation of one's life of limited duration is *mokṣa*.

It may be argued that it is superfluous to postulate the concept of *dharma* and *adharma* to account for the existence of *sukha* and *duḥkha* when it is possible to explain all events in one's life on the basis of certain known factors. Or it may be said that just as what is stated in the Āgamas (Sacred texts) which is eternal, cannot be negated by the other *pramāṇas*, in the same way that what is postulated to explain a phenomena is not to be questioned. But both these arguments stand rejected since perception alone cannot be the final authority in respect of spiritual matters.

The *caitanya* or consciousness which is located in a part of the body cannot also be claimed as *jñātṛ* or knowing self because this is not proved by *pratyakṣa* which is the only *pramāṇa* for the Cārvākas. We sometimes say that a tree in which flowers are seen only in a single branch, is a beautiful tree full of flowers. Citing a few examples, a philosophical theory cannot be conclusively established. If this be possible, then any rival school of thought can advance its own theories and claim that it is sounder than those admitted by others. To overcome all these objections it may be argued that *caitanya* that is present in a part of the subtle body (*sūkṣma-eka-deśa*), is *jīva*. But such a theory when subjected to further scrutiny stands untenable since it cannot be proved by logical arguments. Hence one has to take resort to *śāstra* or sacred text as the only source of authority for providing the existence of *jīva*.

PRĀṆA IS ALSO NOT THE *JĪVĀTMĀ*

The arguments advanced to refute the theory that the physical body itself is the *jīva*, equally holds good in respect of *prāṇa* or vital breath, being regarded as *jīva*. The *praṇa-vāyu* functions in fivefold form under the name of *prāṇa, apāna, vyāna, udāna,* and *samāna* and this combinations of the five junctions constitute an aggregate of physical parts. Such an aggregate being similar to the aggregate of different limbs of the physical body, it cannot become the *jīva*. Some yogis who have acquired some supernatural powers by the control of breath are found to perform extraodinary feats such as standing on the water in a lake (*jala stambhana*), walking on burning coal, etc. and on the basis of this, it is believed that *prāṇa* itself is the *jīva*. But Vedānta Deśika points out that these are were delusions caused by super-natural powers. *Prāṇa* itself is not *jīvātman*, even though *jīva* is associated with *prāṇa* which is an accessory to it. In the Upaniṣad it is clearly stated that *prāṇa* along with sense organs is caused by *Paramātman* (*etasmāt jāyate prāṇo*' *manaḥ sarvendriyāṇi ca*).[8] As a created entity, it cannot be eternal, unlike *jīvātman*. We always speak as "my *prāṇa*," implying distinction between the self and *prāṇa* and not in the form "I am *prāṇa*."

Indriyas also cannot be *Jīva*

For the same reason, even *indriyas*—the sense organs, cannot be claimed to be *jīva*. There are five sense organs, each having a specific function. Either each *indriya* with specific function of the combination of all with different functions cannot constitute *jīva* proper. *Indriyas* are only the instruments of knowledge for the *jīva* but they themselves are not the knower of what is seen or heard. If *indriya* itself is the knower then with the loss of one *indriya* such as eyes, what is seen cannot be recollected or experienced by another *indriya*. The *jīva* is therefore to be admitted as different from the *indriya*.

In the same way, the five cognitive organs cannot be *jīvātman*. As regards the mind (*manas*)—the inner sense organ, it is only the instrument for recollection by *jīva* what is experienced earlier by other sense organs.

Mere *Jñāna* cannot be *Jīvātman*

Some Cārvākas maintain the theory that *jñāna* or knowledge itself is the *jīvātmā* as is evident from the experience "I know" (*jānāmi*). This experience which arises in the mind is itself *jīvātmā* and there is no need to postulate any other entity as *jīva*. Even this theory is untenable. Such a *jñāna* is either momentary in character (*kṣaṇika*), as Buddhists claim, or it is of enduring nature (*anuvṛtta*). In either case, it is not possible to account for recollection of what is seen or experienced earlier, since it cannot be the *jnātā* or knower as distinct from *jñāna* which alone can recollect or recognize what is seen earlier by mere *jñāna*. The Cārvākas do admit that during the state of deep sleep knowledge is not present, whereas during the state of consciousness, knowledge persists. It is not possible to explain the persistence of knowledge without admitting an eternal *ātmā* as the basis of knowledge. Those Cārvākas who admit that *jñāna* is itself *ātmā*, cannot claim that *jñāna* is the repository of the *saṁskāra* or impressions of earlier experiences. If, on the other hand, the heart in the central part of the body is regarded as both the *jñāna* and also the locus for all the *saṁskāras,* it amounts to the formulation of a peculiar theory. It would be more appropriate to subscribe to the theory which is sanctioned by the Sacred texts which are flawless. The theory that *jñāna* itself is *ātmā* is opposed to our experience which arises in the form that "I" (*ātmā*), as the knower, possess the knowledge. Otherwise, with the destruction of knowledge, even *ātman* is destroyed. If, with the death of the body, the *jīvātman* also ceases to exist, then on the same principle, it would follow that during *suṣupti,* according to the Cārvākas, *ātmā* ceases to exist. But it is not so, because after awakening from deep sleep, one feels happy and desires to get such a joy.

Jīvātman is an Eternal Spiritual Entity

After criticizing all the defective views of the Cārvākas regarding the *jīva,* Vedānta Deśika presents the correct and acceptable theories about *jīvātman* with the support of the *pramāṇas.* It is to be admitted that *ātman* is an eternal spiritual entity as distinct from the body. This is proved not only on the basis of the perceptual experience but also on the strength of the authoritative Scriptural texts. As Naiyāyikas explain the instinctive behaviour of a newly born infant and the possibility of recollection of the events of the past by some individuals, also support the theory of continuity of the *jīvas,* through several lives. Theories such as "*jīvātman* endures till the end of one's life (*dehāvadhi*) or till the end of the dissolution of the universe (*praḷayāvadhi*) or till the attainment of liberation from the cycle of births and deaths (*mokṣāvadhi*)" are all opposed to the Scriptural teachings.

That with the death of the body, *ātmā* also ceases to exist is the most unsound theory. This is similar to the view that during the state of *suṣputi* the *ātman* is dissolved. But this is contrary to our experience. The same *jīvātman* which experienced *suṣputi* continues to function soon after waking from sleep. This is well-established by the author of the *Vedāntasūtra* reading as "*sa eva tu karma anusmṛti śabda vidhibhyaḥ.*"[9] On the same basis, the *jīvātman* does not cease to exist with the death of the body but is reborn by assuming another body.

There are a few stray statements in the Upaniṣads which give the impression, prima facie, that *jīvātman* ceases to exist with the death of a person. Thus, in the *Taittirīya Āraṇyaka* it is stated: "who knows what exists and what does not exist in the higher transcendental realm *(paraloka)*."[10] Another text *Bṛhadāraṇyaka* says: "*na pretya saṁjña asti*—One who is dead does not possess consciousness." In the preceding statement, it is pointed out that *ātmā* which is of the nature of knowledge (*vijñānamaya*) raises from this body along with the five elements and perishes like the elements.[11] Even in our empirical usage, we only say that an individual is born and the same dies. Taking all these statements, it is contended that *jīvātman* exists as long as the body lasts and it also ends with the death of that body.

Vedānta Deśika refutes these arguments as unsustainable. If, on the basis of the Scriptural texts, one advances the theory that *ātman* is not eternal, then the same Scriptural texts teach that *ātman* is eternal (*nityo nityānām cetanaḥ cetanānāṁ*) and on the strength of these texts, it is to be admitted that *jīvātman* continues to exist passing from one body to another (*śarīra paramparā*). The *Bhagavadgītā* also reiterated the same by citing the illustration of how a person throws away the worm-cut coat and puts on another new one. It repeatedly emphasizes the eternality (*nityatva*) of *jīvātman* as against the non-permanent body. The scrupulous observance of the prescribed Vedic deeds by men of wisdom for the attainment of higher spiritual goal would be of no value if *ātman* is not eternal. The birth of *jīva* is only associated with a body and its death is separation from the body. It does not perish with the death of the body but assumes a different form by assuming another body.

Jīvātman does not become One with *Paramātman*

The view that *jīvātman* endures till the end of the *pralaya* or dissolution of the universe is also unsound. This theory advanced on the basis of a statement in the *Viṣṇupurāṇa* which states that both *prakṛti* which has manifest and unmanifest forms and also the *puruṣa (jīvātman)* are dissolved in *Paramātman* during dissolution of the universe.[12]

This theory is untenable because of the following reasons. First, it is opposed to Smṛti text which states, that both *prakṛti* and *puruṣa* are without a beginning.[13] What does not have a beginning does not have an end. Besides, the same *Gītā* text says that *jīva* is neither born nor it dies (*na jāyate na mriyate vā vipaścit*). The implication of *anāditva* is that there is a continuous series of births and deaths and for the *jīva* like, the continuous flow of the water of the river (*pravāha nityatā*). If we accept the birth and death to the *jīva*, then *Īśvara* would be subjected to the criticism of partiality and cruelty since He would be destroying the *jīvas* without any consideration to the *puṇya* and *pāpa* acquired by them. Besides, the Smṛti text says that *karma*, in the form of the results of the good and bad deeds, cannot be eradicated even in several *kalpas*, without experiencing them (*na abhuktam kṣīyate karma kalpakoṭi śatairapi*). This statement confirms the fact that *jīvātmā* endures through several *kalpas* or epochs. Further, if *jīva* ceases to exist at the end of an epoch, then the *jīva* born in the next *kalpa*, would not be able to reap benefit of the *karmas* done in the previous *kalpa*. Also, it would acquire *karma* which is not done by it (*akṛtābhyagama kṛtavipraṇāśaḥ*). In view of all these considerations, the *laya* of *jīva* and *prakṛti* in *Paramātman* in the state of *pralaya*, is to be taken in the sense that *jīva* and *prakṛti* exist in *Paramātman* in an unmanifested form, and in indistinguishable manner, similar to the water which is absorbed by the heated iron rod.

The ancient school of Vedānta expounded by Brahmadatta (which is not extant) and Bhāskara, according to which *jīvas* during the states of creation are created and during *pralaya* they are destroyed. These theories are also untenable as they are opposed to the Scriptural teachings which emphasize the eternality of *jīva*. The details of these criticisms will be considered later in the section dealing with the critical review of Vedānta schools. According to the Upaniṣads, the *jīvas* are devoid of birth or origin (*aja*) and also eternal (*nitya*). They are not subject to either creation or destruction at any period.

The theory that *jīvas* exist or endure by assuming several births until they are totally liberated from bondage (*āmokṣasthāyī*) is also unsound. According to this view, there are two kinds of *pralaya* or dissolution, viz., *nitya naimitika pralaya* and *ātyantika pralaya*. The *nitya pralaya* takes place, as described in the *Viṣṇupurāṇa*, at the end of each day of *Caturmukha* Brahmā, which is measured in terms of one thousand human *yugas*. The *naimitika pralaya* takes place at the end of the *kalpa* or epoch of Brahmā (*kalpānto*). Prākṛta *pralaya* occurs after a certain a duration of Brahmā's rule, while the *ātyantika pralaya* or total dissolution happens when *Caturmukha* Brahmā attains *mokṣa* after several *yugas*. When once total *pralaya* takes place, the *jīvātmans* are also dissolved in *Paramātman*. On basis of these details, it is maintained that *jīvas* exist until they attain *mokṣa* (*āmokṣasthāyī*) which by implication means that *jīvas* cease to exist soon after their being merged into Brahman.

This theory is also untenable because the Scriptural texts speak of the difference between Brahman and the *mukta jīvas* even in the state of *mokṣa*. The description of *mokṣa* in terms of *sāmya* or equality between Brahman and *jīvas*, *sādharmya*, or enjoying a status similar to that of *Paramātman*, do not support the view of absolute identity with Brahman. Besides, the Upaniṣads categorically state that *jīvas* enjoy the *ānanda* or glory of *Paramātman* in the state of *mukti*, In view of these, the description of *ātyantika pralaya* is to be understood in the sense that when once *jīvas* attain *mokṣa*, they are totally liberated from *karma* and that there is no possibility of the *jīvas* returning to mundane existence (*punarāvṛtti*) and that the *muktas* enjoy the blissful Brahman fully in a transcendental realm. Hence the view that dissolution of *ātman* is *mokṣa* amounts to the acceptance of the Cārvāka philosophy.

By way of concluding, Vedānta Deśika states that it is appropriate to admit the *ātma-tattva*, or the doctrine of *jīvātman* as a reality as distinct from the physical body, which is well-established by the Sacred texts and which is also evident to our experience. Once should follow the prescribed way of life for overcoming the afflictions in life and also attaining eternal happiness in a higher realm. The Cārvākas defend their philosophy on the assumption that it was taught by Prajāpati, the chief of the celestial deities in the *Chāndogya Upaniṣad* and also by Bṛhaspati, the preceptor of the celestial deities (*devaguru*). But these teachings were intended to delude the demons (*asuras*). The reference to statements made by sage Jābāli, at the assembly of Lord Rāma in the *Rāmāyaṇa,* were not intended to support the theory of Cārvākas, as is clarified by Lord Rāma himself. The presence of some Lokāyatikas in the *yāga* performed by sage Kaṇva mentioned in the *Mahābhārata,* along with other sages, do not imply that they were the followers of the Cārvāka philosophy but, on the contrary, those were the persons well-qualified to refute the arguments of the Cārvākas. Hence it cannot be claimed that Cārvāka philosophy has the support of the Vedas and also of the orthodox Vedic scholars. The Cārvāka philosophy, teaching sensual pleasure as the goal of life, which may appeal as proper knowledge to foolish people, is not acceptable to men of wisdom.

References

1. See *PMB*, chap. 6.
2. See *Ch. Up.*, VIII.8.7.
3. *Rāmāyaṇa,* Ayodhyākāṇḍa.
4. *Mahābhārata,* Ādiparva: *nānāśāstrārtha mukhyaiśca suśrāva svanamiritam; lokāyatika mukhyaiśca samantād abhinaditam.*
5. See *BG,* IV.13: *cāturvarṇyam mayā sṛṣṭam guṇa karma vibhāgaśaḥ; tasya kartārampi māṁ viddhi....*
6. See *Sarvārthasiddhi* on *TMK,* II.1. See also Yāmuna's *Ātmasiddhi,* p. 8.
7. For details of the dialectic, see *TMK,* I.32. Also *FVV,* chap.1, p. 54.
8. See *Muṇḍ. Up.*, II.1.3.
9. *VS,* III.2.9.
10. *Tait. Āra.*, VI.1: *ko hy tad veda yadyamuṣmin loke asti vā na vā.*
11. *Br. Up.*, II.4.2: *Vijñāna-ghana eva etebhyo-bhūtebhyaḥ samutthāya tānyeva anuvinaśyati.*
12. *V.P.: Prakṛtirya mayā ākhyātā vyaktā-vyaktarūpiṇī; puruṣaścāpyubhau etau līyete Paramātmani.*
13. *BG: prakṛtim puruṣam caiva viddhi anādi ubhau api.*

5
Buddhism

After the refutation of Cārvāka, Vedānta Deśika takes up Buddhism for critical examination which is the second important non-Vedic school of thought. Even chronologically it appears to have come into existence later than Cārvāka since there are critical references to Cārvāka teachings in the Buddhist treatises. According to Vedānta Deśika, the justification for taking up Buddhism soon after Cārvāka is that, unlike Cārvāka, it admits *vijñāna* in the form of metal ideas. It also advocates a religion of its own and believes in the concept of the attainment of a higher goal in the name of *nirvāṇa* by the pursuit of a rigorous ethical and religious discipline. Though Buddhism does not accept the Vedas, it owes its authority to the teachings of the Buddha who is regarded as *sarvajña* or the omniscient Being.

Buddhism, as a religion, which is acknowledged as one of the world religions, does not come up for criticism. Vedānta Deśika, like all other critics hailing from orthodox schools, confines his attention to the criticism of the important philosophical and epistemological doctrines of Buddhism which are considered to be untenable, apart from their being totally opposed to the Upaniṣadic teachings.

Buddhism, as a system of philosophy, is also not uniformly the same. In the course of its development during a long period spreading through several centuries since the advent of Buddha, it has undergone several modifications, giving rise to different schools of thought, each one presenting distinctive doctrines. Four major of thought are generally acknowledged as important. These are named as Vaibhāṣika, Sautrāntika, Yogācāra, and Mādhyamika.[1]

The Vaibhāṣika and Sautrāntika admit to the existence of external objects. The Yogācāra denies the existence of external objects. The Mādhyamika, on the contrary, maintains that both internal ideas and external objects are *śūnya* or void in the sense that they are of indeterminable character. All the schools except Mādhyamika maintain that everything in the universe is of momentary nature (*kṣaṇika*), that it does not exist for more than an instant.

These teachings, though conflicting, are considered to have been based on the sayings of the Buddha, who is omniscient and hence are regarded as authoritative. According to the Buddhist tradition, Buddha taught the following four principles: (1) *Sarvam kṣaṇikam kṣaṇikam*; (2) *duḥkham duḥkkam*; (3) *svalakṣaṇam svalakṣaṇam;* and (4) *śūnyam śūnyam.*[2] According to Vedānta Deśika, Buddha advocated the following four doctrines: (1) *kṣaṇa-bhaṅgaḥ*, that is, everything in the universe is momentary in nature; (2) *pratyakṣārtha-bhaṅgaḥ*, that is, the objects of perception do not actually exist; (3) *bāhyārtha-bhaṅgaḥ*, that is, the external objects do not exist apart from knowledge; and (4) *dharma-dharmi-bhāva-bhaṅgaḥ*, that is, apart from attributes (*dharmas*), there is no separate substance (*dharmī*) as such. On the basis of these basic teachings, the four schools have developed their main doctrines. As will be seen later, the first one is accepted by all except Mādhyamika. The second theory is developed by Sautrantika for whom external objects are inferred. The third one is embraced by Yogācāra for whom external objects are the projections of internal ideas. The fourth one is accepted both by Vaibhāṣika and Sautrāntika for whom *svalakṣaṇa* or the bare unrelated being seen in the initial stage of perception is real, whereas what is perceived later as qualified (*savikalpaka*) is false.

Vedānta Deśika confines his attention to the critical examination of these doctrines. He deals with each school separately. As explained in the introduction to the *Mādhyamika-bhaṅgādhikāra*, Mādhyamika is accorded highest priority because it advocates *śūnyavāda* or that everything in the universe is void which amounts to non-existence and marks the climax of Buddha's teachings (*sugatamata-kāṣṭha*). He is regarded as worse than Cārvāka since he does neither accept even *pratyakṣa* as a *pramāṇa* nor the existence of external objects. The Yogācāra makes a concession to this extreme view of Mādhyamika by admitting the existence of *vijñāna* in the form of series of ideas. The Sautrāntika goes a step further and concedes both thoughts and external objects though the latter is to be inferred on the basis of the cognition of the objects. The Vaibhāṣika is far more accommodative since he admits both internal knowledge and the existence of external objects. But all the schools of Buddhism except Mādhyamika uphold the theory that all things in the universe are of momentary character (*kṣaṇika*).

1. Mādhyamika School of Buddhism

Mādhyamika is first taken up for examination. Its central philosophy is summed up in the following verse which is quoted by Vedānta Deśika:

na san-nāsan-nasad-asan-nācā'py-anubhayātmikam
catuṣkoṭi-vinirmuktaṁ tattvaṁ mādhyamikaṁ viduḥ;
buddhyā vivicyamānānāṁ svabhāvo nāvadhāryate
ato nirabhilapyas-te nis-svabhāvaśca darśitaḥ.

It neither 'is' nor 'is not' 'both is and is not' nor 'neither is nor is not.' It is outside the four alternatives that are regarded *tattvaṁ* by the Mādhyamikas.

Even by closer examination, the nature of the object cannot be determined. Hence the nature of the objects is indescribable and is found to be void.

In other words, excludes all conceivable predicates including that of non-existence and the ultimate is accordingly to be viewed as beyond all conception. It is therefore indeterminable.

If this be the main thesis of the Mādhyamika, then the experience we get in the form "I know this" which involves three factors, viz., the knower (*ahaṁ*), the object known (*jñeya*), and the process of knowing (*jñāna*) cannot be explained in any manner. That is, the nature of the objects in the universe is indeterminable, then there would be no difference between the waking experience and the dream experience. They would become almost non-existent (*tuccha*) similar to the sky-flower.

If this be acceptable, our endeavours for attaining higher spiritual goals as heaven, *mokṣa,* etc. would be of no value. All human endeavours for achieving other human goals would be futile. According to such a philosophy, *mokṣa* would amount to the realizaton of mere voidness (*śūnyatāpatti*) in respect of all our experiences.

After making general criticisms against the Mādhyamikas, Vedānta Deśika criticizes their views in greater detail. The first and foremost criticism of this school is that their teachings do not have the support of the valid *pramāṇas.* The claim that these theories are the outcomes of the teachings of the omniscient Buddha, is questionable because one who is omniscient cannot present conflicting theories. There are no well-defined criteria to determine that among the conflicting theories, which one is the correct and final one.

It is wrong to maintain that *tattva* or what is regarded as reality or an object has a real existence outside the four possible logical alternatives, viz., *na sat, na asat, na sadasat, na tadubhayātmikaṁ.* An object can be defined in all four ways from different standpoints. Thus, for instance, a pot exists in a particular place but the same does not exist in another place. It can be regarded as both existence and non- existence and also different from being both existence and non-existence from different stand points. All these facts are evident to our experience. If we say that an object exists and does not exist in the same place and at the same time, it involves a self-contradiction. If, on the contrary, we conceive that an object exists and also does not exist at the same time in different forms, it would amount to the admission of the Anekānta-vāda or manifold nature of the object, advocated by the Jainas. Hence the contention of the Mādhyamikas that an object is indescribable in any manner is untenable.

The Mādhyamikas adopt a different argument to prove the non-existence (*abhāva*) of an object. Every object, prior to its production, does not exist. This is regarded as its prior non-existence (*prāgbhāva*). It does not also exist after it is destroyed. This is known as its posterior non-existence (*pradhvaṁsābhāva*). What does not exist earlier and later, cannot be considered to exist between there two states.

This argument is logically untenable. The prior non-existence of an object ceases to exist as soon as the object is produced. If the concept of non-existence itself is not acceptable on the ground that it is indeterminable (*nirupākhya*), then even the causal factors which produce the object would have to be treated as indeterminable. Again, if an object comes into existence, it would also have an end or destruction (*vināśa*). If an object, whose nature is indeterminable (*nirupākhya*) according to the Mādhyamika, does not have either an origin or destruction, it would become eternal. But it is not so. Hence both *prāgbhāva* and *pradhvaṁsabhāva* are to be admitted as positive concepts in the sense of two different states of an object.

In view of this explanation, *abhāva,* as a logical concept, is not indeterminable or mere non-existence as Mādhyamika says. It only means non-existence of an object. An object has both prior non-existence (*prāgbhāva*) before it is caused and *pradhvaṁsābhāva* after it is destroyed, because that which is produced is also subject to destruction, resulting in its *pradhvaṁsābhāva.*

Hence what comes between *prāgbhāva* and *pradhvaṁsābhāva* does exist during the period of its existence (*svakāla-sattva*).

In this connection, Vedānta Deśika clarifies the logical concept of *abhāva* and *bhāva.* According to Viśiṣṭādvaita, both *bhāva* and *abhāva* are positive concepts representing different states of a substance. According to Nyāya-Vaiśeṣika, these are different logical categories. It is not therefore correct to say that *abhāva* is *nirupākhya* or *nis-svabhāva* (indeterminable).

An object, prior to its production, is *asat* or non-existent, and in that state it is *nis-svabhāva.* After its production, it is regarded as possessing *sattā* or existence, that is to say, it assumes a new character. It is asked: what is the nature of the new character assumed by the *asat*? The non-existence (*abhāva*) of an object which we speak of on the basis of *pramāṇa* is not *nis-svabhāva* or devoid of any intrinsic nature as the Mādhyamika assumes. This *abhāva* is also not the *svarūpa* of the object which becomes manifest after its production. If it is different from the object that is produced, then it is asked what is its nature? This question, Vedānta Deśika argues, is irrelevant because it arises only if it is established that *abhāva*, in some form or the other, exists prior to *kārya*. All that can be said is that prior to the origin of the object, the object we see with its nature did not exist prior to its production. It is therefore not relevant to ask what the nature of the *abhāva* was, prior to its production. This is explained by an illustration. After knowing Devadatta, a person with his characteristics, one can ask where he exists or lives. This question is relevant only when one has known Devadatta, but not in the absence of any knowledge about him. Similarly, if we have the knowledge of the pot in the state prior to its production, then it is possible to ask what the nature of its non-existence was.

There are a few other arguments which are of dialectical nature advanced by Vedānta Deśika to refute the theory of Mādhyamika in defence of non-existence. The main point of criticism is that it is impossible to conceive absolute non-existence. The terms such as *śūnya, tuccha*, etc. which appear to mean total negation (*sarva-śūnya*) do not imply non-existence. Negation (*niṣedha*) necessarily presupposes its counter-correlate. It does not imply total non-existence at any time or at any place. When we say that an object does not exist, it only means that it exists at some other place or at some other time, but not that it is totally non-existent like the sky-flower. Absolute non-existence (*sarvathā-śūnyatva*) is logically untenable. As stated by Vedānta Deśika in the *Adhikaraṇa-sārāvalī*, it is purely a speculative theory without having any support of the *pramāṇas* (*amānataḥ, sveṣṭā-vāda*). Bādarāyāṇa also points out in the *Vedāntasūtra* that the doctrine of Mādhyamika is totally untenable (*sarvathā anupapatteśca*).[3]

2. Yogācāra School of Buddhism

Unlike the Mādhyamika, who denies the existence of everything, Yoḡacāra admits, as if it is an improvement to the Mādhyamika Buddhist philosophy, the existence of *vijñāna* in the form of a series of mental ideas. His doctrine is therefore titled *vijñāna-vāda*. He also admits, unlike the Cārvāka, a concept of causality (*kārya-kāraṇabhāva*). The central theory of Yogācāra is summed up in the following verse quoted by Vedānta Deśika:

> *avibhāgo hi buddyātmā viparyāsita darśanaiḥ,*
> *grāhya grāhaka samvitti bhedavāniva lakṣyate.*
> Knowledge is of one form without any distinction between knowledge and its object. The distinction between the object of experience (*grāhya*) and the knower who cognizes it (*grāhaka*) is all due to illusion.

In support of this view, the following argument is advanced: "*sahopalambha niyamāt abhedo nīlataddhiyoḥ*—There is no distinction between the cognition and the object cognized because there is an invariable connection between the two."

According to the Yogācāra, there is no external object from knowledge. The variegated experience of the object takes place due to the influence of the *vāsanās* or innate mental ideas which are variegated. There is no need for the objects to qualify the knowledge as of a different nature. The series of cognitions themselves are influenced by the *saṁskāras* caused by earlier cognitions from as beginningless time.

This theory comes up for a severe criticism from all the realistic schools of thought which admit knowledge as distinct from the external objects. It is opposed to our perceptual experience. It cannot also be established by *anumāna* or logical arguments.

Vedānta Deśika points out that the Yogācāra cannot uphold the theory of causal relation, that is, the proper relation of cause to effect. According to Yogācāra, all things are of momentary nature (*kṣaṇika*). That is, an object exists only for a moment and in the next moment, it ceases to exist in the same form. What exists for a moment cannot serve as the cause of what is produced in the next moment. Besides, what is considered to be real is only the bare being, technically termed as *svalakṣaṇa* and not that which is qualified with attributes. If everything is of momentary existence and what is considered as an effect is a bare being (*svalakṣaṇa*) then there cannot be a relation between the two since they are of different nature. If any two entities can have a causal relation, then it would amount to saying that the presence of a donkey is related to smoke on the hill. All earlier moments would be the cause of all later moments. It is not possible to adopt an inferential argument since there is no relation between the entities to formulate a logical concomitance between one entity and another, as in the case of smoke on the hill with the fire. Even in respect of a series of ideas as one continuous process, there is no determining factor to establish a correlation between the earlier event and the later one, without the admission of a permanent self as the cognizer (*jñātā*). The illustration of the white cotton which is coloured with redness cited in support of the view that at the same time *saṁskāra* becomes qualified, does not serve the purpose, since there is nothing which endures for more than a moment.

The theory of Yogācāra that other than *jñāna*, nothing else exists, is untenable because *jñāna* as a continuous series of ideas is only momentary and it is not everlasting or *nitya* as Advaitin maintains. What is momentary implies that either in its earlier state (moment) or in its later state (moment), it does not exist in the same form. Following the logic of Mādhyamika, what is non-existent prior to it and also non-existent subsequent to it, also becomes non-existent. Yogācāra does not also accept that *jñāna* is qualified with some attributes. Whatever is qualified (*savikalpa*) is of the nature of illusion. According to Yogācāra, only *svalakṣaṇa* or bare being without any characteristics is true knowledge.

The theory that the external object other than knowledge does not really exist, is also wrong. Though knowledge may be self-revealing, it needs some other means or another knowledge to reveal its nature as momentary (*kṣaṇika*). To say that knowledge itself is the external object involves self-contradiction. If another series of knowledge (*jñāna-santati*) can reveal that the knowledge of the present series is momentary and that it is part of the previous momentary *jñāna* and also that of the subsequent moment, then the individual should be aware that it is a separate series and also truly exists. It is not known then even the difference drawn between the teacher and the taught and also between the exponent of the theory and its opponent cannot be explained. If this be not possible, then the Yogācāra, like Mādhyamika, cannot prove his own theory.

The central theory of Yogācāra is that there is no difference between knowledge (*jñāna*) and the external object (*grāhya*).

This is the most unsound theory because it is generally accepted by all schools, as is also evident to our experience that the knowledge of an object which arises in the form "I know this" (*idam aham jānāmi*) involves three factors; the knower denoted by *ahaṁ* the object denoted by *idaṁ*, and the process of knowing denoted by *jānāmi*. If this is not admitted, the statement of the Yogācāra "*grāhya grāhaka saṁvitti bhedavān-iva lakṣyate,*" which means that it appears that there is difference between *grāhya* or the object, the knower (*grāhaka*), and the knowledge (*saṁvit*), does not stand. It presupposes all the three factors. When an object can exist independent of knowledge and knowledge also exists as an attribute of the knower, it follows that *jñāna* is related to an object on one side and the subject on the other. Hence it is wrong to deny both the object and the subject who knows it. If this theory, which is accepted by all, is rejected, then even the existence of *jñāna* as the only reality, stands refuted by applying the Mādhyamika logic.

It is argued in defence of the Yogācāra theory denying the external objects, that even Vedāntins do not accept the theory of Nyāya-Vaiśeṣika, according to which, *avayavī* or the conglomeration of *avayavas* or parts is not real on the ground that *paramāṇus* which are infinitesimal partless supra-reals and also non-perceptible, cannot combine together since they are partless. Vedāntins should not therefore object to the theory of the Yogācāra denying the existence of external objects. Vedānta Deśika controverts the argument by explaining that according to Viśiṣṭādvaita, *paramāṇus* are the smallest particles and they are perceptible. The combination of these particles constitute a gross object and this is established by cognition.

The *jīvātman*, which is either monadic in size, as Viśiṣṭādvaitins maintain or all-pervasive as Naiyāyikas hold, manifests itself as "I" (*ahaṁ*) and hence it is undeniable. If *ātman* is admitted as a real entity, the object experienced by it is also real.

It cannot be said that *jñāna* or knowledge and *jñeya* or the external object are identical because the two are cognized together (*sahopalambha*). This view conflicts with one's own stand. Besides, all our activities are initiated after we see object as different from *jñāna*. If *jñāna* and *jñeya* are regarded as identical, then it would not be possible to make any distinction between the right cognition and the wrong cognition. Then one has to take resort to either *śūnyavāda* which admits that knowledge and the objects seen do not really exist, or to Jaina's *saptabhaṅgī* according to which an object exists and also does not exist at the same time.

On the analogy of objects seen in the dream state, it is not possible to deny the existence of objects in the waking state, because it is opposed to our common experience. We always experience that object is different from *jñāna.* What does not exist cannot be comprehended. Even in the case of dream objects, they exist in the state of dream according to the Viśiṣṭādvaitin, as these are created by *Īśvara* to be experienced by a *jīva.* Even if objects do not exist in the dream state, they do exist in some other place and at some other time and they are not therefore totally non-existent.

It cannot also be argued that the object exists without any specific intrinsic character (*nis-svabhāva*) because the same is experienced differently by different individuals as in the example of a beautiful damsel seen by an ascetic, a lover, and a dog. Then, even the very *jñāna* which is admitted as really existing would have to be treated as non-existent (*nis-svabhāva*) because it is also regarded by others in different ways such as *satya, tuccha, jaḍa, svayaṁprakāśa, kṣaṇika,* and *nitya.* An object assumes different characters in terms of *liṅga* or gender, number, dimension (*parimāṇa*), etc. because of the limiting or conditioning factors (*sopādhika*). If this is not admitted, it is not possible to regard the same *jñāna* as prior or posterior, as *kārya* and *kāraṇa,* as *nīlākāra* (blue) and *pītākāra* (yellow). Such a position leads to the Mādhyamika theory of *śūnya.*

The Yogācāra, who does not accept the existence of the external objects, attempts, to explain the nature of character of knowledge in the form of a series of ideas on the basis of the influence of the variegated *vāsanās* or the innate tendencies inherent in the previous series of ideas and not with reference to the nature of the external objects. Even the explanation is not logically sustainable. *Vijñāna,* for the Buddhists, is *kṣaṇika,* that is, it changes every moment. In the series of cognitions, when the earlier cognition ceases to exists, the *vāsanā*associated with it is also erased and as such it cannot influence the next momentary cognition. If the series of cognitions is admitted as one continuous cognition, it may be possible to account for the continuation of *vāsanā* and its influence on cognition. Alternatively, the reality of the external objects has to be admitted to account for diversity of experience. Neither is accepted by the Vijñānavādin and his theory of *vijñāna* is therefore untenable.

Bādarāyaṇa sums up the criticisms against the Yogācāra doctrine in the following three *sūtras*:

1. *Na abhāva upalabdheḥ.*[4] It cannot be said that external objects do not exist, because these are cognized by the individual self through the process of knowing.
2. *Vaidharmyācca na svapnādivat.*[5] On the basis of the objects perceived in the dream, it cannot be said that objects do not exist, because there is difference between the dream experience and waking state.
3. *Na bhāvo anupalabdheḥ.*[6] Knowledge as devoid of content is not proved to exist. That is, all knowledge is related to an object and also to a subject.

Thus, it is concluded by Vedānta Deśika, that the doctrine of Yogācāra upholding only *jñāna* as real and that the external object is illusory, is not sustainable.

3. Sautrāntika School of Buddhism

As compared to the Yogācāra who denies the existence of external objects, Sautrāntika goes a step further by admitting the existence of external objects in addition to *jñāna* or knowledge. But the object is not directly perceived but it is to be inferred on the basis of the knowledge having the content in the form of an object. This is a peculiar epistemological theory developed by Sautrāntika and it is subjected to severe criticism. The criticism is mainly directed to prove that the arguments adopted by the Sautrāntika regarding the existence of an external object though it is not directly perceived, are untenable.

The external object admitted by Sautrāntika is not regarded as the *avayavī* or the combination of several parts, as Naiyāyikas believe. What is conceived as *avayavasaṅgātha* or combination of *avayavas* is treated by him as non-existent (*avastu*). The *avayava* is the combination of the *paramāṇus* or subtle particles which are devoid of parts (*niraṁśa*). If *paramāṇus* conceived by him are partless, its combination to form an aggregate whole is also rejected. The idea of the *paramāṇus* becoming a conglomeration is therefore a mere delusion. On further analysis of the *paramāṇus*, it turns out to be a non-existent entity. Only if *paramāṇus* come together, it is possible to speak of the smallest dimension, biggest dimension, and dimension of middle size (*madhyama parimāṇa*). *Paramāṇus* do not possess the dharma of *paramāṇutva.* Hence the combination of *paramāṇus* in any form is not possible. Even *ākāśa* which is all-pervasive is not accepted by Sautrāntika. It is another name for spatial absence (*āvaraṇābhāvaḥ*). It amounts to saying that it does not exist as a separate entity. If these are the views held by Sautrāntika, even the external object which does not exist for him, cannot be inferred. Unless the external object is seen, its inference on the basis of having seen the object by perception cannot be proved. Either it is to be admitted as Vaibhāṣika says, that the collection of *paramāṇus* (*paramāṇus-puñjaka*) is perceptible or as the realists say that objects are always directly perceived by knowledge. There is no other way of proving its existence only on the basis of inference. It cannot be said that objects experienced in the long past or objects to be experienced in the long future leave their impression on the mind by means of which objects of the present are inferred. Just as we infer objects seen in the past by memory, it is not possible to explain on the basis of the inference that an object of the present also exists. There is not one instance which can be cited in support of the view that the existence of an object is inferred.

The denial of *ākāśa* or ethereal space as a real entity, which is so obvious to our perceptual experience, is the most unsound theory. It should be possible for the Sautrāntika to accept it on the basis of inference in the same way as the existence of an external object is admitted on the basis of inference. Instead, it is totally wrong to negate it as a non-entity (*tuccha*). If an entity which is cognizable is regarded as *tuccha,* then even the external objects would have to be treated as *tuccha* or non-existent by adopting the Mādhyamika logic. If *ākāśa* is regarded as *āvaraṇabhāva*, that is, absence of spatial relation, then it is not even possible to include it in the three types of *abhāva* accepted by Naiyāyikas and others such as *prāgbhāva* (prior non-existence), *pradhvaṁsābhāva* (posterior non-existence), and *anyonyābhāva* (mutual non-existence or difference) since all these concepts presuppose the existence of an object.

In the absence of *ākāśa* as a real entity, Sautrāntika cannot speak of either its prior existence or posterior existence. Even the concept of mid-space with reference to which we speak of an object being nearer or farther, is inconceivable. All these criticisms are implied in the *Vedāntasutra* reading as: "*ākāśe ca aviśeṣāt.*"[7] It means that it is not correct to say that *ākāśa* does not exist (*tucchata*) because it is perceptible as in the case of other objects (*aviśeṣāt*).

It is generally believed that the differences existing in the external objects cause the differences in respect of their knowledge. But the Sautrāntika explains the variegated nature of knowledge (*jñāna-vaicitrya*) on the basis of the variations in the nature of the objects (*artha-vaicitrya*). This view is untenable because the invariable concomitance (*vyāpti*) between object and knowledge cannot be established by the Sautrāntika since the two—object and knowledge—are not present at the same time in any given moment. The object is momentary and so also the knowledge which cognizes. it. The knowledge which has grasped a particular object ceases to exist in the next moment. Similarly, the object which is cognized by a knowledge at a particular moment, also ceases to exist. Unless it is proved that there is an invariable concomitance between knowledge and object, it is not possible to say that knowledge cognizes objects and thus it becomes variegated depending on the differences of the objects. If the nature of knowledge itself is conceived as variegated and on that basis it is inferred that objects are different, then there would be a need for another knowledge to comprehend that particular knowledge which is variegated. To escape all these difficulties, the Sautrāntika has to admit, as in the case of Yogācāra, that *jñāna* in the form of a series of mental ideas itself is variegated due to the influence of previous *vāsanās* or innate tendencies and each series of *jñāna* influences the next series. This would amount to the admission of the Yogācāra theory according to which external objects as such do not exist, and that *jñāna* itself projects as objects. This would defeat the stand adopted by Sautrāntika that external objects which are inferred on the basis of knowledge exist. Then there would be no difference between the dream experienced in which objects do not really exist and waking experience in which objects though exist, are to be denied, Such a theory is most unsound epistemologically, since there is difference between the waking state and the dream state as stated in the *Vedāntasūtra* (*vaidharmyācca na svapnādivat*).[8]

The Sautrāntika defends his theory that external objects exist, though it is to be inferred, by stating that an object, when cognized, transfers its *ākāra* or form to the knowledge and on the basis of such a knowledge which is characterized by the object, the object is inferred (*jñānakāra-arpaṇam*). Even this explanation is untenable, contends Vedānta Deśika. The external object does not possess a separate characteristic other than its *svarūpa,* to be transferred to knowledge. Even if it is admitted that it has a characteristic, how does it move out of the object in which it inheres? The *svarūpa* of the being momentary, does not persist for another moment for transferring it to the knowledge.

Both knowledge and object are without qualities (*nirdharmaka*), according to Sautrāntika. How can the *ākāra* of the object be transferred to the knowledge? It may be said that the *ākāra* of the object is reflected in the knowledge which is pure (*svaccha*). Even this explanation does not hold good since, according to the accepted theory of reflection of one object in another, it is necessary that the two should exist at the same time (*samānakāla*) and the entity in which it is reflected, as in the case of a mirror, should be tainted for the reflection to take place (*rūpavattva*). The reflection cannot be explained on the analogy of the heated red iron piece or the heap of black gram in which black colour is mixed, because such a combination of internal knowledge with the external object is not conceivable. It cannot also be explained on the basis of the illustration of a red colour being generated by the combination of white lime with yellow turmeric powder, because according to the Sautrāntika, what is earlier and what is later cannot come together (*saṁsarga*) since each has a momentary existence. In order to offer a satisfactory explanation of *ākāra samarpaṇa*, one has to admit that an external object with its form is perceptible or that the series of knowledge are influenced by the *vāsanās*. Hence the doctrine of Sautrāntika that external objects are inferred, though they do not really exist, cannot be proved.

The author of the *Vedāntasūtra* has summed up the criticism in the following *sūtra*: "*nā-sato adṛṣṭavāt.*"[9] It means: "When the object does not exist, the transfer of its *dharma* (*ākāra*) cannot take place since such a possibility is not perceived anywhere."

4. Vaibhāṣika School of Buddhism

In order to overcome the defects pointed out in the theories advanced by the schools of Mādhyamika, Yogācāra, and Sautrāntika, this school admits both *jñāna* and external objects which are perceptible. But both these are momentary in character. It does not accept *jñātā* or knower as a separate entity. Even this modified doctrine is considered defective and it is therefore open for criticism.

Like the Naiyāyikas, the Vaibhāṣikas also admit *paramāṇus* which are partless, imperceptible, and infinitesimal reals. All the entities, both the external objects and the internal sense organs including mind and body, are the conglomeration of these *paramāṇus*. Though the *paramāṇus* are not perceptible, the combination of these *paramāṇus,* technically named as *puñja*, can become the object of perception. The question is asked: How do these *paramāṇus* which are momentary in character, combine themselves into an aggregate entity? The Vaibhāṣika does not admit any causal factors of enduring nature which can bring them together. There is also no valid *pramāṇa* to prove the existence of the aggregates of *paramāṇus.* According to Vaibhāṣika, the *nirvikalpaka pratyakṣa* which is the first stage of perception reveals the indeterminate and momentary character of the *paramāṇus* and these *paramāṇus* established in *nirvikalpaka* become the object of perception (*savikalpaka*) as aggregates. This view is questioned by Vedānta Deśika. What is claimed to be seen in *nirvikalpaka* cannot itself serve a *pramāṇa* for what is seen in the *savikalpaka* perception. But what is revealed in the stage of *savikalpaka* does not also exist as an enduring entity and hence it cannot be treated as real.

The Vaibhāṣika also does not admit that *vikalpa* or what is seen in the stage of *savikalpaka pratyakṣa* is valid. If this is the case, even *nirvikalpaka* perception cannot be regarded as a valid *pramāṇa*. On the basis of inference, it is not possible to establish that all *savikalpaka pratyakṣa* is invalid, since the inference adopted for this purpose suffers from logical fallacy. If the knowledge derived from *savikalpaka pratyakṣa* is invalid, then what is taught in the Buddhist treatises which are also of the nature of *vikalpa-jñāna*, would also become invalid. As in the case of Mādhyamika, Vaibhāṣika also does not believe in any valid *pramāṇa* to prove his doctrines. In the absence of *pramāṇas*, there would be no distinction between the true theory and the false theory. Even if the knowledge of the aggregate is regarded as false and what appears as aggregate is due to the influence of the *vāsanās*, the external object which is admitted to exist, cannot be considered as perceivable.

The relation of *jñāna* to *jñeya* or the object of perception cannot also be established unless it is admitted that the object really exists. If both *jñāna* and *jñeya* do not exist at the same time and endure for more than a moment, there cannot be any relation between the two. The *jñāna* which cognizes the object at a particular moment ceases to exist. The Vaibhāṣika argues that the previous momentary *jñāna* which cognizes the object, transfers the *ākāra* of the object to the next momentary *jñāna*. The next momentary *jñāna* grasps what is cognized by an earlier *jñāna*. But this explanation is against the generally accepted theory that *jñāna* only cognizes what is actually present at the time of cognition.

The Vaibhāṣika along with the Yogācāra and Sautrāntika, upholds the theory that all entities are of momentary character (*kṣaṇika*). This view is opposed to the theory of *pratyabhijñā* or recognition of an object which is the same as seen earlier.

The Buddhists adopt the following syllogistic arguments in support of the momentary character of an object. "Whatever exists, that is momentary; just as a series of water particles (*jalandhara*) or the continuous flow of the flame of the lamp. In the instance of the flame, we get the idea that it is the same flame that endures, though each moment the flame changes depending on the supply of oil and burning of the wick. In the same way, it should be possible to say that the series of *jñāna*, though being momentary is one. So also in respect of the objects, which are constantly changing, we get the illusion of it being the same one object. This arguments is untenable because in the case of the flame it is obvious to our experience that it cannot be one and the same since we know that the constant supply of oil causes the burning of the flame continuosly. If all things are momentary and since there is no cognizer to recognize that there is similarity between the earlier event and the latter, there is no scope to say that it is the case of *pratyabhijñā* or recognition of the earlier and the latter as the same. Similarly, the individual who has earned *puṇya* and *pāpa* cannot be the recipient of the effect of the good or bad deeds. It would then lead to the position that someone else reaps the effects of *puṇya* and *pāpa*.

It may be said that whatever is done in one series of acts, the fruit of it also becomes applicable to the same series, as in the case of the red colour present in the seed appearing in the cotton grown out of it (*kārpāse raktatā yathā*). But this argument with the illustration cited does not hold good. What is true in the case of objects which endure for some time does not hold good for things which are constantly changing. Things which are totally destructible without any residue cannot have continuous endurance.

The Buddhists believe in the theory of *niranvaya-vināśa* or the total destruction without any residue. In support of this, they cite the example of the flame of the lamp, which when extinguished, does not leave any residue. But this kind of destruction does not apply to objects such as pot. A pot when destroyed does not totally disappear. It exists in some other form as broken pieces of pot. This is called *sānvaya-vināśa*, as contrasted to *niranvaya-vināśa*. On the basis of this, it is more appropriate to accept *sānvaya-vināśa* even in respect of the flame of a lamp. When the flame gradually diminishes and is extinguished, the rays radiating from it spread widely and they gradually become invisible.

The following syllogistic argument is advanced in support of this theory. Destruction does not need a cause because it inevitably takes place (*dhvaṁsaḥ hetu-nirapekṣaḥ; dhruva bhāvitvāt*).

This syllogism, according to Vedānta Deśika, suffers from logical fallacies. The *hetu* "*dhruva bhāvitvāt,*" when subjected to logical analysis, is found to be faulty.[10] The *sādhya* or *probandum* (*hetu-nirapekṣa*) is not admitted by the critic. It should be acceptable to both the disputants but Viśiṣṭādvaitin does not admit *niranvaya-vināśa.* For him, the objects, even after destruction, continue to exist in some other form. As already pointed out, even in the case of the disappearance of the lamp-flame, the subtle elements of light dwindle and spread themselves all over and become invisible. Even if it is considered that in this one instance there is total destruction, it is not possible to assert on the basis of this one example that all physical objects undergo similar destruction, as it is not warranted by our experience.

In order to escape all the criticisms against momentariness (*sarva-kṣaṇikavāda*), a small section of the Vaibhāṣikas, as stated by Vedānta Deśika, holds the theory that there is one *tattva* which is real. In support of it, he quotes the following statement mentioned in Pāli language, which is claimed to have been taught by the Buddha himself: "*atyihi bhikko akadayaṁ, jahaṇatthi edassya jantuṇo sattam; māṇasa suṇṇāvatthā ṇaṁ saṁpajjayi.*" It means: "It is acceptable to the mendicant Buddha that it is desirable to accept one real entity; otherwise if an entity perishes every moment, there would be liberation for *ātman* every moment."

The source of this quotation cited by Vedānta Deśika is not given. It is claimed to have been said by some disciples of Buddha as taught to them. Whatever may be the credibility of this view, it would not conform to the main teachings of Buddhism. If this is admitted, then the central doctrines of Buddhism such as everything is *kṣaṇika* and *vikalpa* or what is cognized in the *savikalpaka-pratyakṣa* is false, etc. cannot be defended. Even if it is accepted as a possible view held by the Buddha, it is not possible on the basis of it, to defend the *kṣaṇikavāda.*

The following syllogistic argument is adopted to prove it. "The things in the universe are momentary because they exist for a moment, as for example the absolute instant (*kṣaṇa*). (*idam vigītam jagad kṣaṇikam, meyatvāt* or *sattvāt, kṣaṇopādhivat*).

The syllogism suffers from logical fallacies.[11] What is sought to be proved stands negated by perceptual experience. The absolute instant (*kṣaṇa*) which is cited as an illustration, is non-existent. It is not accepted as strictly momentary by the Viśiṣṭādvaitin. The word *kṣaṇa* means for Viśiṣṭādvaitin, the conglomeration of various causal factors which have been operative in producing the effect (*kārya-śūnya sāmagrīkṣaṇaḥ*). Thus the word *kṣaṇa* is applicable even to what is permanent. It is not therefore possible to prove by any means that everything is momentary. Vedānta Deśika therefore concludes that it is necessary to admit that all entities are essentially of permanent character (*svarūpataḥ nitya*) and that only the modifications they assume are of varying nature.

References

1. These four schools are divided into two classes as Hīnāyāna who are realistic and Mahāyāna who are idealistic. *Vibhāṣa* is the commentary on the Abhidhamma books and those who accept it as authority are called Vaibhāṣikas. The Sautrāntikas are those who believe that Buddha taught Abhidhamma doctrines only in certain *sūtras* and recognized the authority of these *sūtras*. Yogācāra is so designated since the followers of this school practiced yoga as part of the religious discipline. The Mādhyamikas are those who are stated to have followed the middle course (*madhyama-mārga*).
2. *PMB*. See commentary on *Mādhyamika-bhaṅgādhikāra*,p.87.
3. *VS*, II.2.30.
4. Ibid., II.2.27.
5. Ibid., II.2.28.
6. Ibid., II.2.29.
7. Ibid., II.2.23.
8. Ibid., II.2.28.
9. Ibid., II.2.25.
10. See *TMK*, I.20; also see *FVV*, chap. 6, pp. 68–69.
11. Ibid., I.36; ibid, p. 7.

6
Jainism

JAINISM is the next important non-Vedic school which comes up for critical examination since the philosophical doctrines as well as the religious practices advocated by it are opposed to the Vedānta philosophy established on the basis of the Upaniṣads and the *Vedāntasūtra.* Some of their theories and, in particular, the *saptabhaṅgivāda* or the doctrine of sevenfold description of all entities, are also logically untenable. All the later schools such as Nyāya, Vaiśeṣika, Mīmāṁsā, and Advaita have also criticized the Jaina philosophy.

Vedānta Deśika, at the outset, explains how such an unsound philosophy gained popularity and survived over centuries as a living religion. Like Buddhism, the Jainas do not accept the Vedas as a source of authority but they claim that a person named Arhan who founded Jainism was a *sarvajña* or an omniscient being and whatever was taught by him, as in the case of the Buddha, is to be taken as authoritative. Unlike the Buddha, he categorizes the ultimate ontological entities in a different manner. So also the religious observances. He rejects the Buddhist doctrine of momentaryness but adopts the doctrine of sevenfold description of the nature of all objects and thereby creates the impression that the teachings of Arhan are sounder than that of Buddha.

Vedānta Deśika further points out that in order to impress on the people that he is omniscient, he presents the knowledge of the movement of the planets, stars, and other astrological details which are not normally understood by others. Unlike in Buddhism, he does not deny the existence of external objects. Besides, the remedial measures suggested by Arhan and his followers to ward off evils through the recitation of certain *mantras* are found to be very efficacious. The followers of this religion are thus made to believe that Arhan is an omniscient being and hence all his philosophical teachings should also be accepted as authoritative. He himself claimed that he is a *sarvajña* so that the followers of his religion should accept his teachings without questioning them. Since he lays great emphasis on *satya* or truthfulness and *vairāgya* or non-attachment of worldly objects as the ethical ideals, people are made to believe that Arhan is free from *rāga* or passion and *dveṣa* or hatred towards others and that his teachings are therefore most authoritative. The doctrines advocated by him are also claimed to be in conformity with our experience and logical principles. Hence the philosophy of the Jainas is claimed to be useful for people who aspire for worldly prosperity and also the attainment of a higher spiritual goal.

The first criticism levelled against Jainism is that the denial of authority to the Vedas is not appropriate because these contain eternal truths and also are not ascribed to any human author and as such they are free from defects. These points are brought out in detail in the *Samudāya-doṣādhikāra.*[1] By departing from the fundamental concepts outlined in the Vedas, the Jainas adopt their own novel categories such as *jīva, ajīva, āsrava, bandha,* and *ārjava* which are named as *pañca-āstikāyas.* Even the religious way of life in the name of *tapas* advocated by them does not have any practical value but, on the contrary, some of their religious practices involve the torture of the physical body.

The astrological teachings advanced by them do not have new features other than what are already enunciated in the ancient Indian Astrology. There are five branches of ancient Indian Astrology and of these the Jainas have attempted to develop one branch in greater detail and claim to have promulgated new science of planetary movements.

The claim made that the *mantras* formulated by the combination of certain syllables and letters and that these are efficacious to yield amazingly good results is intended to attract laymen and create in them a faith that Arhan is omniscient.

Vedānta Deśika points out that similar claims are also made by some Buddhists and, on that basis, the Buddha is also regarded as *sarvajña*. If the Buddha is *sarvajña*, how can the Jainas claim that only Arhan is *sarvajña*? If both are *sarvajñas*, then the doctrines of these two schools should not be radically different. If either of them is a *sarvajña*, then how to disprove the claim of the other? If Arhan is claimed to be a *sarvajña* because he advocated the *vairāgya* and *ahiṁsā dharma*, then the same was also taught by the Buddha. In fact *ahiṁsā dharma* advocated by the Buddha is a better type since Buddhist monks do not practise the torture of one's body in the name of *tapas* or penance like Jaina monks do by plucking each hair of the head by hand instead of shaving the head with a razor.[2]

In the guise of the upholders of the theory of compassion (*kāruṇikatva*), the Jainas regard the killing of an animal for the purpose of *yāga* or fire sacrifice as prescribed in the Vedas, as *adharma* and hence Vedas are not supposed to be accepted as authoritative. Then how do they justify the torture of the body by plucking the hairs of the head by hand and defeating the opponents by adopting wrong arguments in debates and thereby wounding the feelings of the rivals (*paravādī*)? If such acts are treated as acts of *dharma*, how would they be justified to regard the killing of an animal for a specific fire sacrifice, the destruction of enemies in the war for the sake of defence of one's country, and the commitment of suicides by jumping into rivers or jumping from the top of a hill on specific occasions, as *adharma*? In fact it is established in the Sacred texts that the killing of an animal for the purpose of sacrifice is for the special benefit of that animal and hence it does not amount to cruelty, just as the surgery performed on an individual is for the benefit of his good health. The punishment caused to individuals who have indulged in theft or murder is not therefore prohibited.

Vedānta Deśika advances a few other arguments in defence of certain rituals prescribed by the Vedas for the purpose of killing an enemy. In all these cases it is contended that these are laid down in certain special circumstances and hence they should not be taken as cases intended for causing injury.

The most important criticism against Jainism is directed towards the enumeration of the *tattvas* or the metaphysical concepts in a wrong way. According to the Jainas there are only two categories of *tattvas,* viz., *dravyas* or substances and *paryāyas* or its modifications or modes (*avasthās*) which are the same as *guṇas* or attributes.[3] Other than these two, there are no other *tattvas.* This is not a correct theory since there are eternal substances such as *Īśvara, jīva,* etc. Such eternal substances possess *dharmas* which are also eternal and these are not subject to changes. All these are established by valid *pramāṇas.* This objection cannot be overcome by merely classifying the *guṇas* into two types, viz., those which exist as part of the substance and those which are accidental (*āgantuka*). The exclusion of *Īśvara* among the eternal *dravyas* stands opposed to Scriptural texts which are *nitya* and free from defects.

The Jainas have admitted six *dravyas.* These are: (1) *jīva* or the individual self; (2) *pudgala* or matter; (3) *dharma* or the principle of motion; (4) *adharma* or the principle of rest; (5) *kāla* or time; and (6) *ākāśa* or ether. Each one of these *tattvas* is defective.

Regarding the doctrine of *jīva,* the Jainas conceive it as of the size of the body it occupies. Vedānta Deśika points out that this is the most unsound theory of *jīva.* One of the reasons advanced by the Jainas for maintaining such a theory is that whenever a person is injured in the leg, he feels the pain in the head. In order to explain such an experience, it is not necessary to conceive that *jīva* is pervasive of the entire body, contends Vedānta Deśika. Such a phenomenon can be explained even by accepting *jīva* as monadic in size (*aṇu*) because experience of pain and pleasure takes place through *jñāna* of *jīva* which is all-pervasive. That *jīva* assumes the size of the body it enters into, would amount to the admission of different dimensions for the *jīva.* But this theory is directly opposed to the Scriptural texts which affirm that *jīva* is *aṇu* and *nirvikāra* or devoid of modification. Further, when the *jīvas* attain the state of *mukti* after liberation, they are devoid of bodies and there is no criteria to determine what kind of body the *jīva* assumes in that state.

According to the Jainas, *jīvas,* after liberation from bondage, keep moving upward continuously (*nityordhva-gamana*). They also believe that certain *jīvas* move upward and enter a transcendental realm called *alokākāśa.* In either theory the *mukta jīva* cannot be regarded as having a dimension. That they can assume a body of a particular size is not philosophically a sound theory.

Regarding *dharma* and *adharma,* these two concepts are understood in Jainism in a different way. They denote the principle of motion and rest respectively. They are regarded as *jagad-vyāpi* or pervasive in the entire universe. The question is asked: Whether they are by their very nature (*svarūpeṇa*) pervasive or by being subtle in nature (*aṇu*) but inherent in all things and in all places similar to the oil in the oil seeds. In either case, *dharma* and *adharma* being eternal (*nitya*), they cannot be regarded as either objects to be acquired by human effort or as common features of all individuals. It can be said that specific modifications or qualities of *dharma* and *adharma* are to be acquired by concerned individuals. But in that case *dharma* and *adharma* are to be restricted to the concerned individuals and they cannot be universal qualities. Then it would follow that *dharma* and *adharma* are nothing other than the observance of prescribed acts and abstaining from the prohibited acts and that these are to be secured by the grace of the concerned deities who are the bestowers of the benefits. If this theory is accepted, then the theory advocated by the Jainas that specific *pudgalas* (conglomerations of several atoms) constitute the *puṇya* and *pāpa,* is not tenable.

Regarding *pudgala,* the postulation of this concept as a separate *dravya* is also untenable, contends Vedānta Deśika. The term *pudgala,* according to the Jainas, means the conglomeration of several atoms to constitute a sizeable whole (comparable to the *prakṛti* of the Sāṅkhyas) which, consisting of the qualities of *śabda, sparśa, rūpa, rasa,* and *gandha,* undergoes modifications into five elements, viz., *pṛthivī, ap, vāyu, agni,* and *ākāśa* each possessing certain specific *guṇas.* The existence of such a *dravya* and also its modification into elements cannot be proved by perception. It cannot be taken as postulate conceived for the purpose of explaining the modification of *pudgala* into elements. If it be a mere postulate for providing certain explanation of evolution into, it is not possible to account for an orderly evolution. *Prakṛti* is accepted by the Vedāntins to explain an orderly evolution on the strength of the Upaniṣadic teachings. It is not so for the Jainas.

Kāla or time which is the fifth *dravya*, is acknowledged by the Jainas as a separate *dravya*. This theory is also defective. *Kāla* as a substance is generally admitted in order to explain that an object existed in the past, or it exists at present or it will come into existence in the future. If according to the Jainas *kāla* is monadic in nature (*aṇu-svarūpa*), it is to be conceived either as of shortest duration or as all-pervasive (*sarva-vyāpi*) like the *ākāśa* and also subtle. Only in that case it is possible to determine the existence of an object in terms of *kāla*. It may be possible to do so by means of *aṇus* admitted by them or through their modifications. Then there would be no need to admit *kāla* as a separate *dravya*. If orthodox Vedic schools accept *kāla*, they do so on the authority of the Vedas and other allied treatises and hence its acceptance as a *dravya* is fully justified. The Digambara sects of Jainas seek the authority of their Āgamas in support of the concept of time. Even then it cannot be proved that it is a separate *tattva*.

Ākāśa is the sixth *dravya* admitted by the Jainas. It is regarded by them as *nitya*, spatially infinite (*ananta pradeśa*) and also all-pervasive (*sarva-vyāpi*). But this view is opposed to the Scriptural texts which speak of the origin for *ākāśa* like other physical elements. The Jainas seek to establish it on the basis of inference and other logical arguments. The *anumāna* adopted for the purpose suffers from logical defects.

DOCTRINE OF SAPTABHAṄGĪ

Coming to the central doctrine of Jainism, viz., the doctrine of *Saptabhaṅgī* or the indeterminable character of the nature of all the six *dravyas* and also their modifications, Vedānta Deśika rejects it as the most unsound theory which is riddled with contradictions. On the basis of the concept of Bhedābheda or difference cum non-difference, the Jainas formulate seven alternatives with regard to the nature of an object. These are: (1) *syādasti* (maybe, it exists); (2) *syād nāsti* (maybe, it does not exist); (3) *syād asti ca nāsti ca* (maybe it exists and it does not exit); (4) *syād-avyaktavyam* (may be it is indescribable); (5) *syādasti ca avyaktavyam* (maybe that it exists and it is indescribable); (6) *syād nāsti ca avyaktavyam* (maybe, that it does not exist and it is indescribable); and (7) *syād asti ca nāsti ca avyaktavyam* (maybe, that it exists and does not exist and is indescribable).

Vedānta Deśika points out that the first five alternatives are somewhat similar to the five alternatives advanced by the Mādhyamikas and on that basis they conclude that the nature of an object is *tuccha* or absolutely indescribable. By the permutation and combination of the five alternatives of Mādhyamika the Jainas add up two more alternatives and come to the conclusion that it is impossible to describe the nature of an object in any specific manner. Even though the Jainas do not use the word *tuccha* or non-existence as the nature of an object, it ultimately ends up in the theory of *tuccha* since the nature of an object cannot be specifically stated. It is possible to evolve more than seven alternatives by adding up a few more by the permutation and combination of *asti, nāsti, asti-nāsti,* etc. The major defect of the presentation of the theory of the *Saptabhaṅgī* which is applicable to all entities and also their qualities (*paryāyas*) is that it is not possible to develop a sound positive theory regarding the nature of an object. Further, there would be no scope to make a distinction between one's own theory (*svapakṣa*) and the theory of an opponent. Nor can the Jainas defend their own theory (*sādhana*) and refute the theory of an opponent (*dūṣaṇa*). It is possible to reconcile the opposition between existence and non-existence of an object with reference to different times and different places (*kālādi-upādhibheda*) as other schools do. Then it cannot be claimed that *anekāntavāda* is the unique theory of the Jainas.

The adherence to the theory that everything in the universe is of manifold nature would end up in complete chaos in the classification of the *tattvas* and so also the observance of the religious practices in a prescribed order. The statement that the entire universe is of the nature of the multiform (*anekānta*) as in the case of divine beings such as Vināyaka (the deity with the combination of a human body and the trunk of an elephant) and Narasiṁha (one of the incarnations of Viṣṇu with human body and the head of a lion) do not serve the purpose of proving the *anekānta* theory.[4] The combination of two forms to constitute one being does not involve any contradiction as in the case of the combination of rice grains with grains of barley (*yava*). *Anekānta* concept in such a sense, viz., having different forms which are not contradictory is acceptable to Viśiṣṭādvaitins also. It cannot be argued that all things are of manifold nature, because they exist, as in the case of *para* and *apara jāti* (*sarvam anekāntam, satvāt, parāpara jātyādivat*). This inferential argument does not support the Jaina thesis that all things are of manifold nature. One and the same object can be regarded as big or small when compared or contrasted to another object of a different nature. For example the *pṛthivī* (the element of earth) is large (*para*) as compared to pot, and the same *pṛthivī* is smaller when compared to the substance (*dravya*). Same is the case with regard to the objects such as human beings as father and son, older and younger, etc. But this is not the case with regard to the Jaina's view of an object possessing different nature since he does not speak of its different nature with reference to what is contrary to it (*pratiyogibheda-nirvāha*).

If it is argued that *Saptabhaṅgī* is confined to the concepts of *aṁśī* or the whole and *aṁśa* or its parts, as well as *dravyas* and *paryāyas* or the *guṇas* which inhere in *dravyas*, the question is raised whether this difference between *aṁśa* and *aṁśī* is due to their own nature or due to the limiting conditions (*sopādhika*). The answers provided contradict his own accepted doctrine. If all entities (*dravya*) by nature possess parts (*svābhāvika aṁśa*), then he will have to admit parts even in respect of *aṇus*. But there would be no separate *aṇu* to determine the difference between the *astikāyas* or that which exists and has parts (*kāya*). The *jīvas* which are similar to other *pudgala dravyas* would become a whole unit comprising internal parts. Such a theory would be as ridiculous as the theory of *jīva* held by Cārvākas. If unity or oneness is the *svābhāvika-dharma* and therefore *ātman* is one entity, then *bheda* also being *svābhāvika*, *ātmans* would be different in nature. Even *ātman*, according to *anekāntavāda* is different and also non-different. In the same way, the other theories of Jainas relating to the *avasthās* of *jīva*, the composition of *jagat* (*jagat-saṁsthāna*), the difference in respect of *devatās*, the offer of worship to them are all riddled with contradictions. Keeping all this in mind, the author of the *Vedāntasūtra* sums up the criticism in one *sūtra-naikasmin asambhavāt*.[5] It means that the doctrine of the Jainas is not sound, because in the same one entity two mutually opposed *dharmas* cannot co-exist.

References

1. See *PMB*, chap.6. See also pp. 52–53.
2. The incident cited by Vedānta Deśika was perhaps an ancient practice and it is not known whether it is still observed in modern times.
3. The classification of *tattvas* as *dravyas* and *paryāyas* is adopted by the ancient Jaina works. But the latter Jaina works classify *tattvas* under two categories, viz., *jīva* and *ajīva* and under *ajīva*, all the five *dravyas* other than *jīva* are included. *PMB*, chap. 6. See also pp. 156–57.
4. *Anekānta jagat sarvaṁ heramba-narasiṁhavat— Jaina-bhaṅgādhikāra* quoted by Vedānta Deśika in ibid.
5. *VS*, II.2.31.

7
Vaiśeṣika School

AMONG THE VEDIC SCHOOLS (*āstika* Darśanas), Vedānta Deśika takes up the Vaiśeṣika school founded by sage Kaṇāda first for consideration, though chronologically it came into existence later than Sāṅkhya and Yoga. The reason for this, as explained by Vedānta Deśika is that some of the doctrines developed by Kaṇāda such as the denial of *apauruṣeyatva* for the Vedas, non-acceptance of primordial cosmic matter (*prakṛti*), admission of *asatkāryavāda,* the acceptance of *avayavī* as distinct from the aggregate of *avayavas,* and the postulation of additional metaphysical categories, etc., are somewhat on the lines of the theories of the non-Vedic schools such as the Cārvāka (Guru-mata), Buddhist (Sugata-mata), and the Jainas (Jina-mata). This observation made by Vedānta Deśika, which reflects the criticisms offered against the Vaiśeṣikas is supported by *Atṛ-smṛti* which states: *kaṇāda-śākya-pāṣaṇḍaiḥ-trayīdharmo-vilopitaḥ; tridaṇḍadhāriṇo pūrvam viṣṇunā rakṣitā trayī.* It means: "The Vedic *dharma* was spoiled (adversely affected) by Kaṇāda (Vaiśeṣika), Śākya (Buddhists), and Pāṣaṇḍis (Pāśupatas); Viṣṇu taking the *avatāra* of Dattātreya holding the *tridaṇḍa,* restored it." Prima facie this may sound as a strong criticism against Kaṇāda, because at the very commencement of the *Vaiśeṣika-sūtras* he declares that he would present an exposition of *dharma* which is the means to attain the Spiritual Goal.[1] But actually he deviates from his declared premise and devotes all his attention to the discussion of the six metaphysical categories, viz., *dravya, guṇa, karma, sāmānya, viśeṣa,* and *samavāya.*[2] Though incidentally he briefly discusses a few points about *dharma,* the *Kaṇāda-sūtras* mainly deal with the nature of the six categories (*ṣaṭ-padārthas*). Hence the following remark is made jokingly by others about Kaṇāda-mata: *Dharmaṁ vyākhyātu-kāmasya ṣaṭpadārthopavarṇanam; sāgaraṁ gantu-kāmasya himavat-gamanopamam*—"One who is desirous of expounding *dharma*, presents the details of six *padārthas*; this is similar to an individual who wishes to go to the ocean, proceeds towards the Himalayas."

After making these general observations about the Vaiśeṣika school, Vedānta Deśika proceeds to examine critically the main theories of Vaiśeṣikas—the metaphysical categories including the concept of *abhāva*, the doctrine of *jīva* and the doctrine of *Īśvara*. He first takes up *abhāva* or non-existence.

THE CONCEPT OF *ABHĀVA*

The Vaiśeṣikas admit *abhāva* or non-existence as a separate category as different from *bhāva* or existence (*bhāva atirikta abhāva*). This is not a sound theory, contends Vedānta Deśika, for the following reasons. In the first place, it is not possible to comprehend it as an entity by perception, just as we see clearly the existence of an object. The existence of an object in a particular place or at a particular time is *bhāva*, which is a positive concept. Similarly, the absence or non-existence of an object in a particular place or time can be regarded as *abhāva*. That is, a different state of *bhāva* itself is *abhāva*. It is also a positive concept. Other than that, it is not necessary to admit *abhāva* as a separate category, *bhāvāntara-abhāva*.

The Vaiśeṣikas conceive four types of *abhāva*: (a) *prāgbhāva* or prior non-existence of an object, a state prior to the production of an object such as a pot; (b) *pradhvaṁsābhāva* or prior posterial non-existence or a state after the destruction of an object; (c) *atyantābhāva* or absolute non-existence, that is, total negation as for instance bare ground with no jar on it; and (d) *anyonyābhāva* or mutual non-existence, that is, difference between two objects, as for example, jar is not cloth. In case of *prāgbhāva* and *pradhvaṁsābhāva* the Vaiśeṣika themselves admit that these are *bhāva-rūpa* or positive concepts. In the same way, *abhāva* can also be regarded as a different state of *bhāva* (*bhāvāntara*) and not a separate category (*padārtha*). *Abhāva* or non-existence of an object means that it exists elsewhere at some other time or in some other form. *Abhāva* is thus a determining characteristic of an object with reference to time, space, and condition.[3]

THE CONCEPT OF *SAMAVĀYA*

The Vaiśeṣikas have admitted the concept of *samavāya* as a separate category (*padārtha*) to explain the relation of inherence that obtains between two separate entities which are invariably connected (*ayuta-siddha*). The *ayuta-siddha* entities are *avayava* (parts) and *avayavī* (whole), *guṇa* (attribute) and *guṇī* (substance), *kriyā* (activity) and that which causes it, *jāti* (generic character) and *vyakti* (object), and lastly, *viśeṣa* (a special quality) that subsists in eternal substances (*nitya-dravyas*) such as *paramāṇus*, souls, etc. Such a relation is regarded *nitya* or eternal and one (*eka*), that is, it is a common feature of all inseparable entities. *Samavāya* conceived as a relation of inherence (*saṁbandha*) relates the two relata (*saṁbandhī*). It does not require another relation to relate it with the two relata. If another principle is needed to relate the *samavāya* with the relata, it would lead to infinite regress. It is therefore regarded as *svapara-nirvāhaka* or capable of relating itself to relatives without requiring another principle to relate it to the relata. This is similar to the illustration of light which reveals the objects but the light itself does not require another light to reveal it.

This theory is subjected to severe criticism. When two entities such as substance and its attributes are inseparably related, there is no need to conceive a separate concept of relation such as *samavāya* and in order to avoid the fallacy of infinite regress, to ascribe to it the capacity of relating itself to the relata without any third factor. In other words, the postulation of the concept of *samavāya* as a separate relation other than the two relata which are already connected by their very nature, is superfluous. When it is well-known that the two *ayuta-siddha* entities are already connected together invariably, there is no need to adopt a third category in the name of *samavāya* to account for their relation. The Viśiṣṭādvaitin therefore uses the expression *apṛthak-siddha* which implies that the two entities are inseparably related as in the case of lotus and its blueness.

When such an entity can give rise to the awareness that it is related (*viśiṣṭa pratyaya-viṣayatvam*), there is no need to postulate a separate concept of *samavāya* to account for their relationship. If *samavāya* as a separate concept of *sambandha* is admitted to explain the relationship between two invariably connected relatives, the fallacy of infinite regress is unavoidable. The principle of explanation adopted as *svaparanirvāhaka* is an additional superfluous postulate.

The admission of *samavāya* as *nitya* and *eka* also leads to problems. If it is *nitya,* then the relata with which it is connected would also have to be *nitya.* But it is not so in respect of *dravya* and its *guṇas* where the relation of inherence exists, since the *guṇas* are impermanent by nature. *Guṇas* come into existence only after the *dravya* is produced. Only when substance and its attribute come into existence, *samavāya* relation is to be conceived and as such it has an origin (*janma*) and it cannot be regarded as *nitya.* If it is argued that the nature of the relation is determined after knowing the nature of *viśeṣaṇa* or attribute and *viśeṣya* or that in which it inheres, then there would be no need to conceive *samavāya* as the relation that exists between the relata. The *viśeṣaṇa* and *viśeṣya* by their very nature can also reveal that they are related together, because *samavāya* as relation, cannot itself determine what is *ādhāra* (supporter) and what is *adheya* (that which is supported).

THE CONCEPT OF *VIŚEṢA*

The Vaiśeṣikas admit a separate category named *viśeṣa* or individually as a special quality that subsists in eternal objects in order to distinguish one eternal object from another (*vyāvṛtti-pratipatti*).[4] It is the differences of ultimate objects which are otherwise alike. The ultimate objects which are supposed to possess the quality of *viśeṣa* are atoms (*paramāṇus*), souls (*ātmans*), time (*kāla*), space (*dik*), ether (*ākāśa*), and mind (*manas*).

Vedānta Deśika criticizes this theory. The *viśeṣa* is not separate quality subsisting objects. The very objects themselves serve the purpose of distinguishing one from the other and it is not therefore necessary to postulate a separate concept for this purpose. It should be possible to distinguish the objects on the basis of temporal as well as spatial factors or with reference to the distinguishing characteristics they possess.

Taking the case of the *muktātmās* or the liberated *jīvas* which are omniscient, they are all alike insofar they all enjoy equally the *bhoga* or bliss of Brahman (*atyanta-sāmya*). Nevertheless, it is possible to distinguish between them on the basis of the functions they perform in the state of *mukti* (*vyāpāra-bheda*). This is determined on the authority of the Sacred texts. Their individuality could also be established on the basis of the types of *karma* with which they were associated prior to liberation (*pūrvopādhi*). It may be asked as to how we come to know this. The answer is, as explained by Vedānta Deśika, that the yogis or those who possess supernormal perception could apprehend such distinctions.[5]

The above explanation is in accordance with the theory *muktātmā* accepted by Viśiṣṭādvaita Vedānta. According to the Vaiśeṣikas, *muktātmā* is totally devoid of all experience similar to a piece of stone (*pāṣāṇa-kalpa*). There is no other basis to distinguish between one liberated *jīva* and another. Hence it would be necessary to admit *viśeṣa* as a special quality inherent in each *jīva*.

Against this argument Vedānta Deśika points out that such a theory advanced by the Vaiśeṣikas on the basis of *anumāna* is untenable since it is opposed to the Scriptural texts which affirm that *jñāna* as a *dharma* of *jīva* is *nitya* and exists even in the state of *mokṣa.*[6]

The Vaiśeṣikas have felt the need to admit the *viśeṣa* as a separate quality in order to account for the distinction between the *paramāṇus* which are the cause of the universe. According to Viśiṣṭādvaita Vedānta, Brahman as associated with *cit* and *acit* in their subtle form, is the cause of the universe. The *paramāṇus* cannot serve as the cause of the universe, since the combination of partless subtle *paramāṇus* is inconceivable. The need of postulating *viśeṣa* as a special quality of *paramāṇus* does not therefore arise. Nor is it justified.

The Vaiśeṣikas have admitted *anyonyābhāva* as a separate concept which stands for mutual difference between two objects and hence there is no need to postulate *viśeṣa* as a quality. If it is argued that *anyonyābhāva* between two objects of the same kind (*samāna-rūpa*) cannot serve the purpose of distinguishing one from the other, it is replied that the concept of *pṛthaktva* or separateness accepted by them as a separate quality can serve the purpose of knowing the difference between two objects of the same nature.

THE CONCEPT OF *SĀMĀNYA*

Sāmānya is another independent category admitted by the Vaiśeṣika. It refers to the feature or property common to two or more things. Thus when we see several cows, we get the notion that they are all the same. This characteristic common to all (*ānugata-dharma*), is called *sāmānya.* The same is also known as *jāti* or generic character. *Gotva* or cowness which is a feature common to all cows is the *jāti,* also known as *sāmānya.* It exists in the three types of *padārthas,* viz., *dravya, guṇa,* and *karma.* Thought it exists in all the three, it is an independent category (*padārtha*). It is one, eternal, of and subsists in many. There are gradations of *sāmānya. Sattā* or existence is the highest universal (*para jāti*) since it belongs to the largest number of entities. The others which are known as *apara-jāti,* follow it in a descending order as *dravyatva* (as substance), *pṛthivītva* (as element of earth), and *ghaṭatva* (as a pot) each one covering lesser number of entities.

Vedānta Deśika criticizes this theory. Though the concept of *jāti,* which is the same as *sāmānya,* is acceptable to the Viśiṣṭādvaitin, it is not regarded as an independent category (*padārtha*) as one and ubiquitous. According to Viśiṣṭādvaita, *jāti* is the *asādhāraṇa-dharma* or the unique characteristic of an object. It is the specific structure of the object (*saṁsthāna-viśeṣa*), as for example, the dewlap in the case of the cow. Apart from this there is no separate entity as *jāti,* aṣ Vaiśeṣikas believe.

The admission of *jāti* as a separate *dharma* than the structure of the object leads to certain difficulties. According to the Vaiśeṣikas, the physical structure of the object (*ākṛti*) is the revealer (*abhivyañjaka*) of *jāti. Ākṛti* itself is a common character found in all kinds of materials and as such it would constitute *jāti.* Then the question arises whether there is something which would reveal this *jāti* in the form of *ākṛti.* If the reply is in the affirmative, it would lead to the fallacy of infinite regress. To overcome this difficulty if it is said that *ākṛti* does not require another *ākṛti* to reveal it but on the contrary it reveals itself as well as the *jāti*, then why accept *jāti* as a separate *dharma* in order to account for similarity (*sādṛśya*)? It may be argues that the principal structure of the subject (*ākṛti*) being different from each other cannot constitute a common character of all objects as *jāti* but nevertheless it can serve the purpose of revealing the *jāti*. It that be the case, it would follow that the special structure of the object (which is the very *ākṛti*) can give rise to the notion of similarity and as such there would be need to admit *sāmānya* as a separate *dharma*. In other words, the very structure of the object which is common to all objects can cause the *anugata-vyavahāra* or the notion of generality and it is not therefore necessary to conceive a separate entity such as *sāmānya*.[7]

The Concept of *Karma*

Karma or action in the form of movement is regarded by the Vaiśeṣikas as a separate category (*padārtha*). According to this school there are five kinds of movement: (1) upward movement (*utkṣepaṇa*), (2) downward movement (*apakṣepaṇa*), (3) contraction (*ākuñcana*), (4) expansion (*prasaraṇa*), and (5) movement in general such as going forward or backward (*gamana*). All kinds of movement (*karma*) belong to *dravya* (substance) and cause the things to move. Their relation to the *dravya* is similar to that of *guṇas* to the *guṇī*. Though *karma* is not perceptible, it is proved by means of inference.

This theory is refuted as unsound. According to Vedānta Deśika, *karma* is that which causes in us the awareness that the object is moving. In other words it is movement itself (*calana*). While he agrees with the Vaiśeṣika with regard to the general nature of *karma*, he questions the soundness of its classification into five kinds. There is no justification criterion on the basis of which such a classification could be maintained. Whatever is the cause of the *karma* as conceived by the Vaiśeṣika, the same may be acceptable to explain the movement of an object from one place to another. The assumption of an additional factor as *karma* besides the movement of an object from one place to another is superfluous.

The Theory of *Guṇas*

The Vaiśeṣikas have enumerated twenty-four *guṇas* or attributes. These are *rūpa* (colour), *rasa* (taste), *gandha* (odour), *sparśa* (touch), *saṅkhyā* (number), *parimāṇa* (dimension), *pṛthaktva* (separateness), *saṁyoga* (conjunction), *vibhāga* (disjunction), *para* (prior), *apara* (posteriority), *buddhi* (*jñāna*), *sukha* (pleasure), *duḥkha* (pain), *icchā* (desire), *dveṣa* (hatred), and *prayatna* (effort). These seventeen *guṇas* are mentioned by Kaṇāda in the *sūtra*. To these are added the following eight *guṇas* by Praśastapāda, the commentator on the *sūtras*: *gurutva* (heaviness), *dravatva* (liquidity), *sneha* (lubricity), *saṁskāra* (latent impression), *adṛṣṭa* (unseen potency), *dharma* and *adharma* (merit and demerit). Each one of this is examined in the *Tattva-muktākalāpa* and proved to be defective.[8] The major criticism against the enumeration of twenty-four *guṇas* is the omission of the three fundamental *guṇas* of *prakṛti*, viz., *sattva*, *rajas*, and *tamas* which are established on the basis of Scriptural and Smṛti texts. The other criticism is that many of these *guṇas* are superfluous and there is no need or justification to regard them as separate qualities. Regarding *buddhi* or knowledge it cannot be a *guṇa* but it is a substance (*dravya*) inseparably related to the individual self according to Viśiṣṭādvaita. The five mental qualities, viz., *icchā*, *dveṣa*, *sukha*, *duḥkha*, and *prayatna* cannot be qualities of the self but are different states of the *dharma-bhūta-jñāna* or attributive knowledge of the *jīvātman*. If *sukha* and *duḥkha* are regarded as separate qualities of the self, then we have to know what causes *sukha* and *duḥkha* in an individual. If the causes of such experiences are the very mental disposition of an individual, then it would be sounder to admit that the very mental states or the states of *jñāna* (according to Viśiṣṭādvaita) are the *sukha* and *duḥkha*. It is therefore superfluous to postulate that these are the qualities of the self.

The Theory of *Dravya*

Coming to the theory of *dravya* or substance which, according to the Vaiśeṣikas, serves as the basis (*āśraya*) for the *guṇas*, is also defective. This is of nine kinds. These are: *pṛthivī* (earth), *ap* (water), *tejas* (fire), *vāyu* (air), *ākāśa* (ether), *kāla* (time), *dik* (direction), *ātmā* (self), and *manas* (mind).[9] Vedānta Deśika points out that this classification of *dravyas* in neither rational nor in conformity to the Sacred texts (*upapatti śāstra-viruddham*). According to the Scriptural and Smṛti texts, the five elements are the evolutes of *prakṛti.* The first four elements, according to the Vaiśeṣikas are the aggregates of *paramāṇus* which are conceived by the Vaiśeṣikas. *Ākāśa,* the fifth element is regarded as *nitya* and also *vibhu. Manas* is also the combination of the *paramāṇus,* which are regarded as *nitya.* Even this view is opposed to the Scriptural texts. The inferential arguments adopted to prove these theories also suffer from logical fallacy.

With regard to the physical elements, the Vaiśeṣikas maintain the view that other than *ākāśa,* these elements exist in two forms: as *avayava* or individual parts consisting of the combination of *paramāṇus* and also as *avayavī* or aggregate of the individual parts which are also constituted of atoms. The postulation of *avayavī* as distinct from *avayava* is considered necessary by the Vaiśeṣikas because there is difference between cause (*kāraṇa*) and effect (*kārya*) on the basis of several factors such as name, number, function, shape and difference in respect of knowledge.[10] This is an unsound theory, contends Vedānta Deśika, as it is opposed to our perceptual experience and also opposed to the Scriptural texts. What is regarded as *kārya* or effect such as a piece of cloth is not different from the threads which serve as the cause. The effect is a modified state of the cause, like the pot made out of clay. The text of *Chāndogya Upaniṣad* dealing with the causation of the universe cites the example of the lump of clay and the products made out of it and states: "*vācārambhaṇaṁ vikāro nāmadheyam mṛttiketyeva satyam,*"[11] which implies that the effects such as the clay products, though they bear different names and forms for purposes of empirical transactions, are the same as clay. The illustration of the scroll of palm leaf and an earring made out of it by just rolling it into shape of an earring makes it clear that the cause and effect are the two states (*avasthās*) of the same substance.[12] Hence it is not correct to hold the theory that *avayavī* is something distinct from *avayava.*

In the same way it is wrong to conceive that *dik* or directions such as east, west, north, south, etc., is one all-pervasive and eternal substance. Such a theory cannot be established by means of inference since the syllogistic argument adopted for the purpose is fallacious. The Scriptural texts do not mention *dik* as a separate *tattva*. The *ākāśa* or the sky itself with the help of the *upādhis* such as the position of the sun can account for the different directional relations such as east and west.

The Nature of *Jīvātman*

Regarding the nature of *jīvātman* which is different from *Īśvara*, the Vaiśeṣikas maintain the view that it is *jaḍa* or non-sentient in the sense that it is not self-luminous. This view is opposed to the well-established theory that *ātman* is self-luminous. Similarly the theory that *jīvātman* is *vibhu* or all-pervasive is also wrong since the Scriptural texts and the *Vedāntasūtra* affirm that *ātmā* is *aṇu*.[13] Besides it is opposed to the teaching of the Vedānta which speak of *utkrānti* or exit of the *jīva* from the body and its movement to the higher realms. What is *vibhu* cannot have movement. Since it is possible for the *jīvātman* to experience pleasure and pain in different distant places through the body with which it is associated wherever an individual goes, it is not necessary to ascribe *vibhutva* to it. It is not necessary for the *jīva* to be actually present in a distant place for the purpose of enjoying the fortune that may arise there. It can reap the reward wherever it exists through the grace of God who is the bestower of the fruits of good deeds in accordance with the previous *puṇya* of an individual.

The Theory of *Īśvara*

This also suffers from some defects. The Vaiśeṣikas admit for *Īśvara* the possession of the attributes of *jñāna* or knowledge, *cikīrṣā* or desire and *prayatna* or capacity to act or function. Some admit only two attributes, viz., *jñāna* and *prayatna*. These attributes are ever present in Him (*nitya*). These serve as accessory causes for the operation of the *adṛṣṭa* of the individuals. If such a view is accepted, then the unchecked freedom (*svātantrya*) that *Īśvara* enjoys has no significance. In that case *Īśvara* would also be subject to the criticism of possessing limited power and capacity (*alpaśaktaḥ*).

So far some of the major theories of the Vaiśeṣika have been criticized. There are other minor matters such as (1) *Pākaja-prakriyā* or that new qualities arise in the physical objects due to their association with fire, (2) *Dvyaṇukādi-prakriyā*, that is, the formation of *dvyaṇuka* or the combination of two single atoms, (3) *Dvi-pṛthaktvādi-prakriyā*, that is, *pṛthaktva* or separateness as a different category and it is similar to *saṅkhyā* or number, (4) *Vibhāgaja-vibhāgādi prakriyā*, that is, separateness as a quality caused by two entities. These are all untenable as in the case of other theories, when subjected to logical analysis.

Vedānta Deśika thus concludes that the Vaiśeṣika teachings on *tattvas* have become a subject of ridicule by others.[14] The author of the *Vedāntasūtra* has summed up the criticisms in the *sūtra*: "*aparigrahācca atyanta anapekṣā.*" It is of no value since their teachings are not acceptable to the exponents of the orthodox schools.

References

1. See *Vaiśeṣikasūtra*: *athāto dharmaṁ vyākhyāsyāmaḥ; yato abhyudaya niśreyasa siddhiḥ sa dharmāḥ; tadvacanāt āmnayasya prāmāṇyam.*
2. The concept of *abhāva* or non-existence was added to these six as a separate category (*padārtha*) at a later period.
3. See *TMK*, V.129: *daśā-deśa-kālādi-bhedāt yah svabhāvam niyamayati saḥ abhāvaḥ.*
4. See *Vaiśeṣikasūtra*: *nityadravya vṛttayo anantāḥ.*
5. See *TMK*, V.125.
6. See *Br. Up.*: *Avināśi vā are ayamātmā anucchittidharmaḥ.* Also *Br. Up.*, VI.3.30: *na vijñātuḥ vijñāteḥ viparilopo vidyate.*
7. See *TMK*, V.118.
8. See *FVV*. chap. 11, pp. 353–67.
9. See *Vaiśeṣikasūtra*: *pṛthivyāpastejovāyurākāśaṁ kālo digātmā mana iti nava dravyāṇi.*
10. For details, see *FVV*, pp. 59–60.
11. *Ch. Up.*, VI.1.4.
12. See for details, *FVV*, pp. 59–60.
13. See *Muṇḍ. Up.*, III.1.9: *Eṣo aṇurātmā cetasā veditavyaḥ.*
14. See above, n.1.

8

Nyāya School

AFTER CRITICALLY EXAMINING the Vaiśeṣika Darśana of Kaṇāda, Vedānta Deśika takes up for consideration separately, the Nyāya Darśana founded by sage Akṣapāda also known as Gautama. Though both ancient and modern scholars on Indian Philosophy treat these two schools as one since most of the doctrines developed by them are alike, they are regarded by Vedānta Deśika as two separate schools founded by two separate authors Kaṇāda and Gautama, respectively. Chronologically also, Nyāya Darśana is later then Vaiśeṣika Darśana.

Nyāya, unlike the Vaiśeṣika school, enjoys the distinction of being included among the fourteen branches of learning called *vidyāsthānas* which serve as supplemental treatises for acquiring spiritual knowledge. Thus states the *Yājñavalkya-smṛti*; *Purāṇa-nyāyamīmāṁsā-dharmaśāstrāṅga-miśritaḥ; vedāḥ sthānāni vidyāyā dharmasya caturdaśa. Manusmṛti* also mentions it in a more explicit way: *Aṅgāni vedāḥ catvāro mīmāṁsā nyāya-vistaraḥ; purāṇam dharma śāstram ca vidyā hyetāḥ caturdaśa.* That is, the four Vedas, its six auxiliaries—Śikṣā, Vyākaraṇa, Chandas, Nirukta, Jyotiṣa, and Kalpa; Mīmāṁsā, Nyāyavistara, Purāṇa, and Dharmaśāstra constitute the fourteen *vidyāsthānas* or the branches of learning which are useful to acquire spiritual knowledge. In view of this, the question arises whether it would be appropriate to criticize the *Nyāyaśāstra.* If this is refuted then all other branches of learning would also be open to similar criticism.

Further, unlike the exponent of the non-Vedic schools whose teachings are unacceptable since they are not based on valid *pramāṇas,* Akṣapāda, a reputed sage compiled the *Nyāyasūtras* which are commented by no less a sage then Vātsyāyana. It would not therefore be proper to criticize what is taught in the *Nyāyasūtras* and the learned commentary on it, even though what is said by the later commentators such as Udyotakara and Vācaspati Miśra are overlooked.

In reply to this objection, Vedānta Deśika clarifies at the outset that it is not our intention to criticize the Nyāya Darśana which is one of the fourteen *vidyāsthānas*. Nor do we question the authoritativeness of sage Vātsyāyana's commentary. If there are any statements or teachings of Gautama which appear to be in conflict with Vedic teachings, these could be explained or interpreted wherever possible in such a way as to overcome the apparent conflict. For this purpose we would also adopt the principles of interpretation laid down in the *Virodha-adhikāra* of Pūrvamīmāṁsā. If there is total opposition, then the teaching is to be ignored. In view of these explanations, Vedānta Deśika adopts for this chapter dealing with Nyāya school, the title "Nyāyavistara-virodha-nistārādhikāra." That is, the chapter devoted to remove the conflicting views found in the *Nyāya-darśana* of Gautama. He avoids the word *bhaṅga* employed in respect of the Vaiśeṣika school to emphasise that *Nyāya-darśana* as such is acceptable to Viśiṣṭādvaita.

There are three ways in which the *sūtras* of Akṣapāda are to be treated so as to avoid the opposition of his teachings with those of Vedānta. In the first place, an attempt is to be made to interpret all the *sūtras* of Akṣapāda in such as way as they would conform to the teachings of Vedānta. If some of the *sūtras* cannot be interpreted to fit with the views of Vedānta, these are to be ignored. If it becomes necessary to interpret some of these *sūtras* in favour of the theories held by Vaiśeṣikas, as contended by later commentators on *Nyāyasūtras*, then these have to be rejected totally as unacceptable as in the case of the Vaiśeṣika theories.

Vedānta Deśika points out that it is not true that Gautama follows the teachings of the Vaiśeṣikas in all matters, since there is no valid proof in support of it. Thus for instance, the *Vaiśeṣikasūtra* at the very commencement states that the investigation into the metaphysical categories, viz., *dravya*, *guṇa, karma, sāmānya, viśeṣa,* and *samavāya* are useful (conducive) to attain the higher spiritual goal.[1] This teaching is ignored by Gautama since knowledge of the metaphysical categories is not a direct means to *mokṣa.*

According to Vedānta Deśika the school founded by the Vaiśeṣikas is different from the school developed by Gautama. The Vaiśeṣika school maintains that Āgama or Scripture is not a separate *pramāṇa* but it is a part of *anumāna,* whereas in the Nyāya school, it is recognized as a separate *pramāṇa.* Similarly for Gautama, *vāyu* is the object of perception (*vāyuḥ pratyakṣa eva*), whereas it is not so for the Vaiśeṣika. When it is found that there is difference of opinion in respect of certain theory, what is to done is to re-examine the theory in accordance with the accepted *pramāṇas* and adopt a modified theory. This is the reason for advancing two differing views by the two commentators such as *Nyāyabhūṣaṇakāra* and Udayana on the same commentary of Gautama.

In the case of the theories which are developed by some of the exponents of Vedānta on the basis of the theories of Vaiśeṣikas, these have to be re-examined and accepted by eliminating the defects found in them. This is explained on the analogy of accepting a piece of impure gold after testing its purity by melting it in fire and eliminating the alloy mixed in it. The *Nyāyaśāstra* which is one of the fourteen *vidyāsthānas* is therefore to be accepted by adopting one of the following methods: If a particular theory of the Nyāya school is found defective, it is to be substituted by a modified theory as in the example of *kuśa,* a specific type of grass (used for religious observances), if not available, a substitute of it (another brand of grass) is to be accepted (*kuśa-kāśāvalambana*).

If any of the theories of Gautama are found totally opposed to that of Vedānta, these have to be rejected. Alternatively it would be better to rewrite the *Nyāyaśāstra* to conform to the *Vedāntaśāstra,* as is done by Nāthamuni who is the forerunner of Viśiṣṭādvaita, by writing a separate treatise under the title *Nyāyatattva* (which is not extant). A similar attempt is made by Vedānta Deśika who has contributed an independent treatise named *Nyāyapariśuddhi* in which the Nyāya theories are modified.

Thus the *Nyāyaśāstra* is to be accepted since it is one of the fourteen *vidyāsthānas*. In the opinion of Vedānta Deśika this is a better course of action than following the theories of Buddhism and Jainism which are totally unsound.

There are however a few doctrines which are not acceptable to the Vedānta. These are: (1) The *paramāṇus* are the source of the universe. (2) *Īśvara* is only the instrumental cause. (3) Vedas are taught by *Īśvara* which means they are not *apauruṣeya*. (4) *Mokṣa* is the state of existence of *jīva* totally devoid of experience of *sukha* or *duḥkha* similar to a piece of stone (*pāṣāṇa-kalpa*). All these are totally opposed to Vedānta. Vedānta Deśika points out that even in respect of these doctrines, the followers of Akṣapāda themselves have attempted to present modified views to conform to the Vedānta doctrines. In the same way it would be appropriate to accept the Nyāya Darśana after modifying its theories, wherever necessary, to conform to the Vedānta doctrines. The *Nyāyapariśuddhi* written by Vedānta Deśika contains the details of how this is accomplished.

References

1. See *Vaiśeṣikasūtra: Dharma-viśeṣa-prasūtāt dravya-guṇa-karma-sāmānya-viśeṣa-samavāyānāṁ padārthānāṁ sādharmya vaidharmyābhyāṁ tattvajñāna nissreyasam.*

9
Nirīśvaramīmāṁsā School

IN THE *PARAMATA-BHAṄGA*, this school comes up for consideration soon after the review to the Nyāya Darśana. The reason for this is that Mīmāṁsā school also, like Nyāya is included among the fourteen *vidyāsthānas* or the branches of learning useful for the acquisition of spiritual knowledge. The *Mīmāṁsāśāstra* is primarily concerned with the interpretation of the Vedas by making use of the logical principles developed by Nyāya Darśana. According to tradition it constitutes one single *śāstra* since the scope of its study covers the entire Vedas. It comprises three parts. The first part is named as Karmakāṇḍa consisting of twelve *adhyāyas* which deal with the nature and manner of performing the various rituals. This is generally acknowledged as Pūrvamīmāṁsā on which Jaimini has formulated the *sūtras.* The second part is known as Devatākāṇḍa consisting of four *adhyāyas* which deals with the nature and status of celestial deities referred to in the Vedas. It is also called Saṅkarṣaṇakāṇḍa named after its author, Saṅkarṣaṇa. The work is not extant but however there are references made to it in other works. The third part of the *Mīmāṁsāśāstra* is the *Brahmasūtra* of Bādarāyaṇa consisting of four *adhyāyas.* The three parts constitute one single treatise, as is evident from the authoritative statement of an ancient commentator on the *Vedāntasūtra*, Bodhāyana, also known as *Vṛttikāra.*[1] Vedānta Deśika has established this fact with sufficient arguments in the *Śatadūṣaṇī* and *Adhikaraṇasārāvaḷi.*[2]

Though Mīmāṁsā is one *śāstra* comprising three parts, the Advaita Vedānta of Śaṅkara has accorded greater importance to the part dealing with Brahman on the basis of the premise that there is opposition between Karmakāṇḍa dealing with rituals, and Brahmakāṇḍa dealing with the knowledge of Brahman. The performance of rituals, the propitiation of deities, the grant of boons by them, etc., are therefore considered as imaginary caused by illusion (*bhrānti-parikalpita*). This view adopted by Śaṅkara is considered as a wrong theory regarding *Mīmāṁsāśāstra* and it is therefore refuted in the chapter dealing with Advaita.[3] On the contrary, another extreme theory is developed by the *Pūrvamīmāṁsā* of Jaimini according to which Karmakāṇḍa or the ritualistic part of the Vedas is of greater importance than the Brahmakāṇḍa dealing with the study of Brahman covered in the Upaniṣads. It is this part of the *Mīmāṁsā-sāstra*, popularly known as *Pūrvamīmāṁsā* as interpreted by the commentators, in particular by Kumārila Bhaṭṭa, that comes up for critical examination. As will be pointed out later the *Pūrvamīmāṁsā* represented by Kumārila which does not accept *Īśvara*, is regarded as Nirīśvaramīmāṁsā. Hence this chapter in *Paramata-bhaṅga* is designated as Nirīśvaramīmāṁsaka-nirākaraṇa.

In his critical review of the Mīmāṁsā of Jaimini, Vedānta Deśika, as in the case of the Nyāya school, does not criticize openly any of their theories. On the other hand, he adopts a compromising attitude and attempts to reconcile the conflicting theories of Pūrvamīmāṁsā with those of Vedānta. Presumably this kind of treatment is adopted for two reasons. First, the *Pūrvamīmāṁsā* of Jaimini is an integral part of *Mīmāṁsāśāstra* as a single treatise dealing with the interpretation of the entire Vedas—both the ritualistic part and the Vedānta part. Secondly, it is acknowledged as one of the fourteen *vidyāsthānas*.

As well established both by Rāmānuja and Vedānta Deśika, there is no opposition between Pūrvamīmāṁsā and the Uttara-mīmāṁsā (Vedānta). In fact, *Pūrvamīmāṁsā* and in particular, the principles of interpretation laid down by Jaimini are very useful for the study of Vedānta. As Vedānta Deśika points out, there is also no difference of opinion between Jaimini and Bādarāyaṇa. There are several *Vedāntasūtras* which Jaimini in by name, is quoted as the supporter of the view of Bādarāyaṇa.[4] In fact, according to the *Mahābhārata*, Jaimini is a disciple of Vyāsa.

Against this background, Vedānta Deśika selects a few important theories advanced by Jaimini as developed by the commentators and re-examines them dispassionately with a view to comprising Pūrvamīmāṁsā with Vedānta. He first takes up the theory of *Īśvara* or the Supreme Being which is the central doctrine of the Vedānta. Though Jaimini himself does not discuss the theory of *Īśvara* in the *Mīmāṁsāsūtras*, his commentators raise the question whether or not *Īśvara* is to be admitted, other than the *karma* or ritualistic sacrifices which are capable of giving the desired fruits. The following statement which refers to the question of *Īśvara*, is quoted by Vedānta Deśika: *Anumānam nirastam, neśvaraḥ.*[5] If it means that the inferential argument (*anumāna*) adopted by the Naiyāyika is rejected and not *Īśvara* as established by the Scriptural texts, then this view of the Mīmāṁsaka is acceptable, since it does not stand opposed to the Vedānta theory. If, on the contrary, the statement is devoted to deny the very existence of *Īśvara* and also the celestial deities as well as their functions as recipients of *havis* (what is offered in the *homa*), then it could be interpreted to imply the importance of *karma* as the cause of the benefits to be derived. Such a view can be tolerated since it does not deny *Īśvara*. If, on the other hand, the denial of existence of *Īśvara* is their conlusive theory (*siddhānta*), then the Mīmāṁsakas have to be treated on par with Cārvākas who also do not admit *Īśvara*.

Though Jaimini himself does not openly deny the existence of *Īśvara* in his *sūtras*, a few *adhikaraṇas* or topical sections of the *Mīmāṁsāsūtras* such as Śabdādhikaraṇa, Arthavādādhikaraṇa, Devatādhikaraṇa, and Apūrvādhikaraṇa contain statements made by the commentators to interpret the *sūtras*, which do not conform to the views of the Vedāntin. Thus, for instance, in the Śabdādhikaraṇa dealing with the question of *nityatva* or eternal character of the Vedas, the commentators adopt the argument that Vedas are *nitya* because the *varṇas* or letters are also eternal. But this is not acceptable to the Vedāntin. Similarly, in the Arthavādādhikaraṇa dealing with the glorificatory Vedic statements, it is argued that only Vedic statements which enjoin the performance of a *yāga* or some other ritualistic deeds are purportful, whereas the statements which deal with an existent as in the case of the Upaniṣadic texts which speak of Brahman, an existent, are not purportful. According to the Mīmāṁsakas these texts have to be taken as glorificatory statements (*arthavāda*) relating to what is enjoined. Vedānta Deśika points out that these views, even though appear to be in conflict with the Vedānta theories, can be interpreted in such a way so as to overcome the apparent conflict.

In the opinion of Vedānta Deśika, Jaimini himself would not have intended to express views as opposed to Vedānta. As pointed out earlier, Jaimini is referred to by Bādarāyaṇa in several *sūtras* of Vedānta as supporting what is taught by him. This demonstrates that Jaimini admits Brahman as the Supreme Reality (*brahma-viṣaya-abhyupagama*). If on certain minor matters there are some differences of opinion, it can be ignored since the two treatises *Pūrva-* and *Uttara-mīmāṁsā* constitute one single *śāstra* (*śāstraikatva*), as stated by sage Bodhāyana.

The Vedic statements are of three kinds—*vidhi* or injunctions, *mantra* or hymns and *arthavādas* or glorificatory statements. With regard to *mantras* and *arthavādas*, if there are conflicting views, these could be ignored and accepted as valid on the basis of the Vedic statements being self-valid (*svataḥ prāmāṇya*), so far as they are not opposed to our experience.

However, in the Apūrvādhikaraṇa, the Mīmāṁsakas mention the concept of *apūrva* or potency as generated by the performance of rituals which is supposed to confer the desired fruits at the appropriate time instead of admitting that the ritualistic deeds themselves have the power to confer the benefits. The postulation of *apūrva* is unwarranted since it violates the Scriptural texts (*śruta hāna*) or imagining a media which is not warranted by Śruti (*aśruta-kalpanā*).

There are a few other wrong theories which are adopted by the Mīmāṁsakas following the Jainas and Vaiśeṣikas such as *bheda* and *abheda, avayava* and *avayavī,* the relation of *samavāya* and the doctrine of *paramāṇus* as the cause of the universe. These are open to criticisms as in the case of Jaina and Vaiśeṣika doctrines which are already refuted in the chapters dealing with Jainism, Vaiśeṣika, and Bhedābhedavāda.

To avoid criticisms against these theories, the best course to be adopted is to admit the classification of the metaphysical categories as *dravya* and *adravya* as formulated by Viśiṣṭādvaita. They should also accept the ontological theory of Viśiṣṭādvaita viz., that performance of *karma* or the prescribed ritual is for the pleasure of the Supreme Being who is the *Antaryāmin* of all beings as taught in the Vedānta. If instead of it, they foolishly stick to the conflicting views of the commentators such as Śabara, Prabhākara, and Kumārila, they would land themselves in a blind alley. The ways and means of reinterpreting the views of the commentators on Jaimini *sūtras* to overcome the conflicts with Vedānta have been fully explained in the treatise titled *Seśvaramīmāṁsā* contributed by Vedānta Deśika.

References

1. See *RB*, I.1.1: *saṁhitametat śārīrakam jaiminīyena ṣoḍaṣakaṣaṇena iti śāstraikatva siddhiḥ.*
2. See *SD, vāda* 3: *ekaśāstra samarthana vāda.* Also see, *The Philosophy or Viśiṣṭādvaita*—A Study based on *AS.*
3. See *PMB*, chap. 11.
4. See *VS*, I.1.2–32; 2.29; 4.18; III.4.40.
5. This statement is found in Bhavanātha's *Nayaviveka.*

10

Sāṅkhya School

THOUGH AMONG the Vedic orthodox schools Sāṅkhya is chronologically the earliest, it is taken up for critical examination by Vedānta Deśika soon after Nirīśvaramīmāṁsā. The reason for this is that one school of Pūrvamīmāṁsā expounded by Prabhākara who accepts the authority of the Vedas and claims to interpret the Vedic texts, denies the importance of *Īśvara*, who is the very essence of all Vedas and also the Lord of the *devatās* or the celestial deities. In the same way, the founders of Sāṅkhya school accept the authority of the Vedas but deny altogether, the existence of *Īśvara*, who is the central doctrine of the Vedas, and admit only two ontological principles, viz., *prakṛti* and *puruṣa*. This school which is designated as Nirīśvara-Sāṅkhya is considered as worse than Nirīśvaramīmāṁsā and therfore it is refuted.

The central doctrine of Sāṅkhya is summed up in the following verse of the *Sāṅkhyakārikā*:

> *mūla prakṛtir-avikṛtiḥ mahadādyāḥ prakṛti-vikṛtiḥ sapta; ṣoḍaṣakaśca; vikārāḥ na prakṛtiḥ na vikṛtiḥ puruṣaḥ.*[1]
>
> The primordial cosmic matter is uncaused and from it evolve seven *vikṛtis* or the evolutes such as *mahat* which serve as the causes of sixteen other evolutes; *puruṣa* or the self is neither caused by any other principle nor does it serve as the cause of anything else.

The evolutes of *prakṛti* referred to here are *mahat, buddhi, ahaṅkāra,* the eleven *indriyas* including *manas* and five *tanmātras* (subtle elements) as well as the five gross elements (*pañca-bhūtas*), thus making a total of twenty-four principles. *Puruṣa* which is distinct from *prakṛti* is the twenty-fifth principle. According to the Sāṅkhya, proper knowledge of the *prakṛti* and its evolutes in their manifest and unmanifest forms serve as the means to the realization of the Self which is known as *kaivalya*, the Supreme Goal (*ātma-kaivalya-sādhana*).

Coming to the details of the theory of *prakṛti*, the Sāṅkhyas maintain that *prakṛti* is constituted of three substances or components (*dravyas*) named *sattva*, *rajas*, and *tamas*, which are eternal and *vibhu* in character. *Sattva* stands for whatever is fine and light (*lāghava* and *prakāśa*) and it causes happiness (*sukha*). *Rajas* represents whatever is active and is the cause of suffering (*duḥkha*). *Tamas* is what is heavy (*gurutva*) and is responsible for ignorance (*moha*). These are also called *guṇas* not in the sense of qualities but as components which forge a chain (like a rope) for binding the self.[2] When these *guṇas* remain in the state of equilibrium (*sāmyāvasthā*), it is known as *prakṛti*. When the equilibrium is disturbed *prakṛti* undergoes evolution.

The admission of three *guṇas* as substances (*dravyas*) is defective, contends Vedānta Deśika. First, this view stands opposed to the teaching of the *Gītā*, which clearly states that these are *guṇas* or qualities.[3] *Prakṛti* is generally regarded as one substance characterized by three qualities. But if it is conceived as a *tattva* containing three components, it becomes four. Besides, if these *guṇas* are *vibhu* or omnipresent (*sarvagata*) at all times, there cannot be any state of equilibrium (*sāmyāvasthā*) and also the state of disturbance (*vaiṣamyāvasthā*). In the absence of these two states, creation and dissolution of the universe cannot take place.

The Theory of Cause and Effect

After criticizing the basic theory of Sāṅkhya that *prakṛti* is constituted of three substances, Vedānta Deśika refutes the Sāṅkhya theory of cause and effect. According to the Sāṅkhyas the effect (*kārya*) is already existent in the cause in a latent form. What is potentially existent is made manifest as effect by the causal operation. The main reason for maintaining this view is what does not exist (*asat*) cannot be produced, as in the example of the oil which cannot be produced from the sand but only from oil seeds in which it is present. The effect is therefore pre-existent in the cause. Hence this theory of causality is called Satkāryavāda, as against the Asatkārya-vāda held by the Naiyāyikas, for whom effect is a new product different from the cause.

This theory is subjected to criticism. Though Viśiṣṭādvaita also subscribes to the theory of Satkāryavāda in a modified form. Vedānta Deśika does not agree with the Sāṅkhya explanation which is defective. It is not necessary that the effect should be pre-existent in the cause. The effect is a modified state of the causal substance, as in the case of the pot produced from the clay. The appropriate causal factors bring into existence the particular effect even without the effect being present in the cause in a latent form. This is evident to our perceptual experience. What is unmanifest becomes manifest. Other than this explanation, it is wrong to assume that the effect actually exists in the cause in an unmanifest form, as in the solitary instance of the presence of oil in oil seeds. The evolutes *mahat, buddhi, ahaṅkāra,* etc., do not actually exist in *prakṛti* in an unmanifest form as in the case of the turtle whose legs, head etc., when withdrawn by it, exist inside its body covered with the shell. This view is opposed to the teachings of the Upaniṣads. The Upaniṣads explain the creation of the element of water from the fire as a modification of the element of fire itself into water (*agni avasthe ca salile*). When the causal state undergoes modification it assumes the state of *kārya* or effect. In connection with the causation of the universe by Brahman, the Upaniṣad cites the illustration of the seed and the huge *nyagrodha* tree. But this does not apply that the *nyagrodha* tree exists in a potential form in the seed but on the other hand, it conveys that the seed contains in it a subtle substance which can grow as a tree.

If Satkāryavāda as conceived by the Sāṅkhyas is accepted, it would involve some difficulty. According to the Sāṅkhyas the effect is latent in the causal substance and what is latent is only made manifest (*abhivyakti*) at a particular time by the causal factors. If the causal substance such as *prakṛti* is *nitya,* then the manifestation of what is latent should also take place all the time. It is not possible to say that *abhivyakti* takes place at a particular point of time. If it is argued that *abhivyakti* takes place only at a particular time by the causal agents, then it would need another operating agent to make it manifest at that particular time and in that way it would lead to an infinite regress. To avoid this difficulty it may be argued that what is latent is not made manifest for which an operating agent is needed, but it is produced (*utpatti*). Even then the problem is not overcome because *utpatti* to take place would need another *utpatti* and in that way it would lead to an infinite regress. The only solution to overcome these difficulties is to admit as Viśiṣṭādvaitins do, that the modification that takes place in respect of the causal substance is the production (*utpatti*) or *abhivyakti* of the effect. In other words, the effect is a passing state of the causal substance (*āgantuka-dharma*). The basic substance (the lump of clay) continues to be the same even if it assumes the form of two halves. The pot when broken assumed the form of potsherd. Thus the effect is a modified state of the cause. The cause and effect are two different states of the same substance. It is not necessary as Sāṅkhyas postulate, that effect is pre-existent in the cause in a potential form.

If the theory of cause and effect is rejected by adopting the dialectial arguments as is done by the Cārvākas and Mādhyamikas, then it would stand opposed to the accepted *pramāṇas* and involve contradiction of one's own teachings (*sarva-pramāṇa-virodha svavacana-virodha*).

THE THEORY OF *PARIṆĀMA* OF *PRAKṚTI*

After criticizing the theory of cause and effect as conceived by the Sāṅkhyas, Vedānta Deśika examines whether *prakṛti*, a non-sentient can undergo modification (*pariṇāma*) without the aid or direction of a sentient being (*cetana*). The Sāṅkhyas who adopt the Pariṇāmavāda, admit this possibility and in support of it cite several instances such as the milk changing itself into curd, water particles becoming hailstones, etc. Not only a non-sentient can undergo modification independently but it can also transform itself into variety of different modifications (*visadṛśa pariṇāma*) and also modifications of similar nature (*sadṛśa pariṇāma*). The water poured out of the clouds assumes different forms such as sweetness, saltishness, sourness, bitterness, etc. when absorbed by coconuts, lemons and other kinds of fruits respectively. Again *prakṛti*, during each evolution in different epochs, evolves itself into the same kind of evolutes (*sadṛśa-pariṇāma*).

Vedānta Deśika refutes these arguments. In all cases cited by the Sāṅkhyas, there is the role of *Paramātman* who has endowed to all the entities, both sentient and non-sentient, *sattā* or existance, *sthiti* or continuance and *pravṛtti* or the capacity to function, as is evident from the Upaniṣadic teachings.[4]

It cannot be said that the mere presence of the sentient being—the self, which is devoid of the *saṅkalpa* or the will to control the event, can cause the evolution as in the example of the conversion of the grass consumed by the cow into milk. On the same analogy the presence of the *puruṣa* by the side of *prakṛti* without the operation of its will, can make the *prakṛti* evolve itself into the manifold universe. The grass consumed by the bullock, in which also the intelligent *jīva* is present, is not converted into milk. If be said that special formation or structure of the physical body of the cow is responsible for the conversion of the grass into milk, then it would amount to the admission of the Cārvāka theory that the special combination of the components of the body itself causes the emergence of *caitanya*.

The Sāṅkhyas attempt to defend the theory of evolution of *prakṛti* on the analogy of the movement of the blind person with the help of a lame person. The blind is enabled to move with the help of the lame person who can guide by telling the direction to go. In the same way, with the mere association or presence of the intelligent *puruṣa*, the *prakṛti* though it is non-sentient, can evolve itself into the universe.

Even this explanation is unsatisfactory, contends Vedānta Deśika. In the case of the blind and lame persons, the lame person is capable of giving proper directions and the blind person possesses the capacity to listen and act accordingly. But in the case of *puruṣa* and *prakṛti* of Sāṅkhyas, both do not possess *jñātṛtva* and *kartṛtva* or the capacity to function. If it be said that mere association of *prakṛti* and *puruṣa* can cause evolution, then the two being *vibhu* or all-pervasive, are associated together all the time (*sannidhi-nitya*).

The purpose of the evolution of the *prakṛti,* according to the Sāṅkhyas is to cause bondage and liberation for *puruṣa.*[5] But his view stands contradicted by their own admission of *puruṣa* as *nitya-mukta* or ever liberated and *nitya-nirlepa* or untouched by any afflictions at all times.

The Sāṅkhyas admit *prakṛti* as a *tattva* on the basis of inference (*anumāna*). What is proved only by means of inference without the support of the Scriptural authority can be open to criticisms. To meet these objections, if they seek the support of the Scriptural texts, they could as well admit *Īśvara* which is well established in the Upaniṣads. If *Īśvara* is rejected because the concept of *Īśvara* also suffers from defects then they could as well reject the theory of *prakṛti* as Vaiśeṣikas have done, by adopting wrong logical arguments.

THE EVOLUTES OF *PRAKṚTI*

Vedānta Deśika criticizes the theory of evolutes and in particular the *mahat-tattva* as conceived by the Sāṅkhyas. The *mahat-tattva* which is the first evolute of *prakṛti* and which is also named as *buddhi-tattva*[6] comprises three functions. These are: (1) *puruṣoparāga,* (2) *viṣayoparāga,* and (3) *vyāpārāveśa.* It becomes *puruṣoparāga* when *mahat,* which represents *buddhi* or intellect, falsely imagines itself as the *puruṣa* or the self which is reflected in it like the reflection of the face in the mirror. When the *mahat* (*buddhi*) flows out through the sense organs and assumes the form of the external objects it is regarded as *viṣayoparāga.* When the *buddhi* wills to do an act after it becomes the ego or the empirical self and also gets into contact with the objects, it is regarded as *vyāpārāveśa.* Thus the *mahat-tattva* has three functions and in view of this, it is regarded as threefold in nature.

According to the Sāṅkhyas, the *mahat-tattva* is also the repository of eight predispositions (*bhāvas*) or instinctive tendencies. These are: (1) *dharma* or merit, (2) *jñāna* or knowledge, (3) *vairāgya* or non-attachment, (4) *aiśvarya* or super-normal powers, (5) *adharma* or demerit, (6) *ajñāna* or ignorance, (7) *avairāgya* or attachment, and (8) *anaiśvarya* or impotence. The first four are the qualities of the *sāttvika-mahat* and the other four belong to the *tāmasa-mahat.*[7] *Adhyavasāya* or the capacity to take a decision is the characteristic feature of *sāttvika-mahat.* Hence it is also designated as *buddhi* or intellect. The five cognitive sense organs (*jñānendriyas*) serve as aids to the *sāttvika-mahat* to perceive directly the five sense data such as *śabda, sparśa, rūpa, rasa,* and *gandha. Manas* or mind subserves the *buddhi* in recollecting the objects and events experienced in the past (*smṛti*) and performing other mental functions such as *cintā* or repeated reflection, *tarka* or reasoning and *saṁśaya* or entertaining doubts.

Ahaṅkāra or ego which is another function of *buddhi,* which stands as the empirical self since Śāṅkhyas do not admit a separate *jīva* in each person other than the transcendental *puruṣa,* serves the purpose of causing attachment (*abhimāna*) to the body. It also causes notions of spatial differences as near and farther, forward and backward, etc., and also the notions of time such as present, past and future in respect of an individual.

All these theories advanced by the Sāṅkhyas are untenable, contends Vedānta Deśika for the following reasons. *Buddhi* is a non-sentient entity being an evolute of non-sentient *prakṛti* and hence it cannot be either the *bodhā* or the subject of knowledge or the *bhoktā* or the subject of experience. If these two functions are attributed to non-sentient *buddhi,* then there would be no need to admit separately the *jīvātmans.* Besides, it would go against their own these viz., that *antaḥkaraṇa* or the internal sense organ (mind) is of three kinds (*antaḥkaraṇaṁ trividham*). These are *buddhi, ahaṅkāra* and *manas. Buddhi* is included among the threefold functions of *antaḥkaraṇa.* The mental functions such as *abhimāna* or developing the sense of attachment, *ālocanā,* or the thinking processes, etc., cannot therefore be attributed to the non-sentient *buddhi.* These are the functions of *jñāna* which is the attribute of the *jīvātman.*

The *mahat-tattva* is of three kinds: *sāttvika mahān, rājasa-mahān* and *tāmasa-mahān.*[8] We have already explained the functions of *sāttvika-mahān* and set aside the views of Sāṅkhya as these are defective. Regarding the *rājasa-mahān,* it is also designated as *prāṇa* which functions by developing on *vāyu.*[9] The five *karmendriyas* subserve it.

This theory of Sāṅkhyas is also untenable as it is opposed to the valid *pramāṇas*. It is also logically unsound. The *Vedānta-sūtra* states that *vāyu* is not *prāṇa* (*na vāyukriye pṛthag-upadeśāt*).

It is maintained by the Sāṅkhyas that the *tāmasa-mahān* is re-garded as *kāla* or time. The moments, hours, days, etc., are its modifications. Time is measured in terms of moments, days, etc., on the basis of the movements of the sun (*sūrya-gati*).

This theory is also defective because it is stated in the Smṛti texts that *kāla* is *anādi* or beginningless and *ananta* or infinite. If this theory advanced by Sāṅkhyas is accepted, then it would follow that prior to *mahat-tattva*, time did not exist and consequently there would be no dissolution and creation of the universe.

The Theory of *Ātman*

According to the Sāṅkhyas, the *antaḥkaraṇa* or internal sense organ is itself the subject of knowledge (*jñāta*) and not the self (*puruṣa*) which is devoid of all functions (*nirvikāra*). The reason for this is that if *jñātṛtva* is attributed to *puruṣa* or the self, it would be subject to modification, whereas *ātman* is *nirvikāra* or devoid of modifications. This theory is directly opposed to the Upaniṣadic texts according to which *puruṣa* or *jīvātman* is *boddhā* or knower.[10] The expressions found in the Upaniṣads such as *vijñāna-ghana-eva* meaning that *ātman* is constituted of knowledge only, *nirguṇa* or devoid of attributes, *niṣkriya* or devoid of all functions, *nirvikāra* or devoid of modifications, etc., bear different import as explained in the chapter or Advaita Vedānta.

Further the notion of "I" denoted by the term *ahaṁ* which is the true self according to Viśiṣṭādvaita, is not identical with the *ahaṅkāra tattva* which is an evolute of *prakṛti*. That *ahamartha* or the notion of "I" is the true self is well established with adequate arguments by Rāmānuja in the *Śrībhāṣya* and also in other works of Vedānta Deśika. For those who deny *kartṛtva* and *bhoktṛtva* for the self on the ground that it is *kuṭastha* or unchangeable, the Vedic injunctions in the form of performing the deeds enjoyed by the Sacred texts and refraining from those acts which are prohibited, would be rendered meaningless in respect of the *puruṣa* or the individual self.

The verses of the *Bhagavadgītā*[11] which deny *kartṛtva* to the *ātman* and ascribe it to the *guṇas* of *prakṛti* bear a different purport as is explained in the *Rāmānujabhāṣya* on the *Gītā*.

The very *Gītā* in a different *adhyāya* admits *kartṛtva* for *jīvātman.*[12] The *Vedāntasūtra* also explicitly states that *jīva* is *kartā.*[13]

Vedānta Deśika further points out that *prakṛti* can never become *kartā* in any sense. If it is argued that *prakṛti* in the form of the physical body which is common to all persons performs all deeds, then it would amount to the admission of experiencing the fruits of the deeds by all individuals. In that case there would be no distinction between bondage and liberation. It cannot be said that the individual bodies are the determinant of experience of pleasure or pain by each individual separately, because the mere bodies cannot serve as the determinant for the experience of the fruits. The argument that *karma* or the results of the past deeds is the determinant, would not hold good because the *karma* associated with *prakṛti* in the form of the body is also common to all. According to the Sāṅkhyas, the *ātman* of an individual is *sarvagata* or omnipresent and as the body of each individual is associated with *ātman,* which is the common feature for all persons, the body alone cannot be the determinant for experiencing the fruits of the deeds by individuals separately. On the other hand if it is argued that the *antaḥkaraṇa* of each individual which is distinct and which when falsely identified with the *ātman,* experiences *bhoga* separately, even then the position does not change because *prakṛti* which is common to all is subject to delusion. Consequently, the *antaḥkaraṇas* of all individuals would become subject to delusion of identity with the self. There is no basis to determine that a particular *puruṣa* in conjunction with a particular individual *antaḥkaraṇa* becomes deluded. Further *puruṣa* who is not admitted as *jñātā, kartā* and *bhoktā* cannot even have any delusion. If such a pure transcendental *puruṣa* is admitted as the subject of delusion, then it would to an *apasiddhānta* or wrong theory.

The theory that *ātmā* is *vibhu* or all-pervasive, is also untenable. The individual experiences pleasure or pain along with the body. When it is possible for an individual to experience *bhoga* even at a distant place through the body with which he is always associated, it is not necessary to postulate for this purpose that *jīvātman* should be *vibhu.* Even when *jīvātman* is devoid of a gross physical body constituted of the three *guṇas* it is possible to have movement on account of the will of *Paramātman* in accordance with the *karma* of the individual as in the case of the *utkrānti* or exit of the *jīva* from the body after death and its movement to higher realms, as stated in the Upaniṣads. It is therefore not necessary to admit *vibhutva* for *jīvātman*.

While concluding the critical review of the Sāṅkhya school, Vedānta Deśika points out that the theories developed by the Sāṅkhyas are mutually oppose. The Sāṅkhyas admit that *prakṛti* is an aggregates of three *guṇas* (*saṅghāta*) and its orderly evolution is for the benefit of the *puruṣa*.[14] This implies that *puruṣa*, for whom *prakṛti* exists, is the *kartā* or the subject of knowing and *bhoktā* or the subject of experience, that is, the enjoyer of the activities caused by *prakṛti* in the form of pleasure and pain.[15] In the same breath they also deny *kartṛtva* and *bhoktṛtva* for *puruṣa* by affirming that *puruṣa* is *niṣkriya* and *nirlepa*.

In another verse of the *kārikā*, it is stated that *prakṛti* functions for causing bondage and liberation for the *puruṣa* (*puruṣasya darśanārtham*).[16] In a more explicit way it is pointed out that just as the milk of the cow is intended for the growth of the calf, in the same way *prakṛti* functions for the purpose of causing liberation from bondage for the *puruṣa*.[17] In one another verse of the *kārikā*, it denies *bandha* and *mokṣa* for *puruṣa* (*tasmāt na badhyate*).[18] Thus all such statements which are of conflicting nature confirm the criticism made by the author of the *Vedāntasūtra* in the words: *vipratiṣedācca asamañjasam.*[19] It means that Sāṅkhya philosophy is most unsound as their teachings are of conflicting nature.

If it is the accepted theory of the Sāṅkhya that *ātmā* is not either *kartā* or *bhoktā*, there would be no need to admit *puruṣa* as a distinct ontological principle other than *prakṛti*. If this position is accepted, it would amount to the theory of Cārvāka that body itself is the self. It *puruṣa* is not *boddhā* or the subject of knowledge and *prakṛti* is devoid of knowledge, there is no scope for a *pramātā* or knower and in the absence of it there are no valid *pramāṇas* to establish a sound philosophical theory. This would bring Sāṅkhyas close to Mādhyamika for whom there are no valid *pramāṇas* either to prove his own theory or disprove the theory of a rival school.

References

1. *Sāṅkhyakārikā*, v. 3.
2. See *Sāṅkhya-pravacanabhāṣya.*
3. See *BG*, XIV.5, *Sattvam rajas-tamaḥ iti guṇāḥ prakṛti saṁbhavaḥ.*
4. *Tait. Up.*, II.6: *Tat sṛṣṭv tadevānuprāviśat, saccatyaccābhavat.* Also *Br. Up.*, Mādhyandina version, V.7.3: *Yaḥ ātmani tiṣṭhan, yamātma na veda, yaḥ ātmānam antaro yamayati....*
5. See *Sāṅkhyakārikā*: *puruṣasya darśanārtham kaivalyārtham tathā pradhānasya.*
6. *Mahat-tattvaṁ-iti proktaṁ buddhi-tattvaṁ taducyate.*
7. See *Sāṅkhyakārikā*: *dharmo jñānam virāga aiśvaryam; sāttvikametad-rūpam, tāmasam-asmād-viparyāstam.*
8. *Sāttviko rājasaścaiva tāmasaśca tridhā mahān.*
9. *Rājasa mahān prāṇaḥ vāyum adhiṣṭhitya dehamādhatte.*
10. *Jānātyeva ayaṁ puruṣaḥ* (quoted by Rāmānuja in *RB*). Also *Praśna Up.*: *Eṣa hy boddha.*
11. *BG*, XVIII.20: *kāryakāraṇa-kartṛtve hetuḥ prakṛtirucyate.*
12. Ibid., XVIII.14.
13. *VS*, II.2.33: *Kartā śāstrārthavattvāt.*
14. See *Sāṅkhyakārikā—saṅghāta parārthattvāt.*
15. Cf. *kaivalyārtha pravṛtteḥ*—the word *pravṛtti* implies *kartṛtva* or effort to be made for attaining *kaivalya.*
16. See *Sāṅkhyakārikā.*
17. *Vatsa vivardhi-nimittam kṣīrasya yathā pravṛttiḥ ajñasya; puruṣa vimokṣa nimittam tathā pravṛttiḥ pradhānasya.*
18. See *Sāṅkhyakārikā.*
19. *VS*, II.2.9.

11

Yoga School

THIS SCHOOL comes up for consideration soon after the examination of the Sāṅkhya school. Though it is allied to Sāṅkhya Darśana insofor as the philosophical theories of the two schools are similar, yet it is regarded as a separate Darśana founded by Hiraṇyagarbha, the Vedic deity entrusted with the task of the creation of the universe. The major difference between the two schools arises on the philosophical side by the admission of *Īśvara* as the third ontological principle besides *prakṛti* and *puruṣa* accepted by the Sāṅkhya. On the practical side, it has developed a comprehensive yogic *sādhana* to be adopted for the realization of the self, which is the spiritual goal to be attained. Hence Yoga school is designated as Seśvara-Sāṅkhya to distinguish it from Sāṅkhya school which is characterized as Nirīśvara-Sāṅkhya.

The title adopted for this chapter in the *Paramata-bhaṅgā* is *Yogasiddhānta-bhaṅgādhikāra.* At the very outset Vedānta Deśika raises the question whether it is necessary to criticize *Yogasiddhānta* since the important philosophical theories of Yoga, which are somewhat similar to those of Sāṅkhya, have already been refuted. More importantly the Yoga Darśana has the distinction of being founded by Hiraṇyagarbha, who is not only a reputed sage like Kapila, the founder of the Sāṅkhya, but also the Vedic deity brought into existence by the Supreme Being and also entrusted with the task of the creation of the universe. Besides he was the direct disciple of the Supreme Being, who taught him the Vedas soon after creation[1] and he was also the guru of Rudra and other celestial deities.

Further, the *Yogaśāstra* promulgated by such a highly respected person, has admitted the three *tattvas*, viz., *prakṛti*, *puruṣa*, and *Īśvara* as taught in the Upaniṣads and also accepted their difference and reality (*satyatva*). The *Yogasūtras* formulated by the sage Pātañjali also mention *Īśvara*, who is described as the Being free from all afflictions and *karma*.[2] It is also stated that *praṇava* or the syllable *Aum* denotes Him.[3] The commentary on the *Yogasūtras* contributed by sage Vyāsa states that the *puruṣa* referred to in the *sūtra* is the *Īśvara* who is the Ruler of the entire universe. The *Mahābhārata* mentions that Hiraṇyagarbha is the promulgator of *Yogaśāstra* (*hiraṇyagarbho yogasya vaktā*). In view of all these facts the entire *Yogaśāstra* is to be accepted as authoritative.

Vedānta Deśika acknowledges all these facts. Nevertheless he considers it necessary to critically examine the Yoga Darśana to determine what teachings or theories of it are in conformity with the Vedānta and what are at variance with Vedānta. According to the statement of the *Mahābhārata*, there were several adherents of the Sāṅkhya and Yoga schools who conducted discussions about Sāṅkhya and Yoga.[4] Naturally it appears that there were differences of opinion among them and consequently different theories were developed later which might have deviated from the original teachings of Kapila and Hiraṇyagarbha. Hence Vedānta Deśika justifies his attempt to critically examine the Yoga school as it was known at that time. Thus he states at the beginning of the review that he attempts to determine what is opposed to Vedānta and what is not opposed to it in the *Yogaśāstra*. With these general remarks he proceeds to examine the main theories of Yoga. Even though Hiraṇyagarbha was a Vedic deity, he too could be subjected to delusion, being an exalted individual self (*jīvātmā*) like other individual selves.

The following are the important theories which are at variance with Vedānta. First, according to the *Vedāntasūtra*, as interpreted by Rāmānuja, Brahman who is organically related to the *cit* (*jīvas*) and *acit* (cosmic matter) is the material cause (*upādāna-kāraṇa*) of the universe. As against this view, the Yoga school maintains the theory that *Īśvara* admitted by them is only the *nimitta-kāraṇa* or instrumental cause of the universe. This

Īśvara, like the *puruṣa* of Sāṅkhya, is devoid of *kriyā* or function and *śakti* or power to create the universe but by his mere presence by the side of the *prakṛti* (*sannidhi-mātra*), He makes the *prakṛti* evolve itself into the universe. Secondly the glory of *Īśvara* (*aiśvarya*) consists in His reflection in *prakṛti* (*upādhi-viśeṣa-prayukta*), similar to the reflection of the face in the mirror placed in front of it.

Thirdly in the matter of the order of evolution of the *tattvas* from *prakṛti*, the Yoga school differs from Vedānta. According to Yoga, from *mahat-tattva* evolve the six evolutes, viz., *ahaṅkāra* and the five *tanmātras* and from *ahaṅkāra* comes eleven *indriyas* and from *tanmātras* arise the five elements. According to the Vedānta the eleven *indriyas* arise from *sāttvika-ahaṅkāra* and the *tanmātras* evolve from *tāmasa-ahaṅkāra*. With regard to the Yogic *sādhana* which is laid down for attaining *mokṣa*, it is not regarded as a form of worship of the *Paramātman* (*paramapuruṣa-ārādhana*) who is to be attained as the goal, but on the contrary it is aimed for the purpose of realization of *jīvātman*. *Kaivalya* or the existence of *jīvātman* in its true form, free from the association with *citta* or the mind and its functions is *mokṣa* and not the attainment of *Paramātman* which is the goal for Vedānta.

All these theories are opposed to the Vedānta doctrines and hence they are refuted. Keeping this in mind, the author of the *Vedāntasūtra* says: *etena yoga pratyuktaḥ*.[5] It means that the Yoga school also stands refuted by the criticisms offered against the theories of Sāṅkhya. The implication of this *sūtra*, as interpreted by Rāmānuja, is that the philosophical theories of Yoga, which are similar to those of Sāṅkhya, stand refuted as they are opposed to Vedānta. But what is not opposed to Vedānta such as the prescription of the Yogic *sādhana* for attaining *samādhi* are acceptable to Viśiṣṭādvaita as this is useful for the purpose of Bhaktiyoga as *sādhana*.

While summing up the review, Vedānta Deśika points out that the original founders of these schools, sage Kapila and Hiraṇyagarbha, were not opposed to the Vedānta doctrines. It is only the later adherents of the schools who created the conflict with Vedānta in respect of the doctrines developed by them. This fact is implied in the statement of the *Mahābhārata*, which reads: *Bahavaḥ puruṣā rājan sāṅkhya-yoga vicāriṇaḥ; naite icchanti puruṣaṁ ekaṁ kurukulodvana.* It means that there were several adherents of Sāṅkhya and Yoga schools who expounded their own theories and they did not like to admit the existence of one Supreme Being (*Paramapuruṣam ekaṁ*). From this point of view the *Mahābhārata* also extols both Sāṅkhya and Yoga.[6] The implication of these statements, as explained by Vedānta Deśika, is that the original founders of these schools were not against Vedānta and hence they are not to be condemned. Only the later followers of these schools who further developed the Darśana by modifying the doctrines, created a conflict with Vedānta teachings. Hence whatever is opposed to the Vedānta is to be rejected and whatever conforms to Vedānta theories is to be accepted.

References

1. *Ch. Up.*: *Yo brahmāṇam vidadhāti pūrvam yo vai vedāṁśca prahinoti tasmai.*
2. See *YS*: *Kleśa-karma vipākāśayaiḥ aparāmṛṣṭaḥ puruṣa-viśeṣaḥ.*
3. Ibid.: *Tasya vācakaḥ praṇavāḥ.*
4. See *Mbh.*: *Bahavaḥ puruṣā rājan sāṅkhya-yoga vicāriṇaḥ.*
5. *VS*, II.1.3.
6. See *Mbh.*: *Sāṅkhyaṁ yogaḥ pāñcarātraṁ vedāḥ pāśupatam tathā; ātma-pramāṇany-etāni na hantavyāni hetubhiḥ.*

12
Pāśupata School

IN THE *PARAMATA-BHAṄGA* this school comes up for critical examination soon after *Yoga-siddhānta*, for the reason that it also admits *Īśvara* as the *nimitta-kāraṇa* or the efficient cause of the universe. Bādarāyaṇa also considers this school along with Sāṅkhya, Yoga, and Nyāya-Vaiśeṣika since the theory of *Īśvara* as only the *nimitta-kāraṇa* of the universe is opposed to the Vedānta theory of Brahman as the *upādāna-kāraṇa*. Besides, many of their religious practices are opposed to Vedic tradition.

There are several schools of ancient Śaivism known under different names based on different Śaiva Tantras. They are: (1) Śaiva, (2) Pāśupata, (3) Saumya, (4) Laguḍa, (5) Pratyabhijña Darśana, and (6) Raseśvara Darśana. Among these, Pāśupata is regarded as the oldest school which existed even at the time of Bādarāyaṇa. All of them are developed primarily on the basis of Śaiva Āgamas and they all admit Śiva as the Supreme Deity as against Brahman or Viṣṇu accepted as the Ultimate Reality in the Upaniṣads and *Vedāntasūtra.*

The *Sarvadarśana-saṅgraha* of Mādhavācārya, a work of the fourteenth century, includes Pratyabhijña Darśana and Raseśvara Darśana besides Nakulīśa Pāśupata Darśana. Following the teachings of Bādarāyaṇa in the *Vedāntasūtra*, and the commentary on it Rāmānuja, Vedānta Deśika confines his attention to the critical analysis of the Pāśupata school only since it is considered fully developed and is the oldest school of ancient Śaivism.

Coming the their doctrines, the Pāśupata Darśana admits thirty-six *tattvas* or ontological principles instead of twenty-five accepted by Sāṅkhya, Yoga and other schools. The primordial cosmic matter named *prakṛti* which is the cause for the evolute known as *mahat,* is conceived as of two kinds, viz., *avyaktaṁ* and *traiguṇyam.* The *avyakta* is the subtle or unmanifest state (*sūkṣmāvasthā*) of the three *guṇas* of *prakṛti,* whereas the *traiguṇya* is the gross or manifest state (*sthūlāvasthā*) of the *guṇas.* There is no Scriptural basis or rational justification for such as division of *prakṛti* into two categories. If it is conceived as a logical possibility or as a postulate, the same kind of division should be made in respect of *mahat* which is the next evolute of *prakṛti.*

Along with *avyakta,* the Pāśupatas also admit five principles. These are: (1) *niyati* or unseen power, (2) *kāla* or time, (3) *rāga* or the principle which causes attachment, (4) *vidyā* or knowledge, and (5) *Kala* or the principle which causes obstruction of knowledge. These are inherent in the *māyā* even during the state of dissolution of the universe along with Śiva and *puruṣa* (*jīvātmā*). According to Śaivism, *māyā, puruṣa* and Śiva exist eternally (*nitya tattva*).[1]

Māyā is conceived in this system as a cosmic power (*śakti*) which binds in accordance with the *saṅkalpa* of Śiva, the souls at the time of creation with the physical body, sense organs, intellect, etc. to enable them to experience pleasure and pain. *Niyati, kāla, rāga,* and *vidyā* serve as accessory causes for *māyā.* In the absence of the support of the trustworthy Āgamas and Scriptural and Smṛti texts, there is no logical justification for admitting these postulates. The concepts of *kāla* (time), *svabhāva* (nature), *niyati* (fate), and *yadṛcchā* (chance) mentioned in the *Śvetāśvatara Upaniṣad*[2] as the possible causes for the creation of the universe cannot be construed in support of the Pāśupata theory because these concepts in the Upaniṣads are mentioned as possible alternative theories to explain the creation of the universe other than Brahman or God. The will of God in accordance with *karma* or the results of the past deeds performed by the *jīvas* in earlier births is responsible for the birth of individuals in the present life and mere *niyati* or any other unknown factor cannot serve the purpose. All the other principles such as *kala, vidyā, rāga,* etc. are superfluous.

Some of the epistemological theories formulated by the Pāśupatas are also defective. They make a distinction between two kinds of knowledge (1) that which reveals the objects directly and (2) that which causes the experience of objects in the form of joy and pain. Such a distinction does not hold good because what is cognized itself leads to the experience of the object.

The theory of bondage or *bandha* and liberation or *mokṣa* for *jīvātman* formulated by Pāśupata is most unsound as it is opposed to the Upaniṣadic teachings. They maintain that the *jīvātman* which is regarded as omnipotent and monadic in nature (*aṇu*) is eclipsed by three kinds of bondage, viz., *mala*, *māyā*, and *karma*. As and when it is liberated by these it becomes omniscient, omnipresent (*sarvagata*), and omnipotent (*sarvaśakta*) and also equal to Śiva in respect of all its glory (*śiva-tulya-aiśvarya*). All these views stand opposed to the Upaniṣadic teachings and the *Vedāntasūtra* which emphasise *sāmya* or equality of the liberated *jīva* with Brahman in respect of certain attributes and, in particular, the enjoyment of the bliss of Brahman (*bhogamātra-sāmya*).[3]

Coming to the doctrine of *Īśvara*, the Pāśupatas conceive it as of five forms. These are: (1) *Īśvara-tattva* (2) *Śiva-tattva* (3) *Śakti-tattva*, (4) *Sadāśiva-tattva*, and (5) *Vidyā-tattva*. The details of the five forms of *Īśvara* and their functions are given in the *Paramata-bhaṅga* based on *Śaivāgamas*.[4] Vedānta Deśika critically examines these details and comes to the conclusion that these are defective since they are mutually opposed (*pūrvāpara-viruddha*).[5]

Under the broad heading of Śaivism, several other schools have been developed with different names such as (1) Śivādvaita or that which upholds the doctrine of Śiva as the only ultimate Reality and that *jīvas* become dissolved in the state of *mukti* with Śiva, (2) Pāṣaṇavādi Śaiva or those who concede the existence of *jīvas* in the state of *mukti* but they are devoid of attributes such as *jñāna*, and (3) Sāmyavādī Śaivas or those who admit equality of *jīvas* with Śiva in the state of *mukti*.

Regarding the Śivādvaita, the criticisms levelled against Pracchanna-Bauddhavāda (Advaita) also apply to Śivādvaita. Regarding the Pāṣaṇavādī Śaiva the criticisms levelled against the Vaiśeṣika theory of *mukti* would apply to it. As regards the Sāmyavādī Śaiva, the arguments advanced against the wrong interpretation of the *śāmya-śruti* would apply to them.

Vedānta Deśika also examines critically a few other important doctrines enunciated in the Pāśupata Tantras. The *tattvas* are classified into four kinds: (1) *Pati* or Śiva, (2) *paśu* or bound selves, (3) *vidhi* or duties to be performed, and (4) Yoga or the attainment of union with Śiva. *Paśu* or *jīvātmās* are classified into six categories, viz., (a) *svābhāvika-kārya-kāraṇas*, (b) *ārabdha-kārya-kāraṇas*, (c) *vyavṛtta-kārya-kāraṇas*, (d) *sammūddha-kārya-kāranas*, (e) *sammūḍha-kārya-kāraṇas*, and (f) *āddhya-kārya-kāraṇas*. Some details of these categories are furnished in the *Paramata-bhaṅga*.[6] According to Vedānta Deśika, these are not supported by the commonly accepted Śruti and Smṛti texts (*sarva-sammata smṛti-itihāsa pūraṇādi-virodha*).

Vedānta Deśika also refers to certain religious observances adopted by the followers of Pāśupata religion such as that a person becomes a Brāhmaṇa by assuming *Śiva-dīkṣā* and that one becomes an ascetic (*yati*) by *Kāpālavṛta*.[7] These are all opposed to the authoritative orthodox Āgamas (*āptāgama virodha*).

According to Vedānta Deśika, the Pāśupata *mata* falls outside the scope of orthodox Vedic religion on several grounds. First, it places Vedas on par with their religious treatises (*tantras*) and also considers Vedas as *pauruṣeya* or as authored by somebody. As the knowledge about Śiva is not adequately available in the Vedas, greater importance is accorded by the Pāśupatas to the Śaiva Āgamas. The existence of *Īśvara* is established on the basis of inference and Śiva is regarded as the *nimitta-kāraṇa* for the universe. The *para* and *apara-tattvas* are not properly presented. The religious observances are laid down as opposed to Vedas.

The stray reference to *Rudropāsanā* in the *Atharvaśiras Upaniṣad* as the means to *mokṣa* cannot be regarded as a Scriptural support to Pāśupata religion since the *upāsanā* referred to here, as explained by Rāmānuja is to be interpreted as *upāsanā* on *Paramātman* as the inner soul (*antaryāmī*) of Rudra (*Rudra-śarīraka paramātmā upāsanā*).

In the same way the casual references made to the greatness of *Umāpati*, *Paśupati*, *Śrīkaṇṭha* as the son of *Caturmukha* Brahmā cannot be taken as the sources of authority for Pāśupata *mata* in the same way as Kapila, though extolled as a sage, who taught Sāṅkhya (*sāṅkhyasya vaktā kapilaḥ*) is not regarded as authoritative.

In the *Mahābhārata*, Pāśupata *mata* is declared to be outside the Vedic religion as it is opposed to the Vedic teachings. It does not also acknowledge Nārāyaṇa as *Paratattva*.

Keeping all these facts in mind, Bādarāyaṇa who is the author of the *Mahābhārata* has stated in the *Brahmasūtra* that the Pāśupata *mata* is unsound (*patyuḥ asāmañjasyatvāt*).[8]

References

1. See commentary on *PMB*, p. 73: *Māyā puruṣa śiva iti etat tritayam mahārtha saṁhāre avaśiṣyate.*
2. *Śvet. Up.*, I.1.1.
3. See *VS*, IV.4.21.
4. See *PMB*, pp. 89, 94: *Śuddhāni pañca tattvāni.* See also commentary on *PMB*, p. 89.
5. Ibid., p. 97: *Ādyanteṣu smaranti śiva tattvam; śakti sadāśiva tattva īśvara-vidyākhya tattve ca.*
6. Ibid., pp. 102–4.
7. Some details of the religious observances of the Pāśupata such as drinking water and eating food by using human skull, smearing the body with the ashes of the cremated dead body (*śavabhasma*) are given in the *Śrībhāṣya*. See commentary on *VS*, II.3.25.
8. *VS*, II.2.35.

13
Pāñcarātra School

IN THE *PARAMATA-BHAṄGA* this school comes up for examination immediately after the critical review of the Pāśupata school. Though it is not intended, unlike the Pāśupata, for refutation, it is included in the treatise with the main objective of defending it against the criticisms levelled by others that Pāñcarātra treatises are not authoritative. As is evident from the *Vedāntasūtra*, even at the time of Bādarāyaṇa there were criticisms against the authoritativeness of the Pāñcarātra on the ground that some of their doctrines were opposed to the Vedānta. One of the major objections which is mentioned by Bādarāyaṇa as a prima facie view,[1] is that the Pāñcarātra admits the theory of the origin of the *jīva* whereas *jīva* according to Vedānta is eternal (*nitya*). In order to answer such objections Badarāyaṇa was required to evaluate the soundness of the Pāñcarātra doctrines and prove their authority. The same task is undertaken by Vedānta Deśika in the *Paramata-bhaṅga.* He examines in greater detail all possible objections against the authoritativeness of the Pāñcarātra and answers them. That is the reason for adopting the title for this chapter "Bhagavat-śāstra-virodha-parihāra" instead of Bhagavat-śāstra-bhaṅga-vāda as in the case of other schools. He states all objections against Pāñcarātra and answers them comprehensively. The importance of taking school for review can be judged from the fact that he has contributed an independent treatise under the title *Pāñcarātra-rakṣā* which presents in much greater detail all the arguments in defence of Pāñcarātra. The chapter (*adhikāra*) included in the *Paramata-bhaṅga* is a briefer account of the important points.

At first Vedānta Deśika points out that the Pāñcarātra treatises enjoy the Supreme authority since the teachings contained in them are promulgated by no less a persom than Nārāyaṇa, who is the Supreme Being and omniscient (*sarvajña*) and omnipotent (*sarvaśakta*) and as such the author of these texts in not subject to any delusion, forgetfulness and incapacity to teach the doctrines. It is stated in the very Pāñcarātra treatise that the Lord Himself imparted these teachings containing the essence of the Vedānta doctrines out of compassion for the benefit of His devotees.[2] These were taught to great sages such as Sanatkumāra, Nārada, Śāṇḍilya, etc. who were devoted to Him. In later epochs these teachings were imparted to other by these very sages. Hence there is no room for questioning their authority, unlike the teachings imparted to the demons and other unqualified persons as in the case of the Āgamas of the non-Vedic schools, for the purpose of deluding them.

The major objection against the authoritativeness of the Pāñcarātra treatises is that some of the philosophical doctrines advanced in them are opposed to those taught in the Vedānta. Vedānta Deśika rules out this possibility by property interpreting the statements of the Pāñcarātra texts in conformity with the Upaniṣadic statements. Thus, for instance, some of the Pāñcarātra treatises speak of seven *tattvas* or metaphysical categories viz., *Īśvara, avidyā, karma, kāla kartavyatā* (duties to be performed), *itikartavyata* (accessories for the *sādhana*) and *saṁyama* (realization of oneness with *Paramātman*). Vedānta, on the contrary, acknowledges only three *tattvas*, viz., *cit, acit*, and *Īśvara*. But this objection is unfounded, contends Vedānta Deśika. The metaphysical categories can be classified as two (*Īśa* and *īśitavya*), or as three or as even five (*arthapañcaka*) and as seven from different standpoints. But the principal *tattvas* are three only, viz., *cit, acit*, and *Īśvara* and these are acknowledged and discussed in the Pāñcarātra treatises. Thus, the following statement of the Pāñcarātra acknowledges the three *tattvas* and discusses their nature: "*acetanā parārthā ca nityā satata vikriyā; triguṇā karmiṇāṁ kṣetram prakṛteḥ rūpam ucyate; vyāptirūpeṇa saṁbandhaḥ tasyāśca puruṣasya ca; sa hi anādiḥ anantaśca paramārthena niścitaḥ.*" It means: *Prakṛti* is non-sentient, eternal and constantly changing, characterized by three *guṇas* and serves as the body for the *jīvas.* It is pervaded by the *puruṣa* (*jīva*) and that *jīva* is beginningless, infinite numerically and eternal. Hence there is no opposition between the teachings of the Pāñcarātra and the Vedānta regarding the principal *tattvas.*

The expression *vyāptirūpeṇa saṁbandhaḥ* in the same verse explaining the relationship between *jīva* and *prakṛti* in terms of pervasion (*vyāpti*) appears to militate against the theory of *aṇutva* of *jīva.* But is not so, explains Vedānta Deśika, because as further elucidated in the Purāṇas, this *vyāpti* of the *jīva* in the body is to be taken in the sense that the *jīva* is pervasive in the body through its *dharma-bhūta-jñāna* similar to the presence of oil in the oil seed, and not by its *svarūpa* which is atomic (*aṇu*).

Similarly, the evolutes of *prakṛti* which is conceived as *śakti,* is counted more than the commonly accepted number by making a distinction between *sūkṣma-avasthā* (unmanifest state) and *sthūla-avasthā* (manifest state). But Such enumerations would not be treated as a conflict with the normally accepted theory.

Another important objection against Pāñcarātra is related to the question of the identity of the *jīva* and *Īśvara* in the state of *mukti.* While the *Vedāntasūtra* clearly states that the liberated *jīva* is devoid of the cosmic functions (*jagad-vyāpāra-varjam*), some of the Pāñcarātra treatises speak of acquisition of *brahmabhāva* or becoming same as Brahman (*Bhāgavata*),[3] Rulership of all (*Sarveśvaratva*) and omnipotence (*Sarvaśaktitva*). These views, Vedānta Deśika contends, are to be understood in accordance with the interpretations of (1) the Scriptural statements which state that a *jīva* who has realized Brahman becomes Brahman, that is, it becomes similar to Brahman (*brahmaiva bhavati*) (2) the texts which state that *jīva,* after the attainment of Brahman manifest with eight attributes of Brahman, and (3) the Upaniṣadic texts which state that it attains *sāmya* or similarly with Brahman (*nirañjanaḥ paramaṁ ṣāmyam upaiti*).

All these statements, if they are properly interpreted, do not speak of identity of *jīva* with Brahman with the cessation of bondage. *Jīva,* after liberation, becomes equal to Brahman in respect of certain aspects only, other than *jagad-vyāpāra.*

In accordance with the will of *Īśvara*, *jīva* enjoys certain freedom (*sa svarāt bhavati*) and performs activities without any obstruction since he is free from the influence of *karma*.

Pāñcarātra treatises admit besides Vāsudeva, three *vyūha* manifestations of the Supreme Being in the names of Saṅkarṣaṇa, Aniruddha, and Pradyumna. They are entrusted with specific cosmic functions. They are also regarded as the presiding deities of *jīva*, *manas*, and *ahaṅkāra tattva*, respectively. Besides, it is also stated that *jīva* in the name of Saṅkarṣaṇa originates from Vāsudeva.[4] This view supporting the theory of the origin and birth of *jīva* is considered as opposed to the Scriptural teaching according to which *jīva* is devoid of birth and origin and that it is eternal (*nitya*).

Vedānta Deśika refutes this objection. He points out that the concerned statement of the *Pāñcarātrasaṁhitā* does not speak of the origin of the *jīva*. On the contrary, it implies, as explained by Rāmānuja in the *Śrībhāṣya*, that Vāsudeva, Saṅkarṣaṇa, Pradyumna, and Aniruddha referred to in the statement are manifestations (*vyūhas*) or *Parabrahma* for the purpose of meditation by devotees seeking to attain Brahman.

Infact Saṅkarṣaṇa is no the name of the *jīva*. Nor does Pradyumna denote *manas*. In the same way Aniruddha cannot be *ahaṅkāra*. The association of the term *jīva* with Saṅkarṣaṇa, *manas* with Pradyumna and *ahaṅkāra* with Aniruddha conveys the idea that these three *vyūha* forms of Vāsudeva are the presiding deities of the three evolutes, respectively. The term *jāyate* does not literally mean "originates" but, on the other hand, it implies *prādurbhāva* or manifestations of Vāsudeva in the form of *Vyūha-avatāra* out of His *saṅkalpa*.

Further the very *Pāñcarātrasaṁhitā* denies the origin of *jīva*. Thus it states that *jīva* is *anādi* and also *ananta* or without end (*jīvo ānādi anantaḥ kathitā*).

After establishing that there are no conflicts between Vedānta teachings and those of Pāñcarātra regarding the major philosophical theories. Vedānta Deśika proceeds to show that even in respect of certain religious practices (*anuṣṭhāna*) relating to the construction of the temples and consecration of a deity etc., laid down by the Pāñcarātra, there is no opposition (*virodha*) between the teachings of the Pāñcarātra and Vedic teachings.

Nor is there any opposition between the *Pāñcarātrasaṁhitās* and other Smṛti texts compiled by sages such as Dakṣa, Gautama, Vyāsa, Parāśara, etc. If in a few cases there appear to be conflicts, these could be easily reconciled by proper interpretation. The *varṇāśrama-dharma* or observance of prescribed rituals in accordance with one's *varṇa* or caste and *āśrama* or stage of life, which is accorded an important place in Smṛti texts (*dharma-śāstra*), are accepted even by the Pāñcarātra texts. The following statement of the Pāñcarātra emphasizes the importance of worship by one who scrupulously observes the *varṇāśrama-dharma*:

varṇāśrama ācāravatā puruṣeṇa paraḥ pumān;
Viṣṇuḥ ārādhyate punaḥ na anyat tat-toṣakārakaḥ.

The Supreme Lord Viṣṇu is worshipped only by persons who scrupulously follow the *varṇa* and *āśrama-dharma.* In no other way He is pleased.

In fact some Pāñcarātra texts acknowledge that *Bhagavad-arcanā* or worship of *Bhagavān*, is also part of *varṇāśrama-dharma.* According to Rāmānuja, *Bhagavad-ārādhanā* is a *nitya karma* or a mandatory *karma.* What is laid down by Dharmaśastra complied by the sages are not overlooked by the *Bhagavadśāstra* (Pāñcarātra treatises) and hence the validity of the Pāñcarātra cannot be questioned on that basis. The Pāñcarātra texts even prohibit the worship of Viṣṇu by those who strictly do not follow the *varṇāśrama-dharma.*[5]

More importantly the *Mahābhārata,* compiled by the sage Vedavyāsa, who is also the author of the *Brahmasūtra,* discusses the greatness of the Pāñcarātra system as compared to Sāṅkhya, Yoga, and Pāśupata and extols it as the Supreme authority. The following verses establish beyond any doubt that these treatises are most authoritative:

idaṁ śreyam idaṁ puṇyam idam hitam anuttamam
bhaviṣyati pramāṇam vai etadeva anuśāsanam.

This (Pāñcarātra teachings) are sacred; they are meritorious and they are most beneficial; this serves as most authoritative and acceptable.

The statement—"*Pāñcarātrasya kṛtsnasya vaktā nārāyaṇaḥ svayam*" which means that the entire Pāñcarātra teachings are taught by Lord Nārāyaṇa Himself, sets aside any doubt regarding its *prāmāṇya*. Yāmuna, a predecessor to Rāmānuja, has contributed an independent work titled *Āgama-prāmāṇya* to establish the authoritativeness of the Pāñcarātra Āgamas. As stated earlier, Vedānta Deśika has also written an independent treatise under the title *Pāñcarātra-rakṣa* in which he defends the Pāñcarātra Āgamas against all possible objections questioning its importance and validity. In view of these facts Vedānta Deśika is perfectly justified to claim that there is no opposition (*virodha*) between the Vedānta and the *Pāñcarātraśāstra*.

REFERENCES

1. See *VS*, II.2.39–40.
2. *Vedānteṣu yathā sāram saṅgṛhya bhagavān ṛṣiḥ; bhaktānukampāya vidvān saṁcikṣepa yathāsukham.* (Quoted in *PMB*, p.139.)
3. See *Muṇḍ. Up.*: *Paramaṁ sāmyam upaiti.* Also, *Tait. Up.*: *Brahma veda brahmaiva bhavati.*
4. See *Paramasaṁhitā*: *paramakāraṇāt vāsudevāt saṁkarṣaṇo nāma jīvo jāyate.*
5. See *PMB*, chap. 21, p.173: *Varṇāśrama-paribhraṣṭaiḥ nārādhyo bhagavān hariḥ.*

14

Śabda-brahma-Vivartavāda of Vaiyākaraṇa

THIS MEANS to be the oldest school of Vedānta which existed long before Śaṅkara. Its chief exponents, as stated by Vedānta Deśika, are Bhartṛhari and Halāyudha who belonged to the school of grammarians (*vaiyākaraṇa*). Though they are primarily grammarians and have contributed scholarly treatises on the subject of grammar (*vyākaraṇa*) including a commentary on *Patañjali Mahābhāṣya* (commentary on *Pāṇini-sūtras*), they have attempted to give a Vedāntic bias or complexion to their theories by conceiving *śabda* or sound (in transcedental form) as Brahman or the Ultimate Reality of the Upaniṣads. Thus states Bhartṛhari: *śabda-brahma* is the only one Ultimate Reality and the entire universe is an illusory manifectation of it (*vivarta*). Halāyudha, on the other hand, states that *śabda-brahma* alone is the life energy of all entities in the universe and the entire universe is a modification (*pariṇāma*) of it. The following statement, which is an invocation verse, and which sums up the central doctrine of Halāyudha, is quoted by Vedānta Deśika in support of this theory:

> *śabda-brahma yadekam yac-caitanyam ca sarvabhūtānām;*
> *yat pariṇāmaṁ tribhuvanam-akhilam-idaṁ jayati sa vāṇi.*[1]
> *Śabda-brahma,* the one Reality without a second, is the life energy of all beings and the entire universe is a modification of it.

As will be seen presently, both these theories are rejected Vedānta Deśika as untenable. In Support of the doctrine of *śabda-brahma,* the grammarians have conceived a novel theory of *sphoṭavāda.* The term *sphoṭa* means that from which the meaning of a word becomes explicit (*sphuṭati asmāt arthaḥ*).

According to this school, words as such do not directly produce the knowledge of the thing. The letters, a group of which constitute a word, generate the essence of sound known as *sphoṭa* which produces the knowledge of the thing. As stated by Vedānta Deśika in the *Tattvamuktākalāpa,* the following argument is advanced in support of it.

A word has several letters. Do these letters convey the meaning individually or collectively? If it be the former, then the very first should convey the meaning. This does not happen. If the letters convey the meaning collectively, then that power not being found in the first letter, how can all the letters of the word combined together get such a power to convey the meaning? Therefore words as such do not convey the meaning. A special potency or essence becomes manifest in letters when they are combined in a particular form and this produces the meaning.[2]

This is the most unsound theory, contends Vedānta Deśika. It is generally acknowledged that words which are the combination of letters (*varṇa-saṅghāta*) and the sentences which are the combination of these words (*pada-saṅghāta*) convey the meaning. This is so obvious to our perceptual experience. By overlooking this commonly accepted principle, the grammarians postulate a special concept named *sphoṭa,* which is supposed to reveal the meaning of a sentence. This cannot be proved by any of the *pramāṇas—pratyakṣa, anumāna,* or *āgama*. It is a mere postulate and it does not help to know whether or not a sentence conveys a sound meaning.

It is important to understand properly the meaning of a sentence in order to determine whether or not it conveys a valid theory. For this purpose the postulation of *sphoṭa* or the sound essence generated by the words is of no use. Even in the absence of it, is possible to know that a sentence or statement bears a proper purport. Perception does not reveal the existence of *sphoṭa* other than the letters and words in the sentences. Even if we carefully and concentratedly hear or contemplate, we do not notice the so called *sphoṭa* or essence of sound in the words or sentences. Nor can it be proved by means of inference (*anumāna*).

The supporters of *sphoṭavāda* argue that it may not be possible to prove the *sphoṭa* or word essence by means of perception. Nevertheless its postulation becomes necessary because letters are not parmanent and it is not possible to explain except through *sphoṭa*, that the same letters always do convey the same meaning of the words. This argument is untenable, contends Vedānta Deśika. Whatever causes the manifestation of *sphoṭa*, the same should be able to convey the meaning of words.[3] If the *varṇas* can as well cause the *śabda*, there is no need to postulate a new concept like *sphoṭa* for the purpose.

Even verbal testimony, neither Scriptural nor Smṛti statements, support the *sphoṭa* theory. The statement of sage Vyāsa in the *Mahābhārata* praising the Lord as *sphoṭa* who is stated to be inherent in the letters (*sphoṭastvam varṇaguṣṭaḥ*) is intended to speak of the glory of the Lord, as in the *Bhagavadgītā*, Lord Kṛṣṇa is being identified as the *rasa* in the water, as *tejas* in the fire, etc. Such statements of Vyāsa cannot be construed in favour of the theory of *sphoṭa*.

Even the statement of Halāyudha,[4] to which we have referred earlier, viz., that *śabda-brahma* is the Reality and the entire universe is a modification (*pariṇāma*) of it, does not lend any support to the theory of *sphoṭa*. Further the *śabda* cannot be treated as sentient Being. *Śabda* normally refers to ethereal sound and it is non-sentient. What is non-sentient cannot be the cause of the universe of living and non-living beings. Such a theory is also totally opposed to the Scriptural teaching. If *śabda-brahma* is taken as personified Deity then it amounts to a glorificatory statement.

Similarly, the statement of Bhartṛhari that *śabda-brahma* is the only Ultimate Reality and it illusory manifests itself in the form of letters and words which denote the objects, does not also lend support to the theory of *sphoṭa* conceived as the essence of *śabda*. Besides, the concept of *vivarta* or illusory appearance of the Reality as the universe, is untenable. The criticisms against the Advaitins, Vivartavāda are equally applicable to Śabda-brahma-Vivartavāda.

Against these objections, it may be argued that the orthodox Vedāntins maintain that the *praṇava* or the latter *Aum* which is recited at the commencement of Vedic recitation, contains the essence of entire Vedas and it denotes the Supreme Being and all that exists is caused by it. If this is acceptable, why should the critic object to the theory that from *śabda-brahma* originates the manifold *śabda-prapañca* or the universe of words and letters?

Against this argument Vedānta Deśika contends that if this theory is advanced on the ground that it is a possibility (*sambhāvanā*) on the basis of the analogy of the Vedic syllable *Aum*, then it lacks any support of the valid *pramāṇas*. If, on the contrary, an inferential argument is advanced in support of the *vaiyākaraṇa* theory, it stands opposed to the accepted *pramāṇas* (*pramāṇa-virodha*). What is regarded as a *sambhāvanā* is also open to doubts and hence it cannot be taken as proof for the theory. The inference may take this form: *artha prapañcaḥ* originates only from *śabda-brahma*, because it is *śabda-brahma* as in the case of the cosmic universe. This *anumāna* stands opposed to the Scriptural statement which states that the entire universe is caused by Brahman.

There is one other view advanced by the grammarian according to which there is close relationship between *śabda* and *artha* or object of perception. This is known as *śabdānuvedha*. Whenever the sense organs are in contact with the objects, the objects are perceived along with the words denoting them, In other words, *śabda* is closely associated with the awareness of the object.

This view is also rejected by Vedānta Deśika, as unsound. Only after the objects are perceived, do the words denoting them become known. As explained in the *Tattvamuktākalāpa*, the idea of the elephant boy comes to the mind only after the elephant is seen. It is only after the object is seen, its name comes to our mind. Further, it is nor correct to say that both *śabda* (sound) and *artha* (object), manifest simultaneously. Thus, for instance, infants, as well as deaf and dumb persons who see the objects do not have any knowledge of the words denoting the objects perceived by them. It cannot be said that such persons have the knowledge of some kind of super normal or subtle sound (*sūkṣma śabda*), because there is no proof in support of the existence of such subtle sound. The mention of subtle sounds in the *mantra-śāstra* under the names of *sūkṣma, paśyanti, madhyamā, vaikharī,* is intended for the purpose of meditation and it has no bearing on the sound as commonly understood. Even if such statements are made by trustworthy persons (*āpta vākya*), *śabda* in the subtle state cannot denote any object or meaning. Such statements regarding the different states (*avasthā*) of *śabda* are intended for different purposes. The adoption of some kind of inference would not find any support of *pramāṇas.*

The Mīmāṁsaka theory of *śabda-svarūpa-nityatva* or that *śabda* is eternal, does not lend support to *śabda-brahma* doctrine. Such as view is also opposed to the Vedānta which does not accept the *nityatva* of letters (*varṇas*). Besides it does not serve the purpose of proving the eternality of vedas. *Śabda* is an evolute of *prakṛti* and it cannot therefore be treated as eternal. That Veda is *nitya,* can be established even without accepting the *śabda-nityatva,* as is explained by Rāmānuja in the *Śrībhāṣya.*[5]

The theory of *śabdādhyāsa* advanced by Bhartṛhari is also not sound. According to Bhartṛhari, the perception of the so-called object takes place through the hearing of the sound of the word (*śabda*) and not independent of it. *Śabda* itself projects or manifests as object. There is no difference between *śabda* or a word and the object denoted by the word. The two are one and the same. Because of such an identity the cognition of the object takes place the moment the *śabda* is known.

This argument is refuted on the ground that *śabda* and object are distinct and can never be identical. The object exists even prior to the origin of *śabda* and it continues to exist even after the cessation of *śabda.*[6] Further, the sound of the word (*śabda*) and the object (*artha*) denoted by it are to be grasped by different sense organs. *Śabda* is known through the ear, whereas the object is perceived through the visual organ. The two do not become manifest at the same time. A word may have different meanings but at the time of hearing a word, we grasp only one particular meaning. If sound and object are identical, then all the meanings of the word should have occurred to our mind when the word is first heard.

This is not so. There are different words which are synonymous but they all refer to the same object. When we get the knowledge of the object, then all the synonymous words should have come to our attention. But this does not happen. *Śabda* and *artha* cannot be identical and hence the theory of *śabdādhyāsa* of Buddhists and Bhartṛhari is untenable.

There is another theory developed by the Buddhists and also Vaiyākaraṇas according to which knowledge itself illusorily manifests in the form of words and sentences. This is known as *pratibhā-vākyārthavāda.* Even this is untenable since it is opposed to our common experience proving that only through the sense organs external objects are directly known.

In view of all these critical observations Vedānta Deśika affirms that the theory of *sphoṭa* and the doctrines of *śabda-brahma* as the sole Reality is the cause of everything in the universe are to be ignored (*anādaraṇīyam*). The Supreme Being (*Parama-puruṣa*) who is the sole creator of the universe is the proper *Para-Brahman* and not the *Śabda-Brahman,* as conceived by the grammarians. The term *brahma* used in other contexts is to be taken in secondary sense. Thus, for instance, the *Gītā* employs the term *śabda-brahma.* The relevant verse reads: "*śabda-brahmaṇi niṣṇātaḥ paraṁ brahma adhigacchate.*" In this context, *śabda-brahma* means the knowledge of Brahman derived from the Āgamas (*āgamotha jñānam*). In another text, we come across another statement: "*jijñasurapi yogasya śabda-brahma ativartate.*" Here *śabda-brahma* stands for *prakṛti* (primordial cosmic matter). The term *brahman* in its primary sense only denotes *Para-Brahman* or the Supreme Being, who according to the Vedānta, is the primary cause of the Universe. Vedānta Deśika further observes that the conclusive theory of Vedānta, viz., the Supreme Being established in the Upaniṣads as qualified by *cit* and *acit* in their subtle form (*sūkṣma cidacit viśiṣṭa*) undergoes modification as Brahman qualified by *cit* and *acit* in the manifested form is acceptable even to the great sages such as Pāṇini, Kātyāyana, Pātañjali (the commentators on *Pāṇinisūtras*). It is therefore not approriate to say that there are certain mutual contradictions in the theories mentioned in the treatises on grammar such as *aindra, candra, maheśa, daurga, kaumāra,* and *piśalya* which came into existence at a later period. Even if some contradictions are found, these can be reconciled by proper interpretation in accordance with the accepted valid theories as in the case of the conflicting statements found in the eighteen Purāṇas, which was compiled and edited by sage Vyāsa, the reputed author of the *Mahābhārata.* Thus it is stated (quoted by Vedānta Deśika): "*Aṣṭādaśa purāṇāni aṣṭau vyākaraṇāni ca; jñātva satyavatīsūnuḥ cakre Bhārata-saṁhitām.*" The principle of reconciliation is adopted by adopting the classification of eighteen Purāṇas into *sāttvika, rājasa,* and *tāmasa.* The same principle can be adopted in the case of eight Vyākaraṇas. The authors of these Vyākaraṇas are also influenced by the *sāttvika, rājasa,* and *tāmasa guṇas* and accordingly, they would have said different things. What is found in *sāttvika* Vyākaraṇas are to be taken as valid and in accordance with it, the correct theories are to be accepted.

References

1. See *PMB,* chap. 14, p.153.
2. See *TMK,* IV.87; also see *FVV,* p.126.
3. See *TMK,* IV.88.
4. *śabda-brahma-yadaikaṁ yaccaitanyam ca sarvabhūtānām; yat pariṇāmaṁ tribhuvanam-akhilam-idam jayati sa vāṇi.* (Quoted by Vedānta Deśika in *PMB,* p.153.)
5. See *RB* on *VS,* I.3.39; also see *FVV,* pp.101–3.
6. See *TMK,* IV.34: *śabdāt prāk paramapi artha siddheḥ.*

15

Advaita Vedānta of Śaṅkara

AMONG THE EXTANT Vedānta schools, Śaṅkara's Advaita Vedānta is the oldest and important living system. But this system of philosophy is the one which is also open to severe criticism by almost all the theistic schools of Vedānta, and in particular Rāmānuja and Madhva. Apart from the elaborate and systematic criticism offered by Rāmānuja in the *Mahāsiddhānta* portion of the *Jijñāsādhikaraṇa* of the *Śrībhāṣya*, Vedānta Deśika has written an independent polemical work named *Śatadūṣaṇī* containing sixty-six *vādas*, each one dealing with a major topic of Advaita. Madhva too has attacked vigorously Advaita doctrines, particularly the *mithyātva* or illusory character of the universe in his *prakaraṇa granthas*. His illustrious follower, Śrī Vyāsatīrtha has written an independent work named *Nyāyāmṛta* in which the major doctrines of Advaita are vehemently criticized. Vedānta Deśika has therefore included as separate chapter in the *Paramata-bhaṅga*, under the title "Pracchanna-bouddha-bhaṅgavāda" (chap. 11), in which he has offered succinct and strong criticisms against a few important theories of Advaita Vedānta. As we have explained earlier, this chapter comes immediately after Mādhyamika Buddhism, for the reason that the concept of *māyā* or *avidyā* adopted by Śaṅkara to explain the illusory character of the universe and *jīvātmans* is similar to the concept of *Saṁvṛti* admitted by the Mādhyamikas to explain empirical transactions in the universe. Though Śaṅkara is an orthodox Vedāntin whose system of philosophy is founded on the authority of the Upaniṣads, the *Vedāntasūtras* and the *Bhagavadgītā*, the doctrines of *Nirguṇa Brahman*, the theory of the identity of *jīva* and Brahman, the view that the universe is illusory (*jagan-mithyātva*) and the postulation of *māyā* would amount in the opinion of Vedānta Deśika, to the admission of the principles of Mādhyamika's *śūnyavāda* or that everything in the universe is void and non-existent. By way of elucidation of this strong criticism, Vedānta Deśika points out that Yogācāra school of Buddhism does not accept either the subject (*boddhā*) or the external object other than the mental series and that all the *dharmas* that we attribute to the knower are falsely imagined to belong to it (*kalpita*). The Vaibhāṣika, which is another school of Buddhism, on the other hand, admit *buddhi* or knowledge as the only reality, while everything else is non-eternal. Similar to these teachings, the Advaita School of Vedānta admit that other than the *Ātman* (Brahman) as the only Reality, everything else is illusory. Hence this school of Vedānta is refuted along with the Mādhyamika Buddhism.

In reply to the objection whether it is appropriate to treat Advaita Vedānta on par with Buddhism, Vedānta Deśika points out that on closer and dispassionate study, the two systems have some common features. Buddhism maintains that *buddhi* or knowledge is *kṣaṇika*, that is, it does not endure for more than a moment. It is also many (*bahu*) in the form of continuous series of ideas. In the case of Advaitin, knowledge (termed as *anubhūti*) is *nitya* or eternal but all the *dharmas* or attributes we ascribe to it are considered imaginary (*kalpita*). That is, it is falsely superimposed on it and these do not really belong to it. Hence, Vedānta Deśika contends, that the two schools of thought have some affinity.[1]

In the *Paramata-bhaṅga* Vedānta Deśika does not take up a detailed criticism of all the doctrines of Advaita, as this task has already been accomplished in the *Śatadūṣaṇī* and other philosophical treatises. He therefore confines his attention to a few crucial topics such as the validity of *pramāṇas* (*prāmāṇya*), absence of valid proofs for establishing the doctrine of undifferentiated Reality, the plurality of the *jīvātman*, the illusory nature of the universe (*jagat*) and the concept of *māyā*. Vedānta Deśika attempts to prove how Advaita is a defective school of Vedānta as it is opposed to the teachings of the Upaniṣads and the *Vedāntasūtras*.

VALIDITY OF PRAMĀṆAS

The question relating to the validity of the *pramāṇas* is first taken up. The doctrines advanced by an exponent of a system require to be well grounded on the valid means of knowledge. In the absence of any valid proof in support of it, it is bound to be rejected as non-authoritative. Like all the other schools of Vedānta, Advaitins have also admitted the three important *pramāṇas*: *pratyakṣa*, *anumāna*, and *āgama* (Scripture). Of these, Scripture is accorded greater validity and it is regarded as the Supreme authority in spiritual matters.

The metaphysical stand adopted by Advaita Vedānta presents some problem with regard to the validity of the *pramāṇas*. According to Advaita, Brahman alone is absolutely real and everything else is illusory. If this is the case, the *pramāṇas* cannot be regarded as real in the proper sense of the term and in the absence of valid *pramāṇas*, the Advaitin cannot that the doctrines advanced by him are sound. This is the main objection raised by Vedānta Deśika. The Advaitin gets over it by arguing that the *pramāṇas* though not real (*pāramārthika*), have empirical reality (*vyāvahārika satyatva*), that is, for practical purposes they are regarded as real and on this basis it is possible to establish one's theories. Vedānta Deśika is not satisfied with this explanation and contends that on final and careful scrutiny, it is found that what is regarded as *vyāvahārika satya*, turns out to be false, similar to the reality of the objects seen in the state of dream (*svapna pramāṇa tulya*).

There are other arguments advanced by the Advaitin in defense of his position but all these are discussed in the *Śatadūṣaṇī* and proved to be untenable. An important point of criticism is that Scripture which is regarded as the Supreme authority for knowing Brahman, cannot be claimed as the source of authority since it being the product of *avidyā*, is not free from defect. The argument that the knowledge of Brahman derived from the Scripture is uncontradicted and hence it is real, is not sustainable, contends Vedānta Deśika, because this is contradicted by the teachings of the Mādhyamikas for whom everything is *śūnya* or non-existent.

THE THEORY OF NIRVIŚEṢA BRAHMAN

After making these critical remarks regarding the *pramāṇas* Vedānta Deśika criticizes the concept of *nirviśeṣatva*, which constitutes the *svarūpa* of Brahman. Following the arguments advanced by Rāmānuja in the *Śrībhāṣya*, while refuting the doctrine of Brahman as *nirviśeṣa* or devoid of all attributes, he points out that none of the *pramāṇas*—either *pratyakṣa*, or *anumāna* or even *śabda* (scripture) can prove the existence of a *nirviśeṣa* entity. According to the Viśiṣṭādvaitin, all entities, both material and spiritual, are *saviśeṣa* or qualified with attributes.

Pratyakṣa does not reveal an entity or even Brahman as devoid of qualification. There are two theories regarding this. According to one theory, there are two kinds of perception known as *nirvikalpaka* or indeterminate perception and *savikalpaka* or determinate perception. In the first stage, that is soon after the contact of the sense organs with the external object, we perceive only bare being and it is only in the next stage, we see the object as qualified. This theory is considered untenable because even in the first stage, we see the object as qualified with some quality (*kenacit viśeṣeṇa*) while in the second stage, we see it as qualified with specific characteristics. According to the second theory, which is advanced by the author of *Brahmasiddhi*, perception reveals only *sat* (*sanmātra*) and the difference that is apprehended later on is superimposed on *sat* due to *avidyā*. Even this theory is refuted as it is opposed to our common experience (*upalambha virodha*).

The Advaitin adopts the dialectical argument to deny the very reality of *bheda*.[2] But such a dialectic can also be advanced to prove that even *abheda* or non-difference is not real. If all differences are considered to be *mithyā* or illusory, it would lead to the position of denial of difference even between *pramāṇa* and *apramāṇa*, *sādhya* and *sādhana*, *svapakṣa* and *parapakṣa*, *sādhana* and *duṣaṇa*, *vādi* and *prativādi*, *jaya* and *parājaya*. Then there would be no human transaction.

Even the *anumāna* or inference and Āgama or the Scriptural texts do not establish the *nirviśeṣa* Reality. The syllogistic arguments adopted to prove that *Anubhūti* (Brahman) is *avedya* and that Brahman is *nirviśeṣa* suffer from the logical defects.

Besides, if the nature of Brahman can be known by means of inference, then it would militate against the stand taken in Vedānta that *śāstra* or sacred text, is the only source of authority for the knowledge of Brahman. The Upaniṣadic texts also do not point out that Brahman is *Nirviśeṣa.* The mention of the terms such as *nirguṇa, niṣkriya, niṣkala,* etc., in a few stray statements convey the idea that Brahman is devoid of *heya guṇas* or defilements.

The following argument is advanced by the Advaitin in defence of his theory of *Nirviśeṣa Brahman*: If according to the Scriptural texts Brahman is devoid of *jāti,* that is, as belonging to particular species, *guṇa* or quality, *śakti* or capacity to function, *vyāpāra* or activities, *vibhūti dravyam* or glorious aspects, etc., is it appropriate to consider such a Reality as *Saviśeṣa* or endowed with attributes? All such conceptions in respect of Brahman are therefore imaginary and caused by ignorance. In the final analysis, the true nature of the Ultimate Reality is to be admitted as absolutely undifferentiated.

Vedānta Deśika controverts this argument. This is not a correct interpretation of the Upaniṣadic texts which negate certain characteristics in respect of Brahman. The Upaniṣads only negate such physical qualities commonly ascribed to the material entitites. They do not deny characteristics which constitute the distinguishing features of Brahman. This point is made more explicit by specifying what is to be attributed to Brahman and what is to be denied in respect of it. The following *dharmas* which are well established by the Scriptural texts dealing with the nature of Reality are to be admitted: (1) designation of *Īśvara* by a name such as Nārāyaṇa or Viṣṇu, (2) the distinguishing attributes such as *satyasya satya, satyatva, jñānatva, anantatva* and *ānandatva,* (3) *ātmatva,* that is, that it pervades everything in the universe, (4) *sarvādhiṣṭhāna śakti* or that it is capable of serving as the ground or source of everything in the universe,[3] (5) *jagat-sṛṣṭyādi-vyāpāra* or that it is the sole cause of the creation, sustenance and dissolution of the universe, (6) the Rulership of both the cosmic and transcendental universe (*vibhūtidvaya*), and (7) *svarūpa vikāra-abhāva,* that is, devoid of any change or modification in respect of its *svarūpa.* All these distinguishing characteristics of Brahman are undeniable, as these are well established by the Upaniṣadic texts. The characteristics which are to be negated in respect of Brahman are: the physical qualities such as *sthūlatva, aṇutva, hrasvatva, dīrghatva,* etc., stated in the *Bṛhadāraṇyaka* text, change or modification in Brahman in respect of its *svarūpa*, experience of pleasure or pain caused by physical body, absence of auspicious attributes (*kalyāṇa guṇābhāva*), since these are not warranted by Scriptural texts.

In the same way, the Scriptural statements which speak of the attributes and negation of the same in respect of *jīvātman* can also be reconciled by interpreting them with reference to the *upādhi* or limiting adjuncts with which they are associated. Thus for instance in the statement "*nāyam devo na martyo vā*" (*jīva* is neither *deva* nor mortal being), its implication is that the *jīva* as far as its intrinsic nature is concerned, is alike but the distinction made as celestial being, human being, etc., is due to the association of the different types of body caused by *karma.*

The very distinction made between *dharma* and *dharmī* is questioned by the Advaitin on the basis of a dialectical argument. But this is refuted as it is not a correct theory. The distinction between the two is to be admitted as it is evident to our experience.[4]

The view of the Advaitin that Brahman is pure, undifferentiated Being devoid of *sajātīya-bheda, vijātīya-bheda,* and *svagata-bheda,* on the basis of the *Chāndogya* text (*sadeva ekameva advitīya*), is not tenable as it is opposed to all *pramāṇas* (*sarva-pramāṇa viruddha*). Thus, it is not possible to establish that Brahman is *Nirviśeṣa.*

It may be argued that there is no need for any *pramāṇa* to prove that Brahman is *nirviśeṣa* because it is *svayaṁ-prakāśa* which implies that it is self-evident or self-established. Vedānta Deśika controverts this argument. Brahman may be *svayaṁ-prakāśa* but the mere *svayaṁ-prakāśatva* cannot prove that it is also *nirviśeṣa* in character. That self-luminous Brahman is *Nirviśeṣa* is to be proved by some other *pramāṇas.* In that case, what is proved by another *pramāṇa* becomes a characterized entity (*saviśeṣa*). If another individual or oneself cognizes the self, he perceives it as a qualified entity (*viśiṣṭa*) and not as devoid of all determinations. In other words, what is *nirviśeṣa* can never become an object of apprehension and even if it is apprehended, it is seen only as a qualified entity. Further, if *svayaṁ-prakāśatva* constitutes the very *svarūpa* of *Nirviśeṣa* Brahman, then the theory that it becomes eclipsed by *avidyā* (*avidyātirohita*) and that there is *adhāyasa* or superimposition on it leading to the *bhrānti* and its removal, etc., are all inconceivable. Only if *ātman* is qualified with attributes, it is possible to explain that it does not manifest fully (*aviśadatva*) due to the false superimposition of *dharmas* which do not belong to it (*viruddhākāra adhyāsa*) or due to some of its *dharmas* being eclipsed.

Further *nirviśeṣa-jñāna* or undifferentiated consciousness cannot be considered as the knower or the subject of knowledge, because cognisership involves change or modification. For this reason, the Advaitin regards the empirical ego or the internal organ (*ahaṅkāra*) as the cogniser. But this theory also suffers from a drawback because what is a non-sentient entity like the physical body cannot be the knower. It would therefore be more appropriate to admit, as the Viśiṣṭādvaitin does, that the entity denoted by the notion of "I" (*ahamartha*) itself is the true self. The inferential arguments advanced by the Advaitin to prove that *ahamartha* or the entity denoted by "I" is not *ātman*, that it is non-sentient, etc., and that only pure consciousness (*saṁvit*) is *ātmā*, *sākṣī*, or mere witness and it is *pratyaktva* or self-revealing, etc. are untenable because these stand opposed to our perceptual experience and the Scriptural texts. That *ahamartha* itself is the true *ātman* is well established by Ālavandār in *Ātmasiddhi* and also by Rāmānuja in the Mahāsiddhānta portion of the *Śrībhāṣya*. If the entity denoted by "I" is not admitted as the self, it would not be possible to explain satisfactorily the Upaniṣadic statements such as "All this is Brahman," "That thou art" which equates the universe and Brahman as well as the *jīvātman* and Brahman.

The Theory of *Mithyātva* of the Universe

The Advaitin contends that, if *Nirviśeṣa* Brahman alone is absolutely real, it would follow that the universe which is generally regarded as real (*satya*) is not so. But this cannot be established, contends Vedānta Deśika. The Scriptural texts which negate the universe such as *neha nānāsti kiñcana* cannot support this theory because such texts, if properly interpreted with reference to the contexts, convey a different meaning.[5] It only implies that there does not exist any other entity which is not inherently related to Brahman (*abrahmātmaka vastvantaram*). If it is attempted to establish the illusoriness by means of *anumāna* or inferential arguments and Āgama or Scriptural texts, then these would stand opposed to perceptual experience (*kalātyayāpadeśa*). Perception which is the foundation for inference cannot be ignored. If by overlooking perceptual knowledge, inference is adopted, it would not be a valid *pramāṇa.*

The description of the universe as *mithyā* in the sense of *sad-asad-vilakṣaṇa,* that is, it is neither *sat* nor *asat* but different from both, involves self-contradiction (*viruddha*), similar to the concept of *sad-asat.* Whatever arguments are offered to defend the theory of *anirvacanīyatva,* these are found untenable when subjected to logical analysis. These concepts can also be satisfactorily explained in a different way. Thus, for instance, taking the instance of the cognition of silver in the conch-shell, the silver which is real and exists elsewhere is seen in the shell due to the eye-defect or some other reason. Since it does not actually exist in the shell, it is being negated. There is no justification to conceive the concept of *sadasat-vilakṣaṇa* to explain this phenomenon.

The Scriptural text *nāsadāsīt* no *sadāsīt* negating both *sat* and *asat,* cannot be taken as a proof for the concept of *sad-asad-vilakṣaṇa,* because this statement is intended to explain how the universe in the state of dissolution cannot be described as *sat* or *asat.* The theory that *māyā* or *ajñāna* which is of the nature of *sad-asad-vilakṣaṇa* is the material cause of the universe (*upādāna-kāraṇa*) is also untenable, because the *jagat* which is its product is not found to be *mithyā* since its existence as real is evident to our experience.

The Theory of Removal of *Avidyā*

Regarding the nature of the means to overcome *avidyā* and the realization of the absolute oneness of the reality, Vedānta Deśika points out that the theory of the Advaitin that liberation from bondage takes place by means of the realization of the knowledge of the identity of *jīva* and Brahman is opposed to the several scriptural texts which affirm that proper knowledge of difference (*bheda*) between *jīva* and Brahman leads to *mokṣa.* If according to the Advaitin the concepts of bondage (*bandha*), the knowledge which removes *ajñāna* causing bondage (*nirvartaka jñāna*), the theory that *jñāta* or the individual self is the aspirant for *moṣka,* that *Īśvara* is the bestower of knowledge (*jñāna-prada*), that the Sacred texts provide the spiritual knowledge (*jñānotpāda-śāstra*), and even the very cessation of *avidyā* (*avidyā-nivṛtti*) are all *mithyā,* then the enquiry or investigation into the nature of Brahman (*brahma jijñāsā*) and the teaching of Vedānta to the disciples by a preceptor are of no value (*niṣphala*). When it is so well established by all *pramāṇas* that the universe is real, the theories such as that *vākyārtha-jñāna,* that is, the *aparokṣa-jñāna* arising from the study of the Scriptural texts, *niṣprapañcīkaraṇa niyoga vāda* or constant meditation on Brahman in the form of dissociating *prapañca* (universe) from Brahman leading to the realization of pure Brahman and *dhyāna-niyoga-janya-sākṣātkāra* or the realization of true form of Brahman after observing the meditation enjoined in the Upaniṣad would not prove the illusory character of the universe (*prapañcabādha*).

Vedānta Deśika briefly mentions a few other inconsistencies involved in the Advaita Vedānta. That the Upaniṣadic texts such as *tattvamasi* (Thou art that) generate *aparokṣa jñāna* or knowledge of immediate nature is a self contradiction similar to the concept of *jīvan-mukti* or that one is liberated though one is embodied. If according to his system *ātman* is *nitya-mukta* or ever free from bondage by its very nature, there is no justification to speak of the *jīvan-mukti.* Similarly, the theory of *bādhitānuvṛtti,* that is, the continuance of the body even after the total cessation of *avidyā,* is untenable. If the preceptor is aware that the disciple is *mithyā,* the teaching of Vedānta to him is unjustified. If the preceptor knows that his disciple is real, he cannot be qualified to teach Vedānta.

THE THEORY OF *JĪVA*

The theory that there is only one *jīva* (*eka-jīva-vāda*), does not allow for drawing distinction between the individuals as *sukhī* or *dukhī*, as disciple and preceptor and as one bound and the other as free from bondage. The theories which speak of the plurality of *jīvas*, also suffer from defects. To overcome this criticism, the plurality of *jīva* is admitted on the basis of the reflection of one Brahman in several internal organs caused by *avidyā* on the analogy of the reflection of a single moon in several waves of watershed. Even this theory is also unsound, as explained in detail in the *Śrībhāṣya* and the *Śatadūṣaṇī*. Besides, the *jīvas* as reflections of Brahman in the *antaḥkaraṇas* become destroyed as in the case of the reflections of the moon, when the watershed is removed.

Ajñāna should have a locus, that is, it should belong to somebody and should also be related to an object. What is the locus of *ajñāna*? There are two views regarding this matter. According to some Advaitins, Brahman is the *āśraya* for *jñāna*. According to others, *jīva* is its locus. In either case, it is untenable. Brahman which is of the nature of *prakāśa* or self-luminous knowledge cannot be the locus since the two are mutually opposed. To avoid this difficulty, if *jīva* is postulated as the locus of *ajñāna*, it involves a vicious circle. If *jīva* is a reflection of Brahman in the *antaḥkaraṇa*, Brahman assumes *jīva-hood* only after the reflection of it in the *antaḥkaraṇa* takes place. Prior to it, there is no *jīva* as such who apprehends *jīva-hood* as a reflection of Brahman. If Brahman itself comprehends, then Brahman is subjected to delusion. If *jīva* apprehends that it is a reflection of Brahman, *jīva* does not exist as such until the reflection is apprehended. In either case, the theory of *jīva* as *pratibimba* of Brahman falls to the ground.

The Concept of *Māyā*

The very difference made between *māyā* and *avidyā* on the ground that *māyā* inheres in Brahman, whereas *avidyā* inheres in *jīvas* is untenable. If on this basis, Brahman as associated with *māyā* is able to see the illusory *jīvas* and the *jagat*, then Brahman would be subjected to *ajñāna* or ignorance, which is not a satisfactory theory.

The term *māyā* does not necessarily mean illusory apprehension of an object. It also bears other meaning as that which is capable of creating the variegated universe. It is in this sense the term *māyā* is employed in the *Śvetāśvatara Upaniṣad* equating it with *prakṛti* or primordial cosmic matter. If in the state of divine incarnation, as human or other beings, the Supreme Lord exhibits grief or ignorance, it is just a mere acting (*abhinaya*) to delude other persons.

While concluding the critical review of the Advaita Vedānta, Vedānta Deśika presents the following correct view which stands established on the unquestionable Scriptural authority and other *pramāṇas*. The Supreme Being creates the universe through the media of *māyā* which stands for the primordial cosmic matter, as is stated in *Śvetāśvatara Upaniṣad*: *asmāt māyī sṛjate viśvametat.*[6] *Māyī* is the Supreme Lord, who is the controller of *prakṛti*, as explained in this Upaniṣad (*māyinam tu maheśvaram*); *māyā* is the primordial cosmic matter (*māyāṁ tu prakṛtiṁ vidyāt*). As part of the creation of the universe, the *jīvas* who are brought into existence by associating them with the bodies, mind and sense organs, are also entangled with *māyā*, taken in the sense of past *karma*. Thus states the Upaniṣad: *tasminścānyo māyayā sanniruddhaḥ*. *Īśvara* is the cause of the bondage (*bandha*) in accordance with the past *karma* of the *jīvas* (*Īśvaraḥ karmānurūpa bandha hetuḥ*). The same *Īśvara* is also the cause of the liberation of *jīvas* from bondage through the observance by the *jīvas* the requisite *vidyās* or the *upāsanās* as enjoined in the Upaniṣads. Thus, the three *tattvas* or the ontological entities, viz., *Īśvara*, *cit*, and *acit* (cosmic matter) are eternally different (*nitya bhinna*), each one possessing the distinctive characteristics (*pratiniyata guṇa viśiṣṭa*). All the three are real and well established by the valid *pramāṇas*. Only such sound philosophical teachings based on the *pramāṇas* and in particular on the authority of unquestionable Scriptural texts become acceptable to those who take their stand on the valid *pramāṇas*.

Other Schools of Advaita

In the *Paramata-bhaṅga* one particular school of Vedānta expounded by Śaṅkara is covered. Vedānta Deśika points out that there are several other types of Advaita taught in earlier times under different names such as Brahmādvaita, Śivādvaita, Vāsudevādvaita, Sphoṭādvaita, Samvid-advaita, and Sad-advaita. Brahmādvaita is the school which upholds that *Hiraṇyagarbha* or *Caturmukha* Brahmā is the only Supreme Reality. Śivādvaita refers to the school which maintains that only Śiva existed prior to the creation of the universe (*Śiva eva kevalaḥ*). Vāsudevādvaita is the school which emphasizes that other than Vāsudeva, no other deity exists (*Paramaḥ pareśaḥ sa vāsudeva no yato anyadasti*). Sphoṭādvaita is the school which accepts that *sphoṭa* or word essence which is called *śabda-brahma* is the only Reality (*Sphoṭastvam varṇa juṣṭaḥ*). This is briefly covered in the *Paramata-bhaṅga* as the school of Vedānta upheld by Bhartṛhari. Saṁvid-advaita is the school of thought advocated by the Yogācāra Buddhist for whom *saṁvit* or series of mental ideas is only real and the external objects are mere projections of it. This is also covered in the *Paramata-bhaṅga* under Buddhism. Sad-advaita is the school of though upheld by the Sāṅkhyas for whom *sat* taken in the sense of primordial cosmic matter is the primary cause of the universe and everything in the universe is constituted of the three *guṇas* of *prakṛti*. According to Vedānta Deśika, all these schools are intended to attract people to join the new type of school founded by those exponents but none of them is philosophically sustainable, as is made evident in the *Brahmasūtras* of Bādarāyaṇa, *Śatadūṣaṇī* and other philosophic treatises.

References

1. Cf. the verse of Yādavaprakāśa quoted by Vedānta Deśika in *Śatadūṣaṇī*: *Vedo' nṛto buddhakṛtāgamo' nṛtaḥ prāmāṇyam tasya ca tasya cānṛtam; boddhānṛto buddhiphale tathā anṛte yūyam ca boddhāśca samānasaṁsadaḥ.*
2. For details see, *Śatadūṣaṇī, vāda* 13.
3. See *Ch. Up., sadāyatanāḥ, sat-pratiṣṭhāḥ.*
4. *SD, vāda* 13; also see *FVV.*
5. See *FVV.*
6. *Śvet. Up.*, IV.9.

16

Dvaita Vedānta of Madhva

AMONG the three principal schools of Vedānta, Dvaita Vedānta developed by Madhva (AD 1199–1278) occupies an important place. Like Advaita and Viśiṣṭādvaita, it presents a distinctive doctrine of Vedānta based on the authority of the Upaniṣads, *Brahmasūtra* and the *Bhagavadgītā*, as interpreted by Madhva. While it is antagonistic to Śaṅkara's Absolutist Vedānta, it has closer affinity to Rāmānuja's Viśiṣṭādvaita, insofar as the fundamental doctrines are concerned. It accepts the Brahman of the Upaniṣads as Supreme Being who is identified with personal God in the name of Viṣṇu and who is endowed with numerous attributes. It also admits the reality of the cosmic universe and the existence of the eternal individual selves as distinct from Brahman. In view of it Vedānta Deśika regards Madhva's Dvaita as *sannikṛṣṭa-mata* or a philosophical system having closer affinity to Viśiṣṭādvaita.[1] Presumably, due to this reason he has not subjected Dvaita Vedānta to a criticism, unlike Śaṅkara's Advaita. Hence it is left out of a critical review in the *Paramata-bhaṅga.* However, he has made a few brief critical remarks in the *Paramata-bhaṅga* and also in his other works on a few important theories of Dvaita Vedānta which stand opposed to the Upaniṣadic teachings and the views of Bādarāyaṇa. We shall consider these points in the present chapter.

With regard to Brahman, which is the central doctrine of Vedānta, the major point of difference between the Dvaita Vedānta and Viśiṣṭādvaita is about the nature of causality of Brahman with reference to the universe. The issue involved is whether Brahman, which is the sole cause of the universe, as stated in the *Taittirīya Upaniṣad* and the *Vedāntasūtra*, is the *upādāna-kāraṇa* (material cause) of the universe or it is mere *nimitta kāraṇa* (instrumental cause) as in the illustration of the potter who makes the pot. In the instances which are cited in the *Chāndogya Upaniṣad*[2] to elucidate the causal relationship between Brahman and the universe, the lump of clay is mentioned as the material cause of pot and other articles made of clay, with reference to the general statement viz. that the knowledge of one (causal) substance leads to the knowledge of all other products made out of it. The general statement is called *pratijñā* and the illustration in support of it as *dṛṣṭānta*. Taking these facts into consideration, Bādarāyaṇa formulates the *sūtra* which reads as: *prakṛtiśca pratijñā dṛṣṭānta anuparodhāt*.[3] The *sūtra* interpreted both by Śaṅkara and Rāmānuja means that Brahman is the material cause, the word *prakṛti* being interpreted as *upādāna-kāraṇa* on the basis of Pāṇini *sūtra*.[4] The adoption of this meaning for the term *upādāna* is considered relevant, as otherwise the general statement (*pratijñā*) and the illustration offered to elucidate it would not be meaningful. This is the view of Bādarāyaṇa, as interpreted both by Śaṅkara and Rāmānuja.

But Madhva, on the contrary, does not admit that Brahman is the *upādāna kāraṇa* of *jagat*, on the ground that the admission of *upādānatva* for Brahman would involve change in respect of the *svarūpa* of Brahman. It is therefore only *nimitta-kāraṇa* of the universe. On the analogy of the potter and the pot produced by him. *Prakṛti* or the primordial cosmic matter is accepted as material cause of the universe, as it evolves into the universe through the will of *Paramātman*. Accordingly he offers a different interpretation for the *Vedāntasūtra* dealing with the material causality of Brahman. By overlooking the *Chāndogya* passage on which the *sūtra* is formulated, Madhva adopts a different Scriptural text as the *viṣaya-vākya* for the *sūtra* in support of his intepretation of the *sūtra*.[5]

As explained by Vedānta Deśika in the *Adhikaraṇa-sārāvalī*, the stand taken by Madhva that Brahman is not the material cause but it is only the *nimitta-kāraṇa* of the universe, is not philosophically sustainable. It is not only opposed to the teachings of the Upaniṣads, particularly the passage of *Chāndogya* and also the views expressed by Bādarāyaṇa in the *Vedāntasūtra.* According to the Upaniṣadic texts dealing with the causation of the universe (*kāraṇa-vākyas*), Brahman itself wills to become many.[6] The *Taittirīya Upaniṣad* specifically states "*tad-ātmānam svayam akuruta,*" which means that Brahman itself evolved into the universe. *Muṇḍaka Upaniṣad* uses the expression *bhūtayoni* for Brahman and cites the example of the spider weaving the web (out of its saliva). All these statements reveal that Brahman itself is the *upādāna-kāraṇa* of the universe. If it were only the instrumental cause, similar to the potter producing the pot, it cannot be the principal cause of the universe as in the case of the potter not being the principal cause of pot. It is therefore obvious that accordingly to Bādarāyaṇa, Brahman which is defined in the *Taittirīya Upaniṣad* as the primary cause of the creation of the universe, is the material cause. If it were the mere instrumental cause, then there would be no justification for Bādarāyaṇa in refuting the theory of *seśvara-sāṅkhya* and the school of Pāśupata which only accept *Īśvara* as *nimitta-kāraṇa.*

The admission of *upādānatva* for Brahman would not effect the *svarūpa* of Brahman as contended by Madhva. The author of the Vedāntasūtras has provided a suitable explanation for it. Brahman possesses *vicitra-śakti* or variegated powers than it can undergo modification without affecting its *svarūpa.* As elucidated by Rāmānuja, Brahman does not directly undergo any transformation but it makes the *prakṛti,* which is the body (*śarīra*) in the technical sense that it is always sustained and controlled by it, evolves itself into the universe. The changes on account of transformation apply to *prakṛti,* which is the body of *Īśvara,* while Brahman which is its *ādhāra* or supporter is not in any way affected. This is illustrated by the analogy of the self of an individual who passes through the states of boyhood, youth, manhood and old age, etc. is not effected by changes taking place in the body. According to the Viśiṣṭādvaita epistemology, the changes in respect of the qualities (*dharmas*) of a substance do not affect the substratum (*dharmī*).

As explained *supra,* chap. 3 on *Para-tattva, upādānatva* is of two kinds. An object is regarded as *upādāna-kāraṇa* when it modifies itself into a different state as in the instance of a pot. An entity is also regarded as *upādāna-kāraṇa* when it serves as the basis for the *avasthās* or different states it undergoes (*avasthāntara yogitvam eva upādānatvam*).[7] The analogy of a boy growing as youth, man, old, etc. is of this type. In this case individual self associated with the physical body is the material cause by virtue of its being the *āśraya* or serving as the substrate for the changes taking place in the body. In the case of the first instance, there is total transformation of the substance (*svarūpa vikāra*) but it is not so in the second instance. Brahman is *ajaḍa-dravya* or spiritual substance and is it capable of assuming different states. The changes taking place in respect of *prakṛti* do not affect Brahman. The concept of *śarīra* is applicable to *prakṛti*, if we bear in mind the definition offered by Rāmānuja for *śarīra* (see *supra*, chap. 1). Thus the Dvaita Vedānta suffers from this drawback by not admitting *upādāna-kāraṇatva* for Brahman.

Another theory of Dvaita Vedānta which needs to be critically examined is the nature of relation of Brahman to the *jīvas* and also the universe (*jagat*). This is of greater importance in Vedānta than that of *upādānatva* of Brahman. All schools of Vedānta have admitted on the basis of the Upaniṣadic teaching, the three metaphysical principles, viz., Brahman, *jīva*, and *jagat*. The *Śvetāśvatara* describes these as *bhoktā* (*jīva*), *bhogya* (object of experience) and *preritāra* or controller of both. What is the nature of the relationship between these three ontological entities? This has engaged the attention of all the schools of Vedānta and divergent views are expressed regarding this matter. Even at the time of Bādarāyaṇa, different views were held on this question by the ancient Vedānta teachers such as Aśmarathya, Auḍulomi and Kāśakṛtsna, as is evident from the references made to them by name in the *Vedānta-sūtra*. The issue involved is whether the relationship between Brahman and the *jīvas* and also Brahman and *jagat* is one of non-difference (*abheda*) or difference (*bheda*) or difference and non-difference (*bhedābheda*). If it is non-difference (*abheda*), is it absolute non-difference (*kevala-abheda*) in the sense of identity (*tādātmya*) or *viśiṣṭa-abheda* in the sense of oneness of a qualified entity. Logically these are three possibilities for explaining the relationship between the three ontological entities admitted in the Vedānta. An answer to this important issue determines the nature of the Vedānta school as Advaita, Viśiṣṭādvaita, Dvaita, and Bhedābheda. Students of Vedānta are familiar with these views and it is not necessary to go into these details. Śaṅkara admits the relation of absolute non-difference (*kevala-bheda*). His Vedānta is therefore characterized as Advaita or Absolute non-dualism. As against this theory, Madhva subscribes to the theory of *kevala-bheda* or absolute difference between the three ontological entities. His Vedānta is therefore designated as Dvaita. Bhāskara and Yādavaprakāśa and the later followers of their doctrine adopt *bhedābheda-vāda* or both difference and non-difference between Brahman and the other two ontological entities. Rāmānuja, on the contrary, accepts both *bheda* and *abheda* relation from different stand points unlike Bhāskara and Yādavaprakāśa. That is, the three ontological principles are absolutely different (*atyantabheda*) but Brahman as inherently or inseparably related to *jīvas* and the *jagat* (*viśiṣṭa tattva*) is one (*abheda*). Hence the Vedānta of Rāmānuja is designated as Viśiṣṭa-Advaita or oneness or Brahman as organically related to *jīvas* and *jagat.* We shall not enter into the discussion of the details of these doctrines. We are at present only concerned with the consideration of the issue whether the stand adopted by Madhva in this regard is philosophically sustainable.

As pointed out earlier, the Upaniṣads speak of both difference and also non-difference between these ontological entities. There are some Upaniṣadic texts which speak of non-difference between Brahman and *jīva* and also Brahman and the *jagat.* There are also several Upaniṣadic texts which point out that the three ontological entities are different by virtue of their intrinsic nature. The Upaniṣads which is the Revealed Scripture cannot teach two different theories. The apparent conflict therefore needs to be reconciled. Each exponent of Vedānta offers his own explanation to reconcile this conflict. Śaṅkara who upholds the doctrine of absolute non-difference (*abheda* or *advaita*) accords greater validity to the Upaniṣadic texts teaching non-difference such as *Tat-tvam-asi*, *Aham brahmāsmi*, *Ayam ātmā brahma* and lesser validity to the texts speaking of difference between Brahman and *jīva* and Brahman and *jagat.*

Madhva, on the contrary, who subscribes to the theory of *bheda* or difference among the ontological entities accords greater validity to the texts speaking *bheda* and lesser validity or importance to the texts teaching non-difference. The *abheda* referred to in the Upaniṣadic texts is taken by Madhva in a figurative sense. As a compromise between these two extreme views, Bhāskara and Yādavaprakāśa as well as other *bhedābheda-vādins* speak of both difference an non-difference. As these two concepts—*bheda* and *abheda*—involve self-contradiction, it has not received serious attention of the Vedāntins.

Rāmānuja, on the other hand, attempts to reconcile the conflict by according equal validity to both kinds of Upaniṣadic texts. He admits both *bheda* and *abheda* between the three ontological entities—from different standpoints. The three ontological entities—*Īśvara, cit,* and *acit*—are different as taught in the Upaniṣad, by virtue of the difference in respect of their intrinsic nature. But at the same time, *abheda* or unity of the three entities is maintained by emphasizing the fact that Brahman as organically related to the *jīvas* and the universe (as a *viśiṣṭa tattva*) is one Reality. This explanation is offered on the authority of *Antaryāmī Brāhmaṇa* of the *Bṛhadāraṇyaka Upaniṣad* which repeatedly points out that Brahman abides in all the sentient and non-sentient entities as their Inner Controller, and all the entities are its *śarīra* or body in a metaphysical sense; while Brahman itself is the Universal Self (*śarīrī*). The merit of this theory is that both the *bheda śrutis* and *abheda śrutis* are accorded equal validity by admitting both *abheda* and *bheda* in their primary sense. That is, Brahman as organically related to the *jīvas* and the *jagat,* is one *viśiṣṭa* Reality, while the three ontological entities are absolutely different by virtue of their intrinsic nature.

This explanation offered by Rāmānuja is in full conformity with the views expressed by Bādarāyaṇa in the *Vedāntasūtras.* There are two *adhikaraṇas* (topical sections) which directly deal with the questions of the relation of Brahman and *jīvas.* The first one is named Vākyānvayādhikaraṇa, in the fourth *pāda* of the first *adhyāya,* in which the relation of *jīvātman* to Brahman is dealt with. The second is called Aṁśādhikaraṇa included in the second *pāda* of the second *adhyāya,* in which the nature of the relation of *jīva* to Brahman is specifically explained by Bādarāyaṇa. As regards the relation of Brahman to *jagat* is concerned, it is discussed in Ārambhaṇādhikaraṇa and Ahikuṇḍalādhikaraṇa included in the second *pāda* of the third *adhyāya*.

In the Vākyānvayādhikaraṇa, as explained both by Śaṅkara and Rāmānuja, Bādarāyaṇa, while discussing the import of the term *ātman* employed in the passage of *Maitreyī Brāhmaṇa*, mentions names of three sages, Aśmarathya, Auḍulomi, and Kāsakṛtsna, who held differing views regarding the relation of *jīva* to Brahman.[8] The *sūtras* containing the views of Aśmarathya and Auḍulomi, as interpreted by Śaṅkara and Rāmānuja, convey that the relation of *jīva* to Brahman is either difference (*abheda*) or difference and non-difference (*bhedābheda*). The view expressed by Kāsakṛtsna is regarded as the view of Bādarāyaṇa both by Śaṅkara and Rāmānuja. The relevant *sūtra* reads: *avasthiteḥ iti Kāsakṛtsnaḥ* (*VS*, I.4.22). It means that the Supreme Self (*Paramātman*) exists in the individual self (*avasthiteḥ*). Śaṅkara interprets the term *avasthiti* in the sense that the highest self exists as if it were *jīva*, to conform to the doctrine of identity of *jīva* and Brahman. But the term taken in the proper sense should mean, as Rāmānuja interprets, that Brahman abides in *jīvātman*. According to the *Antaryāmī Brāhmaṇa* of *Bṛhadāraṇyaka Upaniṣad*, Brahman abides in *jīvātman* (*ya atmani tiṣṭhan*), as its *antaryāmin*. In view of it, the implication of this *sūtra* with reference to the relation of *jīva* to Brahman, is not non-difference, as Śaṅkara interprets, but one of inherent relation and by virtue of Brahman's immanence in the *jīva*, the two as inseparably related is one (*viśiṣṭa vivakṣayā ekatva*), as explained by Vedānta Deśika.[9]

This explanation, though not explicitly conveyed in the Vākyānvayādhikaraṇa, becomes evident in the Aṁśādhikaraṇa, in which Bādarāyaṇa states clearly that *jīva* is an *aṁśa* of Brahman. The relevant *sūtra* reads: "*aṁśo nānā vyapadeśāt anyathā ca.*"[10] It means that the *jīvātman* is part of Brahman on account of difference and otherwise also. Its implication is that some Scriptural texts speak of difference between *jīva* and Brahman (*nānā vyapadeśāt*), while other texts speak of non-difference (*anyathā ca*). In order to reconcile both these conflicting teachings, *jīva* is to be regarded as *aṁśa* or part of Brahman. The term *aṁśa* literally means part but *jīva* cannot be taken as part of Brahman for the reason that Brahman is *niravyaya* or devoid of parts. It is therefore interpreted in two ways: (a) as if it is a part (*aṁśa iva*), as Śaṅkara means and (b) as an essential characteristic of Brahman (*asādhāraṇa dharma*) of a *viśiṣṭa* entity as Rāmānuja explains. The meaning offered by Śaṅkara is not tenable because Brahman and *jīva* are not identical but are different by nature. Hence the other meaning offered by Rāmānuja is more appropriate since it conforms to the views of *bheda* and *abheda* with regard to *jīva*'s relation to Brahman.

These two *sūtras*—"*Avasthiteḥ iti Kāsakṛtsnaḥ*" and "*Aṁśo nānā-vyapadeśāt anyathā ca*" clearly indicate that Brahman and *jīva* are inherently related and in view of it, the two though are different, can also be regarded as non-different by virtue of its immanence in it. If such an explanation is not admitted it would not be possible to uphold the validity of the two kinds of Upaniṣadic texts speaking of both difference and non-difference in the primary sense. The other plausible explanationas adopted by Śaṅkara is that only Brahman is absolutely real, whereas the *jīvas* are illusory being the reflections of Brahman in the *antaḥkaraṇas*. As there is only one Reality which is absolutely real, *abheda* or non-difference stands established. The texts which teach difference between Brahman and *jīvas* are to be taken, according to Śaṅkara, in a secondary sense and these are of lesser validity, as compared to the texts emphasizing *abheda*. But this explanation as pointed out earlier, is untenable, because Scriptural texts speak of both difference and non-difference between Brahman and *jīvas* in the primary sense, as conveyed by the expressions *nānā* and *anyathā vyapadeśāt* by Bādarāyaṇa. The term *vyapadeśa* implies primary sense, according to Pāṇini.

In dealing with the subject of relation of Brahman and *jīvas*, Madhva takes an altogether different stand and in this respect, he deviates from the teachings of the Upaniṣads and also *Vedāntasūtra*. The Upaniṣads explicitly mention that Brahman and *jīva* are non-different in such statements as *Tat-tvam-asi*,

Aham brahmāsmi, Ayam ātmā brahma. Based on the Upaniṣadic texts Bādarāyaṇa also acknowledges *abheda* relation as conveyed in the two *sūtras* to which we have referred. In order to accommodate the teachings of the *abheda śrutis,* Bādarāyaṇa employs the terms *avasthiti* and *aṁśa* in these *sūtras* respectively. Madhva does not admit that Vākyānvayādhikaraṇa deals with the subject of the relation of *jīva* to Brahman. This *adhikaraṇa* and the relevant *sūtras* are explained in a different way without reference to *jīva*'s relation to Brahman. The *sūtra* in the Aṁśādhikaraṇa is no doubt acknowledged by him as dealing with the subject of *jīva*'s relation to Brahman but he offers a different explanation to the term *aṁśa,* to fit with his premise that *abheda* spoken of in the *sūtra* is to be taken in the secondary sense. The term *aṁśa* for Madhva implies *sādṛśya* or similarity between Brahman and *jīva* in respect of some qualities, such as *jñāna* and *ānanda.* Mere similarity between two entities, such as moon and the face of an attractive woman, cannot prove non-difference between the two. To overcome the objection, the followers of Madhva add the qualification of dependence of one on the other (*tadadhīnatva*), as in the example of the jar on the floor. But the dependence of one on the other (*tadadhīna*) also does not convey an inherent relation because such relation is separable. The word *avasthiti* employed by the *Vedāntasūtra* on the basis of *Antaryāmī Brāhmaṇa* refers to a permanent and inseparable relationship between *jīva* and Brahman. Madhva uses the terms *bimba* and *pratibimba* to explain the relation of Brahman to *jīva.* Brahman is *bimba,* while *jīva* is its *pratibimba,* not in the sense of reflection, as Advaitin says but in a technical sense as a dependent reality. Even this explanation does not prove the intimate or inherent relationship that exists between these ontological entities, as conveyed by the terms *avasthiti* and *aṁśa* employed by Bādarāyaṇa to affirm the relation of non-difference (*abheda*) in the sense of organic unity or oneness as a qualified entity (*viśiṣṭa-tattva*). This is the criticism that is leveled against Madhva's theory of *jīva*'s relation to Brahman from the standpoint of Viśiṣṭādvaita.

The same kind of criticism holds good in respect of the relation of Brahman to *jagat.* As pointed out earlier, the

Ārambhaṇādhikaraṇa and Ahikuṇḍalādhikaraṇa of the *Vedāntasūtras* deal with the question of the relation of the universe to Brahman. The *Vedāntasūtra* mentioned in the Ārambhaṇādhikaraṇa deals with the question whether Brahman which is the cause of the universe and the *jagat* which is its effect is different or non-different. The relevant *sūtra* reads: *Tad-ananyatvam ārambhaṇa śabdādibhyaḥ.*[11] This *sūtra* is framed by Bādarāyaṇa on the basis of the *Chāndogya* passage in which the causal relation between Brahman and the *jagat* is discussed on the analogy of the clay and the pot, etc., made out of it. The word *ārambhaṇa* mentioned in the *sūtra* occurs in this Upaniṣadic statement (*vācārambhaṇam vikāro...*).[12] The word *ananyatva* is used to explain that cause and effect are not absolutely different, as Naiyāyikas believe but are non-distinct as otherwise a causal relationship cannot be satisfactorily explained.

This *sūtra,* if properly interpreted, implies that though Brahman as cause and the *jagat* as effect are different they are also non-different (*ananya*) in the sense that it is the same Brahman as associated with *cit* and *acit* in their subtle form becomes Brahman as associated with *cit* and *acit* in, their gross from after the creation of the universe. This is the view expressed by Rāmānuja. It is necessary to adopt this interpretation to explain the non-difference between Brahman and *jagat,* as conveyed in such Upaniṣadic texts as *sarvaṁ khalu idaṁ brahma, ātmevaidam sarvaṁ,* etc., which equate Brahman and *jagat.*

Madhva does not accept this view. This *sūtra* in the Ārambhaṇādhikaraṇa is interpreted in a different way. In the first place he does not make any reference to the passage of the *Chāndogya* in which the word *ārambhaṇa* is used and the same term used in the *sūtra.* He quotes as the *viṣayavākya* a statement from *Ṛgveda* which refers to the origin of the universe, though contextually this passage in not relevant for the *sūtra* formulated by Bādarāyaṇa to discuss the causal relationship between Brahman and *jagat.* Madhva attempts, by adopting a novel interpretation of the *sūtra,* to prove through a double negation (*ananyatva*) that Brahman is the independent cause and all the accessories such as *prakṛti*, *jīvas*, *kāla*, *karma*, etc., are by hypothesis metaphysically dependent on Brahman.[13]

The Ahikuṇḍalādhikaraṇa included in the second *pāda* of third *adhyāya* specifically discusses the question of relation of the universe to Brahman, according to Rāmānuja (the relation of *jīva* to Brahman, according to Śaṅkara). Bādarāyaṇa introduces three *sūtras*[14] in which he refers to the different views regarding the nature of the relation in terms of *bhedābheda* and *abheda* (non-difference) by citing two illustrations: (1) The serpent and its coil (*ahi-kuṇḍala*) and (2) The luminous body and its light (*prakāśa* and *prakāśāśraya*). The illustration of the serpent and its coil conveys the idea of difference-cum-non-difference between Brahman and *jīva*, according to Śaṁkara. As a serpent it is one but if we look at the coils, there is difference. On the basis of this explanation, the *jīva*, prior to its liberation, is different and after liberation, it becomes identical with Brahman. According to Rāmānuja, this illustration conveys the idea of non-difference between Brahman and the non-sentient universe. That is, the non-sentient universe constitutes the special form (*saṁsthāna viśeṣa*) of Brahman, as coil of the serpent. The illustration of light and its substrate indicates both difference and non-difference. The light and its luminous body are different but at the same time they are identical insofar as both are of the same nature of lustre (*tejas*).

Both these *sūtras* are taken to support two prima facie views, both according to Śaṅkara and Rāmānuja, since Bādarāyaṇa offers his view in a subsequent *sūtra*. The *sūtra* in which Bādarāyaṇa conveys his own view reads as *pūrvavad vā*. It literally means as stated previously. The word *vā* implies that the view contained in the present *sūtra* is different from the two prima facie theories referred to earlier which are considered to be defective.

Śaṅkara, as an advocate of the doctrine of identity refers to an earlier *sūtra*,[15] which speaks of non-difference between *jīva* and Brahman as in the case of the luminous body such as the sun and its reflection in the waves. Brahman is one but it appears as many *jīvas* due to the limiting adjuncts.

Rāmānuja, who does not subscribe to the theory of absolute oneness or *tādātmya* of *jīva* and Brahman, refers to the *sūtra* in the Aṁśādhikaraṇa in which the relation of *jīva* to Brahman is explained in terms of *aṁśa*, which property interpreted implies an integral part in the sense of an essential or distinguishing attribute being inherently related to its substance. By virtue of Brahman abiding eternally in *jīva*, as stated in the *Antaryāmī Brāhmaṇa* and also by Bādarāyaṇa by using the expression *avasthiteḥ*. Brahman and *jīva* are non-different in the sense that Brahman as organically or inherently related to *jīva* is one as a *viśiṣṭa tattva*, though Brahman and *jīva* are different by their very nature. Thus the relation of both *abheda* and *bheda* between Brahman and *jīva* as well as Brahman and *jagat* are reconciled without relegating *bheda śrutis* to the category of lesser validity.

Madhva unfortunately does not acknowledge that Ahikuṇḍalādhikaraṇa deals with the relation of either *jīva* to Brahman, as Śaṅkara does, nor that between universe and Brahman, as Rāmānuja interprets. According to him, these *sūtras* deal with the question of the relation of Brahman and its attributes. He raises the issue, claimed as the prima facie theory, whether the attributes such as bliss (*ānanda*), knowledge, power, etc. can also constitute the essence of Brahman. According to Bādarāyaṇa, as interpreted by Madhva, there is no contradiction in Brahman being the essence of these attributes and also it possessing these attributes as its property since both these facts are borne by the testimony of Śruits. The illustrations cited by Bādarāyaṇa are intended, according to Madhva, to prove the identity of the attributes with Brahman on the basis on the doctrine of non-difference between *guṇa* and *guṇī* admitted by Madhva.

Without entering into the discussion of the merit of this interpretation it may be noted that Madhva as an advocate of Dvaita Vedānta does not admit that the Ahikuṇḍalādhikaraṇa establishes that Brahman and *jagat* are non-different in any way. Similarly, he does not admit that the Vākyānvayādhikaraṇa deals with the theory of non-difference between Brahman and *jīva*. Even Aṁśādhikaraṇa, which is devoted to discuss the relation of *jīva* and Brahman, as is evident in the *sūtra*, does not support the difference between the two in the primary sense on the basis of the inherent relationship between the two, as explained by Rāmānuja on the basis of the *sūtra* and the Upaniṣads. Difference between the three ontological entities is of greater importance to Madhva than any kind of oneness (*abheda*) or organic unity. Such a theory of relationship between the three ontological entities, viz., *Īśvara*, *jīva*, *jagat* does not conform either to the Upaniṣadic teachings or the *Vedānta-sūtras* of Bādarāyaṇa. This is a major drawback of Dvaita Vedānta in the same way as Advaita Vedānta of Śaṅkara which suffers from the defect of emphasizing absolute non-difference without acknowledging the real difference that exists between Brahman and *jīva* as well as *jagat*, as warranted by the Scriptural texts and the *Vedāntasūtras*.

The third major theory of Dvaita Vedānta which is also open to criticism is *ānanda-tāratamya* or the gradations of experience of *ānanda* or bliss in the state of *mukti* by the *muktas* or the souls liberated from bondage. This theory is advanced by Madhva on the basis of the premise that *jīvas* including the *mukta jīvas* are different from each other in respect of their intrinsic nature (*svarūpataḥ bheda*) and hence even in the state of *mokṣa* each *jīva* enjoys only its quantum of *ānanda* in accordance with its status. In support of this unusual theory, not accepted by any other earlier Vedānta schools, either Bhāskara, Yādavaprakāśa and Rāmānuja, Madhva seeks the support from a few Upaniṣadic passage and in particular the passage in the *Ānandavallī* of *Taittirīya*, by misconstruing the import of the text in favour of his theory.

Whatever may be the merit of this theory, it does not conform either to the teachings of the Upaniṣads or the *Vedāntasūtras* of Bādarāyaṇa dealing with the status of *mukta*. The major point of criticism against this theory, as explicitly stated by Vedānta Deśika. *Paramata-bhaṅga* also in one of his works,[16] is that it is opposed to the text of *Muṇḍaka Upaniṣad*, which categorically states that the *jīva*, after it is liberated from bondage, attains a status of *sāmya* or similarity with Brahman. The relevant text reads: *nirañjanaḥ paramam sāmyam upaiti.*[17] The *Bhagavadgītā*[18] also reiterates the same by using the expression *sādharmya* or equality. The *Taittirīya Upaniṣad* specifically states that the *muktātmā* enjoys all the auspicious qualities of Brahman along with Brahman (*so' aśnute sarvān kāmān saha brahmaṇā vipaścita*). In view of these Scriptural texts. Vedānta Deśika remarks that Ānandatīrtha (Madhva) in advocating the *Ānandatāratamya*, ignored the *Sāmyaśruti.*[19]

Further, there is no difference between one *mukta jīva* and another in the state of *mokṣa.* The difference between one *jīva* and another is made only in respect of the nature of the body assumed by it. Intrinsically, they are alike. This is well brought out in the verses of the sixth *adhyāya* of *Bhagavad-gītā*, as correctly interpreted by Rāmānuja.[20] With the removal of bondage and dissolution of the body, the *jīvas* are not different. They are all alike in respect of their intrinsic nature. The plurality of *jīvas* is due to the fact that they are infinite in number (*ananta*) and also are eternal (*nitya*), as stated in the Upaniṣads. The postulation of a *viśeṣa* or a special quality as inherent in each *jīva* to distinguish one from the other is logically not sustainable, as it cannot be proved by any of the *pramāṇas.* This point is brought out in the criticism levelled against the theory of *viśeṣa* postulated by the Vaiśeṣika as a separate concept.[21] If one *jīva* is to be distinguished from another, it is done on the basis of the *upādhi* or limiting conditions such as time factor (*kāla*), place (*deśa*) and functions performed and more importantly with reference to the type of the body with which it is associated due to past *karma*, during the state of bondage. In the state of *mokṣa*, if a distinction is drawn between one *mukta* and another *mukta* and such as Viśvaksena, Ādiśeṣa, and Garuḍa, who perform special services for the Lord, these are due to the functions they perform in accordance with the *saṅkalpa* or *Paramātman.* Hence Madhva's doctrine of *Ānandatāratamya* is unsound philosophically and logically.

References

1. See *SD*, opening verse.
2. *Ch. Up.*, VI.1.4.
3. *VS*, I.4.24.
4. Pāṇini, *sūtra* I.4.30: *Janikartuḥ prakṛtiḥ.*
5. See Madhva, *Brahmasūtrabhāṣya*, I.4.24.

6. See *Ch. Up.*, VI.1.3: *Tad aikṣata bahusyām prajāyeyeti.* Also see, *The Philosophy of the Vedāntasūtra*, 5, p. 68.
7. See *SD*, *vāda* 52. Also *FVV*, p. 247.
8. *VS*, I.4.20–22. See also *The Philosophy of the Vedāntasūtra*, pp.106–9.
9. See *Nyāyasiddhāñjana*, opening page.
10. *VS*, II.3.43.
11. Ibid., II.1.15.
12. *Ch. Up.*, VI.1.1.
13. See B.N.K. Sharma, *Brahmasūtras*, vol. I, pp. 368–69.
14. *VS*, III.2.27–29.
15. Ibid., III.2.25: *Prakāśādivacca avaiśeyam prakāśaśca karmaṇyabhyasat.*
16. See *Rahasyatrayasāra*, chap. 22. See also p. 23.
17. *Muṇḍ. Up.*, III.1.3.
18. *BG*, XIV.2: *Idam jñānam upāśritya mama sādharmyam āgatāḥ.*
19. See *RTS*, 22.
20. See *BG*, VI.29–31.
21. See chap. 8.

17

Bhedābheda Vedānta of Bhāskara and Yādavaprakāśa

AS DIFFERENT FROM Advaita Vedānta of Śaṅkara, a few other schools of Vedānta were developed by the exponents such as Bhāskara, Yādavaprakāśa, Nimbārka, and the followers of Caitanya. Chronologically Bhāskara and Yādavaprakāśa came soon after Śaṅkara but earlier than Rāmānuja and Madhva, whereas Nimbārka came after Rāmānuja and Madhva.[1] The followers of Caitanya came long after Madhva. Though all these schools are categorized under the heading of the Bhedābhedavādins or the upholders of the doctrine that the relationship between Brahman and the *jīva* as well as Brahman and the *jagat* is one of difference and non-difference, they are acknowledged as distinct schools of Vedānta and designated differently as Aupādhika-bhedābhedavāda (Bhāskara), Svābhāvika-bhedābhedavāda (Yādava and Nimbārka) and Acintya-bhedābhedavāda (Caitanya). Earlier than Śaṅkara, Bhāskara, and Yādavaprakāśa, Bhartṛprapañca had advocated Bhedābhedavāda. He is stated to have upheld Brahma-pariṇāma-vāda or transformation of Brahman itself as *jagat* and also the *bhedābheda* relation between Brahman and *jīva* as well as Brahman and *jagat*. Except the extensive references made to his views by Śaṅkara and Sureśvara, we do not have any of his works.

As the literature on Bhartṛprapañca is not available, it is not taken up for examination. As regards the extant Bhedābheda schools, Vedānta Deśika has included a separate chapter for Bhāskara and Yādavaprakāśa under the title Bhāskarādi-bhaṅgādhikāra (*adhikāra* 13). The word *ādi* implies all other

Bhedābhedavādins. The objective of including these schools in the *Paramata-bhaṅga* is to prove that the concept of *bhedābheda* is not logically tenable and the system of Vedānta based on this doctrine is totally opposed to Viśiṣṭādāvaita Vedānta. The later schools founded by Nimbārka and the followers of Caitanya are not included in the *Paramata-bhaṅga* for the obvious reason that they came into existence long after Vedānta Deśika. However, as these are modified forms of the Vedānta of Bhāskara and Yādavaprakāśa, the criticisms offered against Bhāskara and Yādavaprakāśa would also be applicable to them. We shall therefore present a critical review of the schools of Yādavaprakāśa and Bhāskara in detail and mention briefly about other later schools of Bhedābheda, though not dealt with by Vedānta Deśika.

In the *Paramata-bhaṅga* the school of Bhāskara comes up for critical examination soon after the examination of Jainism in the same way as the Advaita of Śaṅkara follows soon after Buddhism. Though both Advaita of Śaṅkara and the Bhedābheda of Bhāskara are orthodox Vedānta schools based on the Upaniṣads and the *Vedāntasūtra,* the justification for consideration of these schools along with the unorthodox non-Vedic schools—Buddhism and Jainism is that in the opinion of Vedānta Deśika, both these schools have some common features in respect of their main tenets with that of Buddhism and Jainism respectively. Though prima facie such a treatment accorded to Advaita and Bhāskara's Vedānta is not fair, it is not considered inappropriate by Vedānta Deśika for the main reason that Advaita has adopted the postulate of *avidyā* to account for the phenomenal character of *jīvas* and *jagat* in the same way as the Mādhyamika Buddhists adopt the concept of *saṁvṛti* to explain the existence of the phenomenal universe. Similarly Bhāskara has admitted the concept of Bhedābheda of Jainism, ignoring the self-contradiction involved in it, to explain the nature of the relation of Brahman to *jīvas* as in the case of Jainas for whom the relation of *dravyas* to the *paryāyas* (attributes) is one of *bheda* and *abheda.* Hence Vedānta Deśika characterizes Advaita as *Pracchanna-bauddha* and Bhāskara as *Jaina-gandhi-vedāntī.* Though this phraseology may sound as a strong criticism, it is employed to indicated the defective nature of both these schools of Vedānta, since the concept of *avidyā* in the sense understood by Advaita as *sadasad-vilakṣaṇa* has no basis in the Upaniṣads or the *Brahmasūtras.* Similarly the description of the relation of Brahman to *jīvas* as one of *abheda* and *bheda* logically involves a self-contradiction. This is a general criticism applicable to all schools of Bhedābheda in whichever form it is presented.

Criticism of the Doctrine of Yādavaprakāśa

Coming to the detailed criticism of the Bhedābhedavādas, Vedānta Deśika first takes up the main doctrine of Yādavaprakāśa because the criticisms levelled against this school are also applicable to Bhāskara. According to Yādavaprakāśa, Brahman which is conceived as *sat* is the only ultimate Reality. It is of the nature of self-luminous knowledge (*svaprakāśa*) and omnipotence (*sarva-śakti*). It comprises three parts (*aṁśas*). These are *Īśvara* or God, *puruṣa* or the *jīva* and *prakṛti* or the primordial cosmic matter. All these are eternal and non-different from Brahman.

Vedānta Deśika points out that such a conception of the ultimate Reality is most unsound, because it is opposed to the teachings of the Upaniṣads which categorically state that Brahman is *niraṁśa* or devoid of parts and that it is different from *prakṛti* as well as *puruṣa* and that *Īśvara* is the very Brahman.[2] It may be objected that, the three principles, viz., *Īśvara, jīva* and *prakṛti* as *aṁśas* of Brahman are different from the *sat* and hence it cannot be claimed that *sat* is one Reality. This objection is ruled out by Yādavaprakāśa on the ground that the element of *sat* is recurrent in all the three and as such all the three principles are not different from Brahman. This is explained on the analogy of the ocean and the foam (*phena*), bubbles, waves, etc., arising from the calm sea water. Though the modifications of the calm sea are different from the sea, these are not actually different from the sea.

This explanation does not hold good, contends Vedānta Deśika. When all the modifications of the sea water become re-absorbed in the sea, it is not possible to determine the part of the sea in which these are absorbed and the part from which they again arise (*avyavasthitabhāga*). If this position is accepted it would follow that each time the *jīvas* come into existence similar to the rise of the waves. Such a theory would militate against the theory of eternality of *Īśvara*, *jīva* and *prakṛti*. Besides, the new *jīvas* would be subjected to the experience of the effects of *karma* not experienced in earlier births and also the destruction of the effects of deeds acquired in earlier births. If it be argued that the origin of these *tattvas* takes place from a separate fixed part of *sat* (*vyavasthita-bhāga*), then it would amount to the admission of four parts in *sat* instead of three. Another difficulty arises with regard to explaining the relationship between the fourth part and the other three parts and in terms of *bheda* or *abheda*. The admission of both *bheda* and *abheda* involves contradiction. If it is both *bheda* and *abheda*, then the criticism offered against the Jaina theory of *bheda* and *abheda* would also apply to this case.

Coming to further details of the threefold nature of *sat*, Vedānta Deśika points out that the concept of *Īśvara* as an *aṁśa* of Brahman is defective. *Īśvara* as part of Brahman is regarded as possessing unsurpassing *jñāna*, *ānanda*, *aiśvarya* (glory) and that these qualities become eternally manifest (*āvirbhūta*) in Him. This view cannot be sustained. If these qualities are already present in Brahman which is comparable to the calm ocean free from waves, etc., then these should be present at all times in Brahman since these are not eclipsed by anything else. In that case, if they become newly manifest in *Īśvara*, then these attributes become newly revealed in *Īśvara*. If it is argued that their manifestation in *Īśvara* is due to the fact that He is part of Brahman, then they should also be manifest in the *jīvas* and *prakṛti* since these are also *aṁśas* of Brahman. But it is not so.

Yādavaprakāśa admits that *Īśvara* is also of threefold nature viz., *vijñānamaya*, *manomaya*, and *prāṇamaya*. If this means that the *svarūpa* of *Īśvara* comprises three forms, then it would militate against the several Scriptural texts which emphasise the unitary character of *Īśvara*.

There are a few other arguments advanced in support of the concept of *Īśvara* as threefold. But these, when subjected to critical analysis, fall to the ground.[3]

The theory of *jīva* as part of Brahman is also open to criticism. According to Yādavaprakāśa, the difference between *jīva* and Brahman is not caused by *upādhi* or limiting adjuncts as in the case of Bhāskara, but it is *svābhāvika*, that is, it is real and natural. In such a theory, only one, the *samaṣṭi-puruṣa* or the aggregate of all *jīvas* known as Hiraṇyagarbha, is regarded as *bhoktā* or the subject of all experiences and all the other individual *jīvas* who are different, are the modifications of the *samaṣṭi-puruṣa*. Such individual selves are separate from each other with their own bodies. They are *aṇu* in nature and numerous. They are also eternal (*nityas*). Such an explanation offered by Yādavaprakāśa is defective because it militates against the Scriptural teaching which emphasizes the eternality of *jīva* (*jīva nityatva*). This is according to the view that *jīvas* are modifications of the *samaṣṭi-puruṣa*. If, on the other hand, the individual *jīvas* are also taken as different part of the aggregate *puruṣa* (*samudāya ekadeśa-viśeṣa*) similar to the trees of the jungle (*vana*) and the individual trees (*vṛkṣādīnām vana*), then there would be no difference between *samaṣṭi-puruṣa* and single individual *jīva*, just as the trees of the jungle are not different from the individual trees.

It may be argued that *jīvas* are parts of Brahman and hence some attributes of Brahman are manifest in some *jīvas* while some are eclipsed. Therefore the *samaṣṭi jīva* and manifested *jīvas* differ from each other. But such an explanation does not hold good. If the feature of *jīva* being an *aṁśa* of Brahman is common to all *jīvas*, then the *guṇas* of Brahman should be equally present in all *jīvas* at all times. It is possible to explain that these differences in the *jīvas* are the natural qualities of the *jīvas*, similar to the general qualities such as *rūpa, rasa,* etc., in objects. But such *guṇas* cannot constitute the attributes of Brahman as *sat* which is recurrent in all *aṁśas*.

The classification of *jīvas* into three main categories such as *siddhas, baddhas,* and *muktas* and further classification of *siddhas* into two groups as *ajñānasiddhas* and *yogasiddhas* is also defective as it is not warranted by any Scriptural and Smṛti texts. In the same way the description of *ajñānasiddhas* as aids or those that are serviceable to *Īśvara* (*upakaraṇa-bhūta*) and the *yoga-siddhas* as those who possess supernatural powers such as *aṇimā, garimā,* etc., is also defective. This view also stands rejected since the *yogasiddhas* have been included among the category of *baddhas.*

The theory of three types of bondage, viz., *prakṛti-bandha, vaikārika-bandha,* and *dakṣiṇa-bandha* with which *baddha jīvas* are associated is also unsound as it is opposed to the commonly associated theory of bondage in the form of *puṇya-pāpa-rūpa karma.*

In the case of *mukta jīvas,* it is believed that only seven *guṇas* (attributes) become manifested in the state of *mukti.* This is also opposed to the Scriptural text according to which eight *guṇas* which are inherent in *jīvātman* become manifested in the state of *mukti.*[4] If *muktas* are free to enjoy *ānanda* or bliss of Brahman there should be no objection to admit *satya-saṅkalpatva* too, which is the eighth *guṇa,* in the state of *mukti.*

There are a few other details regarding the relationship between Brahman and *jīva* in the state of *mukti.* All these are unsound, contends Vedānta Deśika.[5]

The views advanced regarding the nature of *prakṛti* which is a part of Brahman according to Yādava are also untenable. If *prakṛti* is part of Brahman, it is not appropriate to regard it as *acetana* on the ground that *brahma-guṇas* are eclipsed in it. According to the Smṛti texts, it is *acetana* by its very nature.[6] According to Yādavaprakāśa *prakṛti* itself is of three kinds, viz., *kāla* (time), *paramākāśa* (transcendental world) and *avyaktam* (unmanifest *prakṛti*). This view is untenable because it is opposed to the commonly accepted *pramāṇas* according to which *prakṛti* is different from *kāla* and *paramākāśa.*

Coming to the evolutes of *prakṛti,* Yādava makes a distinction between *jñānendriyas* and *karmendriyas.* The *karmendriyas* are regarded as having been produced for each body separately. There is no *pramāṇa* in support of this view. Such an explanation is opposed to the statements which mention the origin and dissolution of all *indriyas.* This is also opposed to the *Vedānta-sūtra* and Smṛti texts which teach about the nature of *indriyas*—both *jñāna* and *karmendriyas.*

In conclusion Vedānta Deśika refers to the following invocatory verse of *Kātyāyanakārikā* which is considered to be the basis for Bhedābhedavāda of Yādavaprakāśa and which is claimed as the view of a sage:

Īśvara avyākṛta prāṇa virat bhūtendriyormibhiḥ;
yat pranṛtyadiva ābhāti tasmai sad-brahmaṇe namaḥ.
I offer my salutation to that *sat* which is Brahman and from which emanate like waves (from the calm sea) *Īśvara,* unmanifest *prakṛti* (*avyākṛta*) and *prāṇa, buddhi, ahaṅkāra,* and *indriyas* as well as elements.

Even if this is considered as a doctrine promulgated by a sage, it is to be ignored since it is opposed to the Scriptural teachings.

In the same way, the doctrine advanced by Brahmadatta (claimed to be an exponent of Bhedābhedavāda and *svarūpa-pariṇāma* for Brahman, stands rejected on the basis of the criticisms advanced against Yādavaprakāśa. If Śruti and Smṛti texts speak of *bhedābheda* between ontological entities, these are to be explained on the basis of *bheda* and *abheda* from different standpoints (*viśiṣṭa ākāra bheda*).

Criticism of the Doctrine of Bhāskara

Similar to the doctrine of Yādavaprakāśa, Bhāskara also maintains that *sat* which denotes Brahman is the only one ultimate Reality. It contains in it *Īśvarāṁśa* or the aspect of *Īśvara* which is eternally Omniscient and Omnipotent (*sarvaśakta*). It is also associated with *upādhi* or the limiting adjunct named *avidyā,* which unlike in Advaita Vedānta is real and which transforms itself into *prakṛti* and its evolutes such as *mahat, ahaṅkāra,* etc. It is always *acetanā* or non-sentient in character. *Īśvara,* who is eternal and *anādi,* takes the form of *jīvas* due to the association with *upādhi* in the form of bodies caused by *avidyā.* When *jīvas* become free from the limiting conditions, they become one with *Īśvara.* This is explained on the analogy of ether (*ākāśa*) which is one, becomes many when conditioned by several pots, but with the destruction of the pots several *ākāśas* become one.[7]

Vedānta Deśika points out that all these arguments advanced by Bhāskara to establish his doctrine of *behdābheda* are untenable when these are subjected to critical analysis. In other words, the main teaching of Bhāskara, viz., that *sat* denoting Brahman alone is one Reality and that it comprises two parts, viz., *cit* and *acit* in the form of *Īśvara* and that these are different and non-different from the *upādhi*, are opposed to Śruti and Smṛti texts. Besides as in the case of Jaina doctrine of *bhedābheda* relation between *dravya* and *paryāyas* or qualities, it is logically untenable since *bheda* and *abheda* are mutually contradictory.

According to Bhāskara, *jīva* and *Īśvara* are essentially non-different (*svābhāvika-abheda*) but they are different due to the limiting condition (*aupādhika*). That is, *jīva* is considered different due to the association of *avidyā* with Brahman. This is similar to the ocean and the waves, etc., arising from it. Though the waves and the ocean are essentially the same, the waves as such are regarded as different from the ocean. When the waves subside, the two become one.

The distinction drawn between *svābhāvika abheda* and *aupādhika-bheda* between Brahman and *jīva* cannot be established either by *pratyakṣa* or *anumāna* due to the fact that both these ontological entities are beyond the scope of perception. In the absence of perception, inference which is dependent on the basis of invariable concomitance (*vyāpti*) between *sādhya* and *hetu* cannot also be formulated to prove the theory. The Scriptural texts also do not reveal that there is *svābhāvika-abheda* and *aupādhika-bheda* between these two ontological entities. The Scriptural texts which speak of both *abheda* (*tat-tvamasi*) and *bheda* (such as *jña ajña*) and also texts referring to the relationship between the two in terms of *śarīra* and *śarīrī* do not explicitly convey the idea of *aupādhika-bheda* between *Īśvara* and *jīva.* If some Scriptural texts refer to the oneness of *jīva* and Brahman in the state of *mukti,* it is to be understood in the sense of *sāmya* or *sādharmya* or equal status in respect of certain attributes but not absolute.

The *Muṇḍaka* text[8] which states on the analogy of the rivers flowing into the ocean becoming one with it, do not imply absolute dissolution or absorption of river water with sea water. It signifies that the river water is mixed with sea water and the two become indistinguishable but not totally lost. This is to be understood in the same way as in the illustration cited in the *Kaṭha Upaniṣad*[9] about the water in a small vessel, when poured into pure water contained in a jug becomes the same (*tādṛgeva-bhavati*). This does not mean that water of the small vessel becomes absorbed or lost in it, but on the other hand, it only means that it remains mixed with it and also becomes pure. This is evident from the fact that the level of water in the jug increases with the mixing of water of the small vessel.

The illustration of the *ākāśa*, conditioned by the pots of different sizes, becomes one with the all-pervasive *ākāśa* with the destruction of the pots, does not support the theory of Bhāskara, viz., that the *jīvas* which are conditioned by the bodies become identical with Brahman because conditioned *ākāśas* do not acquire any new character of identity (*svarūpaikyāpatti*). The *jīvas* by their very nature are the same as Brahman, according to Bhāskara. The characteristic of their being different from Brahman caused by limiting conditions ceases to exist. In the same way, *jīva* which by its very nature is one with Brahman, assumes the same condition as it was before with the cessation of *karma*.

There are similar statements in the *Viṣṇupurāṇa*[10] which prima facie lend support to the theory of Bhāskara. But these texts, if properly interpreted with reference to the context, emphasise the difference that exists between *jīvas* and Brahman and they do not prove absolute identity.[11]

If, according to the central doctrine of Bhāskara, *jīva* is the very Brahman conditioned by the limiting adjunct, it is not possible to speak of difference between the two ontological entities of different nature only on the basis of *upādhi*, on the analogy of the limited *ākāśa* and the all-pervasive ethereal *ākāśa* conditioned by the pots. Besides, it would militate against the *Gītā* teaching which describes *jīva* as *acchedya* or non-divisible. If that part of the all-pervasive Brahman becomes *jīva* when it is conditioned by the *upādhi* in the form the body, then with the change of the bodies new *jīvas* which condition other parts of Brahman, would not be able to carry with it the experiences of the deeds performed earlier. Besides, every time a *jīva* comes into existence with the association of Brahman with a new *upādhi*, bondage and similarly *mokṣa* or liberation from it with the cessation of the association of the body with Brahman would take place (*pratikṣaṇam bandha-*

mokṣa prasaṅgaḥ). If that part of Brahman which becomes associated with *upādhi* becomes free from bondage, the same becomes associated with another *upādhi* and thus becomes again bound. It cannot be said that only a particular fixed part of Brahman becomes associated with *upādhis* and as such Brahman is not subject to bondage and release all the time since there is no basis to postulate such a theory. Nor can it be said that *upādhi* is *vibhu* or all-pervasive and such a Brahman conditioned by *upādhi* becomes *jīva.* This goes against the theory of *jīva* as *aṇus* or monadic, accepted by Bhāskara. Further, all the *upādhis* in the form of bodies which experience *sukha* and *duḥkha* would become applicable to Brahman also. This would be opposed to the theory of *Īśvara* being free from all afflictions. If it is argued that *jīva* is *upādhi-viśiṣṭa* Brahman and such a Brahman is not affected by suffering, which actually applies to *upādhi* and not to Brahman, then it would amount to the admission of Cārvāka doctrine. To escape these criticisms it is safer to accept the theory that *jīvas* as associated with bondage in the form of bodies and sense organs experience pleasure and pain and with the removal of bondage, these *jīvas* attain the status of Brahman. Such a theory is sounder and is in accordance with Śruti and Smṛti texts.

After criticizing the doctrines of Yādava and Bhāskara separately, Vedānta Deśika points out the common defect of both the schools of Bhedābhedavādins—(1) those who maintain that *Īśvara* and *jīvas* are by their very nature different and also non-different and (2) those who uphold that both these entities are by their very nature non-different (*abheda*) but they are different (*bheda*) due to *upādhi.* If *Īśvara,* according to these schools, is an *aṁśa* of Brahman and He is by nature omniscient (*svataḥ sarvajñaḥ*), the question is raised whether or not this *Īśvara* is aware that *jīva* which is either an *aṁśa* of Brahman or the very Brahman conditioned by *upādhi*, is non-different from Him? If He is not aware of it, then He cannot be regarded as *sarvajña.* If He knows this fact, then He would be experiencing all the afflictions of *jīvas* and consequently He too would be going through the cycle of births and deaths endlessly. Similarly if *Īśvara* and *jīva* are non-different, then the special (exclusive) characteristics of *Īśvara* such as *ānanda* would also be applicable to *jīva*.

References

1. According to some scholars, Nimbārka is claimed to have existed before Madhva.
2. Cf. *Śvet. Up.*, VI.11.19: *Niṣkalam, niṣkriyam, śāntam niravadyam nirañjanam.* Also I.10: *Pradhāna-kṣetrajñapatiḥ, kṣaraṁ pradhānaṁ amṛtākṣaram haraḥ kṣarātmānau īśate deva ekaḥ....*
3. See for details, *PMB*, pp. 116–18.
4. See *Ch. Up.*, VIII.1.5: *Apahatapāpam vijaraḥ vimṛtyuḥ viśokaḥ vijighatsuḥ apipāsaḥ satyakāmaḥ satyasaṅkalpaḥ.*
5. See *PMB*, pp. 123–24.
6. *VP*: *Acetanā parārthā ca nityā satata-vikriyā.*
7. See Viṣṇudharma: *Ghata-dhvaṁse ghatākāśo na bhinno nabhaso yathā.*
8. *Muṇḍ. Up.*: *Yathā nadyās-syandamānāḥ samudre astam gacchanti nāma-rūpe vihāya; tathā vidvān nāmarūpādvimuktaḥ parātparaṁ puruṣaṁ upaiti divyam.*
9. *Kaṭha Up.*, II.1.15: *Yathṭodakam śuddhe śuddham āsiktaṁ tādṛgeva bhavati.*
10. *VP*: *Vibhedajanake ajñāne nāśam-ātyantikam gate; ātmano brahmaṇo bhedam asantam kaḥ kariṣyati.*
11. See *RB*, I.1.1.

18
Other Bhedābheda Schools

Svābhāvika Bhedābheda Vedānta of Nimbārka

Nimbārka was born in south India about the middle of fourteenth century. According to modern scholars he belongs to the period later than Rāmānuja and Madhva.[1] Though like other theistic schools of Vedānta, he admits three *tattvas*—Brahman, *jīva*, and *jagat*, he differs from them in advocating the relation of *bheda* and *abheda* between Brahman and *jīvas* and Brahman and *jagat*. This relationship, according to him is also not *aupādhika*, that is, it is not caused by *upādhi* or limiting adjunct as in the case of Bhāskara but it is *svābhāvika*, that is, the three ontological entities are different (*bheda*) by their very nature and also they are non-different (*abheda*) by their very nature (*svābhāvika*). Hence his Vedānta is designated as Svābhāvika Bhedābhedavāda, as different from Aupādhika Bhedābhedavāda of Bhāskara. As we have seen earlier, the Bhedābhedavāda advocated by Yādavaprakāśa is also *svābhāvika*. That is, the relationship between *Sat* or Brahman and three *tattvas* named *Īśvara*, *cit* (*jīva*), and *acit* (cosmic matter) which are regarded as *aṁśas* or parts of *Sat* is one of both *bheda* and also *abheda* by their very nature (*svābhāvika*). The theory of Brahman as both non-difference and also different from *jīva* and *jagat* by its very nature (*svābhāvika*) at all time involves self-contradiction. It may be possible to overcome the self-contradiction by admitting absolute non-differene or identity of the three principles as is done by Śaṅkara. But this theory is not acceptable to Nimbārka since it militates according to him, against Scriptural texts speaking of real difference between them. The other alternative to overcome the criticism is to admit absolute difference (*atyanta bheda*) between the three ontological *tattvas*, as upheld by Madhva. This theory also is not acceptable to Nimbārka since several Scriptural texts speak of *abheda*, such as *Tat-tvam-asi*, *Ayam ātmā brahma*, etc. The theory of Yādavaprakāśa, according to which *Sat* is different and non-different from *Īśvara*, *jīva* and cosmic matter which are the parts (*aṁśa*) of *Sat*, is also considered to be defective. Rāmānuja admits three *tattvas*—*Īśvara* (Brahman), *jīvātman* or individual self and *jagat* or primordial cosmic matter and adopts the relation of body to the soul (*śarīra-śarīrībhāva*) between Brahman and the *jīvas* as well as cosmic matter. On the basis of this logical principle of inherent or organic relationship, he reconciles the conflict between the *bheda-śrutis* and *abheda-śrutis* and accepts both *bheda* and *abheda* between Brahman and *jīvas* as well as Brahman and *jagat* from different standpoints. The three ontological entities are different because they are of different nature. But Brahman as organically related to *jīvas* and *jagat* is one (*viśiṣṭaikya vivakṣayā ekatva*). But the concept of *śarīra-śarīrī* relation is not acceptable to Nimbārka. He therefore advocates *svābhāvika abheda* and also *svābhāvika bheda*. The question to be considered is whether this theory is philosophically and logically tenable.

If we go by the criticisms levelled by Vedānta Deśika against Yādavaprakāśa, who also admits Svābhāvika Bhedābheda, this doctrine is untenable. As stated earlier, the main point of criticism is that both *bheda* and *abheda* cannot co-exist. They are mutually opposed, like light and darkness. On this ground the Jaina's doctrine of *Saptabhaṅgī* (Anekāntavāda) is refuted by the Vedāntins. For the same reason the Vedānta expounded by Bhāskara and Yādava has been vehemently criticized by Śaṅkara and Rāmānuja. By merely qualifying Bhedābheda concept with the terms such as *svābhāvika, aupādhika*, it is not possible to escape the criticism against the Bhedābheda-vāda. In order to overcome this criticism, one has to accept either Abhedavāda or Absolute oneness of Brahman by denying the reality to the *jīvas* and *jagat* and regarding them as illusory manifestations of Brahman, as Śaṅkara has done or absolute difference between the three ontological entities, as Madhva has done. The other alternative is to admit *bheda* as well as *abheda* from different standpoints, as Rāmānuja has advocated. The Bhedābhedavāda, in whatever form it is formulated, cannot escape the criticism of self contradiction and other philosophical and logical defects pointed out by Vedānta Deśika against Yādavaprakāśa.

Now coming to the details of specific defects of Nimbārka philosophy, if *bheda* and *abheda* cannot coexist because of mutual opposition, how can *svābhāvika bheda* and *svābhāvika abheda* can coexist? If Brahman and *jīvas* are essentially (*svarūpataḥ*) are non-different, they cannot also by their very nature (*svarūpataḥ*) be different. They can be regarded as different only when Brahman becomes many when the same is conditioned by *upādhi* in the form of several bodies such as in the case of all-pervasive *ākāśa* becoming many by being conditioned by several pots. Nimbārka does not subscribe to this view of Bhāskara. The example of sea and the waves arising from it does not serve his purpose. Sea water and waves are essentially the same but as waves, it is regarded as different. But waves are caused by the wind or some other factor, which is the *upādhi* or conditioning factor for causing the waves. If *svābhāvika abheda* is accepted, *svābhāvika bheda* cannot be maintained.

Further if the *jīvas* and Brahman are essentially non-different (*svarūpataḥ abheda*), then the afflictions and other defects of the *jīvas* would also be applicable to Brahman. But Brahman by its very nature is free from all defects. It does not stand to reason to say that though Brahman and *jīvas* are essentially non-different (*svarūpataḥ abheda*), the defects of *jīvas* do not apply to Brahman. Hence the relation of *svābhāvika bheda* and *abheda* in respect of Brahman, *jīva* and *jagat* as advocated by Nimbārka is philosophically untenable. It is also not warranted by Scriptural texts. If *svābhāvika bheda* exists, as stated in the Upaniṣads, then *svābhāvika abheda*, in the sense of identity (*svarūpaikya*) cannot be maintained.

Nimbārka defends the *svābhāvika abheda* between three different ontological entities, by arguing that *abheda* is not to be taken in the sense of absolute identity (*svarūpaikya*), as Śaṅkara interprets, by accepting Brahman as the only Reality, whereas *jīvas* and *jagat* are illusory in character which amounts to the denial of their existence as real entities. If all the three entities are real and different in nature, their absolute identity is logically untenable. To overcome this objection, Nimbārka argues, as in the case of Madhva, that the *jīvas* and *jagat* do not have independent existence (*svatantra-sattā bhāva*) but on the contrary, they are dependent on Brahman for their existence (*paratantra sattā bhāva*). Since the *jīvas* and *jagat* are dependent on Brahman for their existence, they are regarded as non-different from Brahman.

In reply to this argument it is pointed out that mere dependence of *jīvas* on Brahman does not prove the theory of the two entities being non-different. Thus, for instance, the physical body is dependent on *jīvātman* for its *sattā* and *pravṛtti* (functions). But the relation between the two cannot be treated as one of *abheda*. The dependence on Brahman (*tadadhīna sattā*) or even similarity between the two (*tat śādṛśya*) in respect of certain attributes such as *jñāna* and *ānanda*, as maintained by Madhva, does not mean *abheda* or even *svābhāvika-abheda* a term used by Nimbārka, following the logic of Madhva between the two ontological entities in the primary sense. The theory of *svābhāvika bheda* and *svābhāvika abheda* is not therefore tenable since the two logical concepts are mutually opposed like *bheda* and *abheda* unless these are conceived from different standpoints, as Rāmānuja has explained. As stated in the *Antaryāmī Brāhmaṇa* and also in the *Vedāntasūtra*, Brahman abides in *jīvātman* as its *Antaryāmin* and controls it from within. By virtue of Brahman's immanence in *jīva*, the latter is regarded as non-distinct (*ananya*) and so also Brahman and *jagat*. Though *jīva* and Brahman are different by their very nature, the two are non-distinct in the sense that Brahman as inherently related to *jīva* is non-different as a *viśiṣṭa* entity, similar to a substance (*dravya*) as inherently related to its essential attribute is one. Only on the basis of such an explanation, *bheda* and *abheda* can be maintained for two ontological entities without contradiction.

ACINTYA-BHEDĀBHEDA VEDĀNTA OF CAITANYA SCHOOL

Kṛṣṇa Caitanya, popularly known as Caitanya Mahāprabhu, who was born in AD 1486 in Navadvīpa (West Bengal) is the founder of Bengal School of Vaiṣṇavism, also called Gauḍīya Vaiṣṇavism. Though he did not personally compose any literature, his followers, Jīva Gosvāmī and Baladeva Vidyābhūṣaṇa developed the philosophy of this school under the name of Acintya-Bhedābheda Vedānta. The concept of Acintya-Bhedābheda is adopted to explain the relation of God (Lord Kṛṣṇa) to the material world. This term was first conceived by Jīva Gosvāmī, one of the close disciples of Caitanya, who has mentioned in his book *Sarva-saṁvādinī* which is a commentary on *Bhāgavata-sandarbha.* It was also employed later by Baladeva Vidyābhūṣaṇa in two of his books *Siddhānta-ratna* and *Prameya-ratnāvalī.* The Vedānta philosophy expounded in these works is mostly influenced by the teachings of Rāmānuja and also Madhva. We do not propose to discuss these philosophical and religious teachings. We shall confine our attention to the critical examination of the main issue relating to the relation of God to *jīvas* and the *jagat* in terms of *acintya-bhedābheda.*

The word *acintya* means "inconceivable" *acintya-bhedābheda,* means "the relationship between God and the universe as well as the *jīvas,*" which is one of *bheda* or difference and *abheda* or non-difference, is inconceivable. As stated earlier, the Bhedābhedavāda was first developed in the area of Vedānta by Bhāskara and Yādavaprakāśa. Even long before Bhāskara and prior to Śaṅkara, Bhartṛprapañca and Brahmadatta, the ancient Vedānta exponents, are believed to be the advocates of Bhedābhedavāda to explain the relation of Brahman to the two ontological entities, viz., *jīva* and *jagat. Bheda* and *abheda* are two logical concepts to describe the relationship between two entities. These two are mutually opposed like light and darkness. The description of the relation as both *bheda* and *abheda* is therefore a self-contradiction. In the area of Vedānta, it became necessary to explain the relationship between Brahman and *jīva* as well as Brahman and *jagat.* Yādavaprakāśa as against Śaṅkara's *abheda-vāda* or absolute oneness of Ultimate Reality by the denial of the reality of *jīvas* and *jagat,* adopted the doctrine of Svābhāvika-Bhedābhedavāda or natural difference and non-difference. As this was found defective, Bhāskara adopted the doctrine of Aupādhika-Bhedābhedavāda, that is, Brahman and *jīvas* as well as *jagat* are non-different by their very nature, while difference among them is caused by limiting adjunct in the name of *avidyā,* which is real, unlike in Advaita Vedānta. Both these schools were vehemently criticized by Rāmānuja and other Vedāntins. To overcome the criticisms, Nimbārka, who is also a Bhedābhedavādin, described the relationship among the three ontological entities by adopting the doctrine of Svābhāvika Bhedābhedavāda, that is, Brahman and other two ontological entities are non-different by their very nature and so also difference between them is natural (*svābhāvika bheda*). Even this theory was open to criticism. It is not basically different from the theory adopted by Yādavaprakāśa.

Caitanya school of Vedānta, which came into existence much later than Nimbārka, has introduced the concept of Acintya-Bhedābhedavāda. The term *acintya* is employed by Jīva Gosvāmī in place of the term *svābhāvika* used by Nimbārka.

According to Jīva Gosvāmī, Brahman is by nature pure and perfect. But it there is natural non-difference between Brahman, who is Lord Kṛṣṇa, and the *jīvas,* the defects of the latter would also exist in the former. By the same logic, the qualities of Lord, such as omnipotence, would also belong to the *jīvas.* But this is not the case. Brahman, who is pure, does not possess any of the imperfections of the *jīvas* or of the world. Therefore the relation must be taken as *acintya* or inconceivable. According to Jīva Gosvāmī, this is more satisfactory explanation than all other explanations offered earlier by other Bhedābhedavādins since it resolves the puzzling problem of the relation among the three ontological entities. By way of elucidation of the term *acintya* it is pointed out that it is inconceivable to logic but it is understandable on the authority of Scripture. *Śabda* or Scripture is the sole authority for knowing the nature of the Supreme Lord. The Scriptural texts point out that the Lord possesses inconceivable powers and that he is the repository of conflicting qualities. Yet these conflicting qualities abide harmoniously in Him because of this inconceivable powers. The Scriptural texts which are quoted by Jīva Gosvāmī in support of his theory is the statements in the *Māṇḍ. Up.* and the *Kai. Up.* (1–6).[2]

The question to be considered is whether the theory of Acintya-Bhedābheda overcomes the criticisms levelled against Nimbārka, who maintains Svābhāvika Bhedābhedavāda. On closer and objective examination, our answer is in the negative. If Svābhāvika Bhedābhedavāda of Yādavaprakāśa and also that of Nimbārka are untenable, Acintya-Bhedābheda cannot also be sustained. As pointed out earlier, if logical concepts of *bheda* and *abheda* cannot co-exist because they are mutually opposed, the same criticism applies to Svābhāvika Bhedābhedavāda and the Acintya-Bhedābhedavāda. By substituting the term *svābhāvika* by *acintya* the mutual opposition (*paraspara vyāghāta*) between *bheda* and *abheda* cannot be overcome.

The argument that the Lord possesses *vicitra śakti* and that there is no opposition between His being different and non-different from *jīvas* at all times does not stand to reason.

Further the Upaniṣadic texts do not explicitly state that the Lord is both different and non-different from *jīvas* and the universe by virtue of his *sarvaśakti.* The *Māṇḍūkya* and *Kaivalya* Upaniṣads employ the term *acintya* along with other negative forms to describe Brahman as an inconceivable Reality but these cannot be taken as a support to the theory of Acintya-Bhedābheda relation between Brahman and the universe. Brahman can be one and also many from different standpoints. The only solution to this puzzling problem of absolute difference and the texts speaking of oneness or *abheda* among the three ontological principles is to resort to the explanation of *śarīrātma bhāva* or the relation of the body to the self, as adopted by Rāmānuja. Brahman as inherently or inseparably related to *jīvas* and *jagat* is non-different or one entity as a *viśiṣṭa tattva.* But the three entities, by virtue of the difference in respect of their intrinsic nature, they are also different. The merit of this theory would be discussed later.

Śuddhādvaita of Vallabha

In the preceding sections we have examined the various schools of Vedānta which uphold the doctrine of Bhedābheda relation among the three ontological *tattvas*—Brahman, *jīva,* and *jagat.* Along with these we may also consider the school of Vedānta designated as Śuddhādvaita expounded by Vallabha. Vallabha was born in the middle of fourteenth century in Andhra Pradesh and he has written a commentary on the *Vedāntasūtra* under the name of *Aṇubhāṣya.* In this and a few allied works, he has presented his views on the Vedānta doctrines. The term *śuddhādvaita* may give the impression that he, is an exponent of another form of Advaita. But actually, he, as a theist with passionate love for Lord Kṛṣṇa, admits that Brahman is qualified with attributes and it is identified with Lord Kṛṣṇa who is the Supreme Reality. He also maintains that *jīvas* and *jagat* are the manifestations of Brahman and as such these are real. Nor does he admit Dvaitavāda, that is, absolute difference or *atyanta bheda* among the three ontological entities as in the case of Madhva, though he is largely influenced by Madhva's teachings. He does not also accept Viśiṣṭādvaita of Rāmānuja, though many of his teachings in his *Aṇubhāṣya* are similar to those of Rāmānuja.

Though he admits the reality of all the three *tattvas,* he does not accept the *śarīrātma-saṁbandha* or body-soul relation between Brahman and *jīvas* as well as *jagat.* He does not also admit the doctrine of Bhedābheda as advanced by Bhāskara, Yādavaprakāśa, and Nimbārka. But while explaining the relationship between Brahman and *jīvas,* which are real and many, being the manifestation of Brahman, similar to the sparks emanating from the fire, he maintains the view that they are non-different (*abheda*). Though he does not claim to be a Bhedābhedavādin, like Nimbārka, he comes closer to the school of Bhedābhedavāda insofar as he speaks of *abheda* or identity between Brahman and *jīvas* and also *bheda* between the two by virtue of their difference in respect of their intrinsic nature. Hence it would not be wrong to classify this school under the category of Bhedābhedavāda and examine it along with other schools of Bhedābheda.

We shall not go into the details of all the doctrines of Vallabha. A fairly good account of the philosophy of Vallabha is given in the book *The Vedānta*[3] and in an article[4] by Sudananda Y. Shastry. We shall confine our attention, as in the case of Nimbārka and others, to the critical examination of the ontological relationship between Brahman and *jīvas* as well as *jagat* in terms of *bheda* and *abheda.*

According to Vallabha, both the *jīvas* and the non-sentient *jagat* are the manifestations of Brahman similar to the sparks emanating from the fire. Just as the fire and sparks are non-different, both being of the nature of fire, Brahman and *jagat* are essentially non-different. This is also explained on the analogy of the serpent and its coil (*ahikuṇḍala*), cited by Bādarāyaṇa in the *Vedāntasūtra* (III.2.26) while discussing the nature of relationship between Brahman and the non-sentient *jagat*. In the same *adhikaraṇa*, two other *sūtras* (III.2.27–28) are mentioned which discuss two other alternative views regarding the nature of relation viz., *bhedābheda* by citing the example of the sun and its *prakāśa* and *viśeṣaṇa-viśeṣya bhāva* or the relation of the substance to the attribute. This is according to Rāmānuja's interpretation.

The *sūtra* which cites the illustration of *ahikuṇḍala*, is taken both by Rāmānuja and Bhāmati as a reference to the Bhedābheda theory, and also the *sūtra* referring to the illustration of *prakāśa* (light) and *prakāśavat* (that which possesses light). Both the views are rejected by Bādarāyaṇa because the concept of *bhedābheda* is mutually opposed. The illustration of *ahikuṇḍala* (serpent and its coil) and fire and its spark (*agni* and *visphuliṅga*) which are cited by Vallabha as supporting the *abheda* between Brahman and *jīva* is not therefore tenable.

Vallabha contends that *jīvas* are also *brahma-svarūpa*, since these are emanations from Brahman and hence the two are essentially non-different. This amounts to the acceptance of *svābhāvika abheda* advocated by Yādavaprakāśa and Nimbārka. If this is the case, then the defects of *jīva* would also be applicable to Brahman. Then, Brahman cannot be regarded as *Śuddha*. The argument that Brahman is not touched by the defects of *jīva* or *jagat* even though they are non-different by nature does not stand to reason. Further the question arises whether Brahman, who is the *Īśvara* or God and who is also omniscient (*sarvajña*) knows that He has become *jīva*? If He is not aware of it, He cannot be regarded as *sarvajña*. If He knows it, He too would be subjected to the experience of the afflictions.

These criticisms can be escaped by admitting absolute identity (*tādātmya* or *svarūpaikya*) between Brahman and *jīva* and maintaining that the *jīvas* are mere reflections of Brahman, caused by *avidyā,* as admitted by Śaṅkara, or by postulating a real *upādhi,* as conceived by Bhāskara. But such theories are not acceptable to Vallabha because Brahman becomes *Aśuddha* with the association of illusory *māyā* or even *upādhi.* Then the doctrine of Śuddhādvaita has to be given up.

If, on the other hand, *atyanta-bheda* between Brahman and *jīva* is accepted, as is done by Madhva, these criticisms levelled against *svābhāvika abheda* can be escaped. But even the theory of *bheda-vāda* is not acceptable to Vallabha. The only way of maintaining the purity of Brahman and also its difference as well as non-difference as declared in the Scriptural texts, is to adopt the theory adopted by Rāmānuja, viz., Brahman as organically related to *cit* and *acit* is one Reality and the three ontological entities are different by virtue of their intrinsic nature.

The explanation offered by Vallabha that the same one Brahman manifests itself as *jīvas* and *jagat* out of his will and that they are made to exist as different, as a *līlā* or sport of the Lord, is not logically tenable. Nor is it supported by Scriptural texts. Both *jīvas* and *jagat* are *anādi* and *nitya.*

They are not created or produced. They exist always either in their subtle form or unmanifest form with Brahman during the state of *pralaya* and in gross or manifest form after creation. This view is supported by the Scriptural texts. The *Bṛhadāraṇyaka* says: the universe including *jīvas* exist as *avyākṛta* or unmanifest during dissolution and the same becomes manifest after *sṛṣṭi.*[5] Vallabha also admits that Brahman is the *upādāna-kāraṇa* of the universe. If Brahman Itself transforms into universe, then It would affect its *nirvikāratva.* That is, if direct *pariṇāma* is accepted, it would cause change in respect of *brahma-svarūpa*, as in the case of the lump of clay into pots. To avoid this criticism, *pariṇāma* or modification is to be explained through a media. Śaṅkara admits the association of *māyā* with Brahman and on account of *māyā* Brahman illusorily manifests itself as *jagat.* This is known as *vivarta-vāda* as against *pariṇāma-vāda.* Viśiṣṭādvaita maintains *prakṛti* which is regarded as the *śarīra* of Brahman as the media through which *jagat* is caused by the process of evolution. Vallabha does not admit either *māyā* or any other media such as *prakṛti* for the creation of the universe. According to him, maifestation of the universe is out of the *śakti* of Brahman. If *śakti* or potential power is part of the *Svarūpa* of Brahman, then Brahman would be subject to modification. If *śakti* is taken as the *saṅkalpa* of Brahman, it would serve as an instrumental or efficient cause (*nimittakāraṇa*). It cannot itself manifest as *jagat*, just as the knowledge and capacity of the potter do not produce the jug. He is only instrumental cause and the clay is the material cause. Hence the view of Vallabha that out of *śakti*, souls and *jagat* which are same as Brahman are made to manifest amounts to saying that Brahman itself becomes universe, which is philosophically unsound.

References

1. According to some scholars Nimbārka belongs to a period earlier than Madhva.
2. See *Manḍ. Up.*, 7: *Adṛṣṭam avyavahāryaṁ agrāhyaṁ alakṣaṇaṁ acintyaṁ avyapadeśaṁ*.... Also, *Kai. Up.* (I.6): *Hṛtpuṇḍarīkaṁ virajaṁ viśuddhaṁ vicintya madhye viśadam viśokam; acintyaṁ avyaktaṁ anantarūpaṁ śivam praśāntaṁ amṛtaṁ brahma yonim.*
3. V.S. Ghate, *The Vedānta*, Poona, 1981.
4. Sunanda Y. Shastri, "Philosophy of Vallabhacharya," in *Theistic Vedānta*, New Delhi, 2003.
5. See *Br. Up.*, I.4.7.

19

Schools of Śivādvaita and Navya Viśiṣṭādvaita

WHAT WE HAVE EXAMINED so far are the schools of Vedānta which were developed during the post-Rāmānuja and post-Madhva period and which are based primarily on the Upaniṣads and the *Vedāntasūtra* in a modified form by adopting the theories advanced either by Rāmānuja or Madhva. There are few other schools which came into existence against the background of the theology of Śaivism and Vaiṣṇavism. These are also claimed to be Vedāntic as far as their philosophical doctrines are concerned. To complete our critical review of Vedānta schools, these are taken up for consideration. The following are the schools which are influenced by Śaivism and Vaiṣṇavism:

1. Kāśmīra Śivādvaita expounded by Abhinavagupta.
2. Śivādvaita of Śrīkaṇṭha also known as Śakti-viśiṣṭādvaita—expounded in the *Śrīkaṇṭhabhāṣya* on the *Vedāntasūtra* with the commentary of Appayya Dīkṣita (fourteenth century) titled *Śivārkamaṇidīpikā*.
3. Śivādvaita of Śrīpatipaṇḍita expounded in the *Śrīkarabhāṣya* on *Vedāntasūtra* from the standpoint of the Vīra-śaiva religious sect.
4. Navya Viśiṣṭādvaita developed by Swāminārāyaṇa belonging to the Uddhavi Vaiṣṇava-saṁpradāya by mostly following Rāmānuja's Viśiṣṭādvaita philosophy.

KĀŚMĪRA ŚIVĀDVAITA

This was developed by Abhinavagupta about eleventh century AD. The term *advaita* may give the impression that it is a

Vedānta school, somewhat allied to Śaṅkara's Advaita Vedānta. But it is far from it in many respects. First of all, it is not developed, as in the case of the other major Vedānta schools, primarily on the basis of the Upaniṣads and *Brahmasūtras*. Secondly, it does not accept Brahman of the Upaniṣads as the Supreme Reality. Following the teachings contained in the Kāśmīra Śaiva Āgamas callsed Tantras, Śiva is the Supreme Being. The universe is the projection of Śiva-Śakti and it is not an illusory manifestation of the Supreme Being due to *māyā* as in the case of Śaṅkara's Advaita. Actually, it is one of several theological schools of Śaivism. Rāmānuja in his commentary on *Vedāntasūtra*, mentions four schools: Kāpāla, Kālamukha, Pāśupata, and Śaiva. The Pāśupata school, which is one of the oldest schools of Śaivism, which existed even at the time of Bādarāyaṇa has been separately criticized both in the *Bhāṣyas* of Śaṅkara and Rāmānuja and also by Vedānta Deśika in the *Paramata-bhaṅga*. Hence Kāśmīra Śivādvaita does not need separate examination. The criticisms offered by Vedānta Deśika in the chapter Pāśumatabahiṣkāravāda on the ground that the teachings of Pāśupata falls outside the scope of Vedic philosophy and religion hold good in respect of Kāśmīra Śivādvaita.

Śivādvaita of Śrīkaṇṭha

The Śivādvaita of Śrīkaṇṭha, though it is based on the *Brahmasūtra*, unlike the Kāśmīra Śivādvaita, is not acknowledged as a system of Vedānta either by the followers of Śaṅkara or Rāmānuja. In a critical study of *Śrīkaṇṭhabhāṣya* as commented by Appayya Dīkṣita, by Mm. K.S. Varadacharya, a traditional scholar of Parakala Mutt, Mysore, it is shown that this work is of dubious nature written by some Śaivite under the name of Nīlakaṇṭha. The *Śrīkaṇṭhabhāṣya* is on the pattern of *Rāmānujabhāṣya*. In place of Nārāyaṇa, Nīlakaṇṭha uses Śiva. Śiva is the Supreme Reality and He is only the *nimitta-kāraṇa*, while *Śiva-Śakti* is the *upādāna kāraṇa* of the universe. This school is therefore called Śakti-viśiṣṭādvaita. Vallabha has remarked that Śrīkaṇṭha is *Rāmānuja-cora* (a thief of Rāmānuja). As the doctrines of this school are opposed to the Upaniṣads and the *Vedāntasūtra*, as interpreted by Rāmānuja, it does not deserve any consideration.

Śivādvaita of Śrīkara

The Śivādvaita conceived by Śrīkara from the standpoint of Vīra-śaivism which is a contemporary sectarian movement in Karnataka state, is worse than *Śrīkaṇṭha-bhāṣya*. As rightly observed by Prof. N.G. Mahadevappa, a modern scholar on Vīra-śaivism, that Śrīpati Paṇḍita who, as a Vīraśaiva, vehemently condemns the Vedic teachings and Vedic religious practices, should have written a laudatory commentary on the *Vedāntasūtra* "looks not merely amusing but ludicrous."[1] The admission of Para Śiva as the Supreme Being in place of Brahman is opposed to the teachings of the Upaniṣads and the *Vedāntasūtra*. It also accepts Śiva as only the *nimitta kāraṇa*[2] of the universe as in the case of Pāśupata school which is outright rejected by Bādarāyaṇa as well as Śaṅkara and Rāmānuja.

Navya Viśiṣṭādvaita of Swāmī Nārāyaṇa

This is the latest school of Vedānta developed during the nineteenth century in the background of the influence of Vaiṣṇavism. The founder of this school is Swāmī Nārāyaṇa born in 1781 in a village near Ayodhyā. He was a disciple of Rāmānanda who himself was a follower of Rāmānuja. He established a new tradition known as Uddhava Vaiṣṇava Saṁpradāya. He has followed two small works titled *Vacanāmṛta* in Gujarati which is a manual on the religious duties to be followed by his disciples and *Śikṣāpatrī* (in Sanskrit), an epistle of precepts covered in 212 verses. In the latter work, he has expressed briefly his views on the philosophy and religion of his school.

As a devoted follower of Rāmānuja, he has closely followed the teachings of Rāmānuja. He himself states in the *śikṣāpatrī* that Viśiṣṭādvaita is his system of philosophy (*matam viśiṣṭādvaitam me*).[3] He also states that the commentaries written by Rāmānuja on *Vyāsasūtra* (*Brahmasūtra*) and the *Bhagavadgītā* are accepted by him as sole authority on the philosophical theories (*Rāmānujārya kṛtam bhāṣyam adhyātmikī mama*).[4] It is thus obvious that the Navya Viśiṣṭādvaita founded by Swāmī Nārāyaṇa is not basically different from Viśiṣṭādvaita Vedānta of Rāmānuja.

However, the later followers of Swāmī Nārāyaṇa have introduced a few novel philosophical concepts as different from Rāmānuja's system. Instead of three fundamental *tattvas* or metaphysical principles viz., *Īśvara, cit* and *acit,* the Swāmī Nārāyaṇa school admits five eternal realities, namely, (i) *Para-Brahman,* the Supreme Being who is identified with *Nārāyaṇa,* (ii) *Akṣara-Brahman,* (iii) *māyā-prakṛti,* (iv) *Īśvara* (cosmic Self), and (v) *jīva* (individual selves). It is claimed that the doctrine of fivefold realities is supported by the Vedas, Prasthānatraya, Smṛti, Itihāsas, Purāṇas, Pāñcarātra, etc. Presumably, in view of the introduction of such doctrines, this school of Vedānta is named as Navya Viśiṣṭādvaita.

As a new school of Vedānta, it may be justified to incorporate into it, some novel theories, provided these are warranted by the Upaniṣadic texts and the authoritative *Vedāntasūtras* of Bādarāyaṇa as interpreted by Rāmānuja. But, the admission of additional ontological principles such as *Akṣara* Brahman, *Īśvara* as cosmic Self in addition to Brahman identified with *Nārāyaṇa* is not warranted by the Scriptural and Smṛti texts including the *Brahmasūtra.* Rāmānuja, while defining the term *brahman* clearly states that Brahman is *Puruṣottama,* the Supreme Self and He is *Sarvésvara.*[5] The term *akṣara* employed in *Bṛhadāraṇyaka Upaniṣad* denotes the *Para Brahman.* This term appearing in the *adhyāya* VIII of the *Bhagavadgītā,* according to Rāmānuja, denotes the *jīvātman* in the context of the *upāsanā* on *jīvātman.* Thus there is no justification to introduce these additional metaphysical principles and use the title of Navya Viśiṣṭādvaita for the school founded by Swāmī Nārāyaṇa except the fact that it is a new religious movement or *sampradāya* started two centuries ago. If, on the other hand, they follow faithfully the principles and religious teachings of Rāmānuja, as claimed by its founder, this school would not be open to any criticism, from the standpoint of Viśiṣṭādvaita Vendānta.

References

1. See the article on Vīraśaivism in the volume on the *Theistic Vedānta* by the Centre for Studies in Civilization, New Delhi.
2. See *Br. Up.*, 1.4.7.
3. See *Śikṣāpatrī*, V.121.
4. Ibid., V.100.
5 See *RB*, I.1.1: *Brahma-śabdena svabhāvato nirasta-nikhila-doṣaḥ asaṅkhyeya kalyāṇa-guṇa viśiṣṭaḥ Puruṣottamo abhidhīyate; sa ca sarveśvaraḥ....*

20

The Doctrine of *Upāya*

THIS CHAPTER is devoted to the critical examination of the *upāya* or the means laid down for attaining a higher Spiritual Goal (*parama puruṣārtha*) as conceived by the different Indian philosophical systems including Viśiṣṭādvaita. In the preceding chapters Vedānta Deśika confined his attention to the critical review of the *tattvas* or the philosophical doctrines of these schools. The study of the *tattvas* constitutes an important part of a Darśana or a system of philosophy. A Darśana should also deal with the question of the main purpose (*prayojana*) for which philosophical investigation is undertaken. In the Indian philosophical background it is called the *puruṣārtha* or a higher goal to be achieved by the study of philosophy. If a specific goal is admitted then the ways and means or what is called *upāya*, to be adopted for attaining the goal is also to be laid down. Thus the Darśana or a system of philosophy should cover all three topics—*tattva, upāya* (also named *hita* in Vedānta) and *puruṣārtha* or goal. The present chapter examines critically the views or theories advocated by different schools of thought including Viśiṣṭādvaita. It is titled "Parokta-upāya-bhaṅgādhikāra." The subsequent chapter will deal with the nature of the objective to be accomplished or what is technically called *puruṣārtha* to be attained, as presented by different schools of thought. It is therefore titled "Parokta-prayojana-bhaṅgādhikāra."

At the very outset, Vedānta Deśika makes a critical remark that all the non-Vedic schools and also most of the Vedic schools including Advaita and Bhedābheda schools have been proved to be defective since their doctrines are opposed to the accepted *pramāṇas* and also not supported by sound logical arguments (*sat-tarka*). He will now attempt to show that these schools have also not presented a satisfactory theory of *hita* or the ways and means to be pursued to achieve the desired Spiritual Goal. He briefly mentions how each school has developed a defective theory of *upāya.*

Taking the school of Cārvāka first, Vedānta Deśika points out that the Cārvākas do not accept any *pramāṇas* other than *pratyakṣa.* Nor do they admit causal relation (*kāraṇa-kārya-bhāva*). In the absence of these, they cannot present any authoritative philosophical treatise which can be taught to others and also establish their own doctrines by refutation of the theories of rival schools. Regarding *artha* or the acquisition of wealth and *kāma* or sensual pleasure, which are considered by them as goals of life, there are no ways and means laid down for achieving these goals in any authoritative texts. Their teachings such as that consciousness (*caitanya*) is generated by the combination of the five physical components on the analogy of the emergence of intoxicating quality out of the admixture of certain ingredients and also the maxim that one should live happily until the end of life (*yāvajjīvaṁ sukhaṁ jīvet*), do not serve the purpose of making an endeavour to achieve the happiness of the future which is not perceptible *(apratyakṣa)*

Coming to the Buddhist schools, the Mādhyamikas maintain the theory that everything in the universe is *śūnya* and hence they cannot claim to have any valid *pramāṇas.* In the absence of it, they cannot establish their own doctrine and advocate a *sādhana* for obtaining the knowledge of *śūnyatva* (*śūnyatva-sādhana*).

The other three Buddhist schools admit the theory of *kṣaṇa-bhaṅga,* that is, nothing exists for more than a moment. If what exists at one moment does not persist in the next moment, then the *sādhana* or *upāya* adopted in the earlier moments do not have any bearings on the results that accrue out of it in the next moments since there is no continuity of the two together. What one individual accomplishes cannot be reaped by another individual in the next moment. If a specific goal enduring for a long duration does not exist, there would be no need to endeavour to attain it.

In the case of the school of Advaita Vedānta, which upholds that everything other than Brahman is lillusory (*mithyā*), a satisfactory theory of *upāya* for *mokṣa* cannot be formulated. According to Advaita, the direct to *mokṣa* is the intuitional knowledge of the identity of the self with Brahman, generated by the Scriptural texts such as *tat-tvam-asi,* which is capable of removing the *ajñāna* that causes bondage. If a person is not aware that everything other than Brahman is *mithyā,* he does not endeavour to acquire such a knowledge that would eradicate *ajñāna.* If he already possessed such a knowledge, there would be no need to acquire a separate knowledge which can remove the *ajñāna.* It cannot be argued that even though the knowledge of identity is acquired, traces of *ajñāna* persist (*bādhitānuvṛtti*) and in order to eradicate it totally, the knowledge of identity of *jīva* and Brahman is to be acquired. But such a view cannot constitute the *sādhana* as an acceptable theory of Advaita. On the analogy of the potter's wheel which, though continues to move even after the production of the pot comes to a stop on its own, the *ajñāna* which though persists even after the dawn of the knowledge of identity of *jīva* and Brahman, should cease to exist, there is no justification to observe rigorous penance through *saṁnyāsa-yoga* for this purpose.

The theory that verbal testimony, that is, study of the Scriptural texts teaching the identity of *jīva* and Brahman generates *aparokṣa-jñāna* or knowledge of immediate nature which is the means to *mokṣa,* is untenable.[1] The knowledge derived from *śabda* is of mediate character and it cannot remove the cosmic illusion leading to the direct realization of Brahman. Similarly the theory of *dhyāna-niyoga,* that is, the *niyoga* or a special potency in the form of *adṛṣṭa* generated by the observance of continuous meditation on Brahman removes the cosmic illusion and that one should pursue this *upāya* for attaining *mokṣa* is also untenable. There is another theory known as Niṣprapañca Niyogavāda, according to which the continuous meditation on Brahman as devoid of *prapañca* or the universe which is falsely super-imposed on it, can serve as the *upāya* for *mokṣa.* Even this theory is untenable as it is not supported by valid *pramāṇas.* Thus according to Vedānta Deśika, the pursuit of any kind of *upāya* for attaining a higher Spiritual Goal does not hold good in Advaita Vedānta.

Coming to the Jaina school, Vedānta Deśika points out that the admission of Anekāntavāda or the theory that all things in the universe are of indeterminable nature, does not allow for the formulation of a constructive theory of *upāya* or *sādhana* to be pursued for a higher goal. If the religious or spiritual discipline prescribed for a higher goal is of the nature of both *dharma* and *adharma* according to the Anekāntavāda, it is not worthwhile pursuing for a higher goal, whose nature is also indefinite.

The Bhāskara school of Vedānta suffers from a similar defect. According to Bhāskara, *karma* or the performance of prescribed deeds and *jñāna* understood in the sense of *upāsanā* on Brahman, together (*samuccaya*) serve as the means to *mokṣa.* According to Yādavaprakāśa both *karma* and *jñāna* play important parts—the former removes the obstruction in the way of attaining *mokṣa* and the latter actually leads to *mokṣa.* Both these views are opposed to the Upaniṣadic teachings. *Jñāna* understood as *upāsanā* aided by *karma-yoga* and *jñāna-yoga* is the direct means to *mokṣa.*[2] That is, *upāsāna* is the principal means to *mokṣa,* whereas *karma* is subordinate to it. Bhāskara and Yādava accord equal importance to both by upholding Jñāna-karma-samuccayavāda.

The school of Vaiyākaraṇa which maintain the theory that *Śabda-brahma* either illusorily manifests as the universe (view of Bhartṛhari) or it undergoes modification (*pariṇāma*) as *jagat* (view held by Halāyudha) suffers from the same defect as pointed out earlier in respect of Advaita. If an individual has already come to know that *jagat* which is an illusory manifestation of *Śabda-brahma* is illusory, there is no need to seek any further remedy to overcome the ignorance by seeking *tattva-jñāna.* Same is the situation in respect of the Śabda-brahma-pariṇāmavāda of Halāyudha for whom *jagat* is *satya* or real. If an individual already knows this fact, there would be no need to pursue the means such as *śravaṇa, manana* and *nididhyāsana,* etc., for obtaining such a knowledge.

Taking the Vaiśeṣika school, though the Vaiśeṣikas have accepted the Vedas as the Supreme authority, they do not admit that *adṛṣṭa* or unseen potency acquired through the observance of Vedic rituals which confer the fruits of *karma*, is in the form of pleasure caused to *Īśvara* (*Īśvara-prīti*), which alone confers the fruits of our deeds. Further they do not admit as taught in the Vedānta, that the grace of God earned by the meditation on *Paramātman* confers *mokṣa*. Instead of it, they accord greater importance to the meditation on *jīvātman* and regards the meditation on *Paramātman* (*Īśvara-praṇidhāna*) as one of the accessories for securing *adṛṣṭa* or the unseen potency which is helpful for overcoming the obstacles in the way of *mokṣa*. Such a distorted theory of the *upāya* or the ways and means to *mokṣa* is of no use for securing *mokṣa*.

Naiyāyikas also follow the same teachings as far as the means and goal are concerned. Hence their theory is also defective.

In the case of Nirīśvara-mīmāṁsā school, the doctrine of *sādhana* advocated by them suffers from serious defects. In the first place they question the very existence of the celestial deities who are the objects of worship in the various rituals enjoined in the Vedas and so also their capacity to confer boons. Such a view is adopted in order to give importance to *karma* or the sacrifical rituals. Secondly, they do not accept that the devoted meditation on Brahman, as enjoined in the Upaniṣads, is the direct means to *mokṣa*. Hence whatever other religious observances are laid down by them for the purpose of attaining *mokṣa* are futile.

With regard to the Sāṅkhya school, the philosophical tenets adopted by them do not allow for a satisfactory formulation of *upāya*. In the first place they have admitted only two metaphysical principles, viz., *puruṣa* and *prakṛti*. The *puruṣa* is neither the subject of knowledge (*jñatṛ*) nor the agent of action (*kartā*). Such a *puruṣa* or *jīvātman* cannot have any functions in the form of either enjoyment of happiness while in bondage or the experience of joy in the state of liberation from bondage (*apavarga*). The *dharma* and *adharma* as well as the results accruing from them are common to all *jīvas* as these are the effects of *prakṛti*. Since both *puruṣa* and *prakṛti* are devoid of *jñātṛtva*, there is no scope to pursue any prescribed means laid down by *śāstra* (*śāstrādi pravṛtti*).

Yoga Darśana does admit *Īśvara* besides *prakṛti* and *puruṣa*. But the spiritual discipline laid down by Yoga Darśana is aimed at the realization of one's own *jīvātmā*, which is not regarded as an integral part of *Paramātman*. Hence it stands opposed to the Yoga taught in the Upaniṣads according to which *Paramātma-sākṣātkāra* is the Supreme Goal.

Coming to the Śaiva schools, Pāśupata in particular which is included in the *Paramata-bhaṅga*, Vedānta Deśika points out that the meditation on Śiva, who is the Supreme Deity for them, cannot lead to *mokṣa* since Śiva too, like *Caturmukha* Brahmā and other higher celestial deities, is an exalted soul and not the *Para-Brahman* or *Para-tattva* referred to in the Upaniṣads. Such an exalted individual, however great he may be, cannot confer *mokṣa*. Besides, the religious observances prescribed by the Pāśupata school are opposed to the Vedic practices (*veda-viruddha-ācāra*). Besides, in all these Śaiva schools the philosophical theories relating to the three fundamental *tattvas*, viz., *Īśvara*, *jīvātman*, and *jagat* (*cid-acid-Īśvara tattva*) are of different nature from what is taught in Vedānta. Hence the observance of *upāya* or the means to the attainment of higher spiritual goal is not of any value (*niṣphalam*).

The Doctrine of *Upāya* in Viśiṣṭādvaita

After critically examining the theory of *upāya* presented by other schools of thought, both non-Vedic and Vedic including Advaita and Bhāskara, Vedānta Deśika briefly outlines the doctrine of *upāya* as enunciated by Viśiṣṭādvaita Vedānta on the basis of the authoritative Scriptural and Smṛti texts including the *Bhagavadgītā*. At the very commencement of the *Paramata-bhaṅga*, he has presented the three fundamental philosophical doctrines of Viśiṣṭādvaita, viz., *cit* or *jīvātman*, *acit* or cosmic universe and *Īśvara* or the Supreme Being in three separate chapters. This is done with the main objective of providing a sound philosophic background against which the philosophical tenets of rival schools of thought could be compared and their defects known.

The two other important doctrines of Viśiṣṭādvaita, viz., (1) *upāya* or the ways and means for attaining a higher goal and (2) *Parama-puruṣārtha* or the nature of the Supreme Goal are now outlined at the end of the *Paramata-bhaṅga* in two separate chapters (chaps. XXII and XXIII) along with a brief critical review of the theories of *upāya* of other schools of thought. Though these five chapters on one's own *siddhānta* should not be normally included in a treatise primarily devoted for the refutation (*bhaṅga*) of rival schools, these are presented with a view to highlight the soundness of the Viśiṣṭādvaita doctrines as compared to the defective doctrines of other schools.

As in the case of the three metaphysical doctrines discussed at the beginning, Vedānta Deśika does not present a detailed narrative account of both the *sādhana* and *puruṣārtha* as is generally found in other philosophical treatises. He confines his attention to a few important points relating to the *sādhana* which have been open to criticism not only from the camps of rival schools but also from the followers of Rāmānuja belonging to a different sect. This can be conspicuously noticed in connection with his presentation of the doctrine of self-surrender (*prapatti*) which, according to Rāmānuja, is an alternative direct means to *mokṣa.* The interpretation of the single verse in the concluding portion of the *Bhagavadgītā* (XVIII.66), which specifically enjoins *Śaraṇāgati* as a means to *mokṣa,* has become a subject of controversy. Vedānta Deśika therefore devotes special attention to this matter and explains the correct theory.

If the theories of *upāya* advanced by other schools of thought are proved to be defective, the question then arises: what then is the correct theory? By way of answering this question, Vedānta Deśika briefly states the correct view regarding *sādhana.*

According to the Hindu Religion, there are four human goals for which individuals aspire. These are *dharma, artha, kāma,* and *mokṣa.* Those who crave for *mokṣa* which is the Supreme *Puruṣārtha,* are categorized as *mumukṣu.* Those who aspire for the other three *puruṣārthas* are classified as *bubhukṣu.* Of these, *mokṣa* is accorded an important place as it is considered the highest goal. In accordance with one's desire and also eligibility, an individual aspiring for either *svarga* (heaven) or *mokṣa* or total liberation from bondage leading to the enjoyment of the bliss of Brahman, is required to adopt the ways and means as laid down by the Vedas and other Sacred texts. The means enjoined by the Scriptural and Smṛti texts for attaining these two goals are *yāga* or ritualistic sacrifices, *dāna* or giving charity and *upāsanā* or devoted meditation on *Paramātman* (Brahman). Only such means, as enjoined in the Sacred texts, which should take the form of worship of *Paramātman* (*Parama-puruṣa-samārādhana*) alone can serve as the means to attain the desired goals.

If *upāsanā*, also known as *Bhakti-yoga* in the *Bhagavadgītā*, is the direct means to *mokṣa*, how can it be said that *Karma-yoga* and *Jñāna-yoga* are the means to *mokṣa*, mentioned in the *Bhagavadgītā*? Vedānta Deśika answers this minor objection by explaining that *Karma-yoga* and *Jñāna-yoga* are subsidiary means to *Bhakti-yoga* which alone is the direct means.

The *Bhagavadgītā* and other religious treatises also mention methods to be adopted as means to attain God. Vedānta Deśika enumerates all these and explains that these are not to be taken as direct means to *mokṣa*, but they serve as accessories to the prescribed *upāya*. The other methods are:

1. *Adveṣābhimukhyam*,[3] that is, one should not entertain any hatred towards *Paramātman* and always look forward to receive His grace.
2. *Avatāra-rahasya-jñāna*,[4] or proper knowledge of the significance of the incarnations of *Paramātman*.
3. *Puruṣottama-vidyā* or the knowledge of *Paramātman* as *uttama-puruṣa* referred to in the *Gītā*,[5] that is, He is the Supreme Being as distinct from *baddha-jīva* and also the *mukta-jīva*.
4. *Sambandha-jñāna-mātram*, that is, the mere knowledge of the intimate relationship that exists between *jīva* and *Paramātman* (a view held by a sect of Vaiṣṇavas).
5. *Adhyavasāya-mātram* or the unshakeable faith that the Almighty surely protects one who has totally surrendered to Him (*prapattiḥ viśvāsaḥ*).
6. *Saṅkīrtana-mātram* or the mere recitation of the names and glory of *Paramātman*.[6]
7. *Ukti-mātram* or the mere ardent prayer addressed to God seeking His protection.[7]
8. *Viṣayavāsādi-mātram* or the mere thinking of the Lord all the time as the sole protector.[8]

9. *Svapravṛtti-nivṛtti,* that is, to remain neutral without making any special effort for the sake of attainment of God since it comes out of His grace, whose concern it is to protect as in the case of an infant by the mother.[9]
10. *Vaiṣṇavābhimānam,* that is, to remain devoted to a Vaiṣṇava.[10]
11. *Ācārya-parigraham* or to secure the grace of an *ācārya.*[11]
12. *Puruṣakāra-viśeṣam* or to obtain the grace of Goddess Lakṣmī who acts as a mediator (*puruṣakāra*) for securing *mokṣa.*
13. *Īśvara-svātantrya-kṛpā* or to unchecked freedom and compassion of *Īśvara* as the main cause for liberation from bondage.
14. *Nirhetuka-viṣayīkarādi* or securing the protection from *Īśvara* without His imposing any specific condition.[12]

All these various methods which are mentioned in the religious treatises give the impression that there are various other means for attaining *mokṣa.* Vedānta Deśika clarifies that these are to be understood not as direct means to *mokṣa* but as aids to either *upāsanā* or *prapatti* which are specifically enjoined in the sacred texts as the means to *mokṣa.*

The Upaniṣads mention several *vidyās* or *upāsanās* such as *Sad-vidyā, Dahara-vidyā,* etc., as the means to *mokṣa.* But there is no mention of *Nyāsa-vidyā* which is the same as *prapatti* or self-surrender to God, as the direct means to *mokṣa.* Hence the question is raised whether such a *vidyā* named *Nyāsa-vidyā* as *upāya* exists? In reply to this objection, Vedānta Deśika states that just as *upāsanā* is enjoined in the *Bhagavadgītā* in the words, *bhajasva māṁ* or "meditate on Me," in the same way the *Gītā* also enjoins *śaraṇāgati* or self-surrender to God as the means to *mokṣa* in the words—*māmekam śaraṇam vraja*— "Surrender to Me as the sole refuge." Hence the two are distinct alternative pathways to *mokṣa* in accordance with the eligibility of the person. That is, for those who are incapable of observing the rigorous *Bhakti-yoga,* they can resort to the method of total surrender of oneself to God for protection. That *śaraṇāgati* is an alternative direct *upāya* to *mokṣa,* is well established in the Pāñcarātra Saṁhitās, *Śaraṇāgati-gadya* of

Rāmānuja and many Vaiṣṇava religious treatises such as *Rahasya-trayasāra* and *Nikṣepa-rakṣā* of Vedānta Deśika.

In this connection Vedānta Deśika discusses the controversial issues rising from the different interpretations of the single *Gītā* verse dealing with this matter as offered by other commentators including Śaṅkara.

The relevant verse which is the subject of controversy reads:

Sarvadharmān parityajya māmekaṁ śaraṇaṁ vraja;
Ahaṁ tva sarva-pāpebhyo mokṣayiṣyāmi ma śucaḥ.[13]

Its general meaning is: "By Relinquishing all *dharmas*, seek Me alone for refuge. I shall release you from all sins. Do not grieve."

The implication of this verse according to Śaṅkara, is that by the total renouncement of all *karmas* (the word *dharma* being understood as the performance of prescribed deeds), one can attain *Paramātman* in the sense of realizing his identity (become one) with Him who is the same in all beings. The performance of *karma* is opposed to the realization of one's identity with Brahman, which is the *mokṣa* for Śaṅkara. The knowledge of the identity of *jīva* with Brahman (*ātmaikya-jñāna*) is therefore the means to *mokṣa*.

This is not a correct interpretation, according to Vedānta Deśika, because such a view is opposed to all the *pramāṇas*, particularly the Scriptural texts which speak of real *bheda* or difference between *jīva* and *Paramātman* and enjoin the performance of the prescribed deeds as mandatory and as such these should not be given up. Even contextually it is not appropriate that the *dharmas* in the form of *Karma-yoga, Jñāna-yoga,* and *Bhakti-yoga* taught in the earlier chapters of the *Gītā* are to be given up totally.

Yādavaprakāśa offers a different interpretation. According to him, this verse does not advocate the abandonment of the prescribed deeds but, on the contrary, it is intended to highlight the importance of *śaraṇāgati*. That is, it implies that even if one has to give up all *karmas*, it is important for him to seek *śaraṇāgati* in *Paramātman*.

This is also not an appropriate view since there is no need to offer such an explanation by adding the unnecessary word *api* after *sarvadharmān parityajya*.

There are several other interpretations on the statement "*sarvadharmān partityajya.*" Vedānta Deśika mentions these views in the *Paramata-bhaṅga* and refutes them as untenable. These discussions which are of technical nature, do not have a direct bearing on the nature of *upāya* to be adopted for attaining a higher goal, We need not therefore go into these details. It would suffice to note the final view of Vedānta Deśika regarding these issues, as summed up by him in a brief statement.

According to him, there are two ways on which the *Gītā* verse is to be understood. By taking into consideration the nature of *prapatti* as explained in various other treatises, it is to be taken as a *nirapekṣyādi-viśiṣṭa-vidhi.* That is, it is a *vidhi* or injunction demanding the surrendering of oneself to the Lord for refuge, without requiring to observe the rigorous observance of *Bhakti-yoga* as aided by *Karma-yoga* and *Jñāna-yoga* as taught in the *Gītā* in the earlier chapters. This *vidhi* is intended for persons such as Arjuna who regretfully feels his utter incapability of following the rigorous *Bhakti-yoga* aided by *Karma-yoga* and *Jñāna-yoga.* This is a state of *ākiñcanya* or the utter incapacity of oneself to follow *Bhakti-yoga* or any other means for attaining *mokṣa.* This is one of the eligibility requirements for *śaraṇāgati* as taught in the *Pāñcarātra Saṁhitā.* This fact is conveyed by the expression *mā śucaḥ*—"Do not grieve," stated in the later part of the verse.

The other alternative interpretation of the verse is to take it as *adhikārī-viśeṣa-anuvāda pūrvaka yathāvasthita prapatti-vidhi.* That is, it is a straightforward *vidhi* or injunction addressed to the individuals who fulfil the eligibility requirements for following the *śaraṇāgati* as the means to *mokṣa.* The eligibility requirements, as explained in the *Pāñcarātra* texts, are *akiñcanya* or not capable of following any other means and *ananyagatitva* or not having anyone else (any other deity other than Viṣṇu) to protect the individual. The word *sarvadharmān parityajya* reiterates these eligibility requirements (*adhikārī-viśeṣa-anuvāda*). The word *mamekaṁ* in the verse implies that other than the Supreme Being, no one else is able to protect the individual.[14]

If either of the interpretations is adopted, there would be no room for conflict with the *pramāṇas* and also with the teachings contained in the earlier *adhyāyas.* All the controversial issues relating to the interpretation of the *Gītā* verse referring to *prapatti* as a means to *mokṣa* have been fully discussed and answered in other works of Vedānta Deśika and in particular *Nikṣepa-rakṣa* and *Rahasya-trayasāra* (chap. 29). The chapter in the *Paramata-bhaṅga* is therefore mainly confined to prove the untenability of the theories on *upāya* advanced by different schools and how the Viśiṣṭādvaita theory is sound.

References

1. See *SD, vāda* 7: *Śabda-janya pratyakṣa-bhaṅgavāda.*
2. See *Īśa. Up.*: *Avidyayā mṛtyum tīrtvā vidyayāamṛtam aśnute.*
3. *Viṣṇoḥ katākṣam adveṣam* (quoted by Vedānta Deśika in the *RTS*).
4. *BG.*
5. Ibid., XV.18–20.
6. *Mbh.*: *Saṅkīrtya nārāyaṇa śabda mātram vimukta duḥkhāḥ sukhino bhavanti.*
7. *Sakṛd uccāraḥ saṁsāramocanam bhavet.*
8. See *Rāmāyaṇa*: *Te vayam bhavatā rakṣyā bhavat-viṣaya vāsinaḥ.*
9. Cf. Ibid., *garbhabhūtāḥ tapodhanāḥ.*
10. See *Paśurmanuṣyāḥ pakṣī vā ye ca vaiṣṇava saṁśrayaḥ; tenaiva te prayāsyānti.*
11. See *RTS*: *Ācāryavattayā muktau.*
12. *Nāham puruṣakāreṇa na cā'pyanyena hetunā; kevalam svecchayaiva ahaṁ kañcit kadācana.*
13. *BG,* XVII.66.
14. See *RTS,* chap. 29: *Adhikāram puraskṛtya upāyasya nirapekṣatām; eka śabdena vaktīti kecit vākyavido viduḥ.*

21
The Doctrine of *Puruṣārtha*

AFTER CRITICALLY examining both the *tattvas* or the philosophical doctrines and the theories relating to the *upāya* or the means of attaining a higher goal as presented by other schools, Vedānta Deśika proceeds to examine the theories advanced by them relating to the *puruṣārtha* or the nature of the goal to be attained for which purpose philosophical investigation or study of a Darśana is undertaken. At the very outset, he states that both the non-Vedic as well as Vedic schools do not serve any useful purpose (*anukūla-phala*) in this regard insofar as they do not help an individual to attain a higher spiritual goal such as *mokṣa* soon after his death. This sweeping and storing criticism by Vedānta Deśika is supported by the following Smṛti text of sage Manu, who is highly respected as an authority in respect of all spiritual matters[1]:

> *Yo vedabāyāḥ smṛtayaḥ yāsca kāśca kudṛṣṭayaḥ;*
> *Sarvāstāḥ niṣphalāḥ pretya hi tāḥ smṛtaḥ.*
> The teachings of those schools which do not accept the authority of the Vedas and also of those schools which are developed as opposed to accepted valid *pramāṇas* and also based on fallacious logical arguments, are of no value because they do not serve the purpose of achieving a spiritual goal by an individual soon after his death.

In the chapter titled "Parokta-prayojanādhikāra" Vedānta Deśika substantiates this criticism by briefly stating the position of each school.

The Cārvāka school does not admit any *pramāṇas* except *pratyakṣa* nor the causal relationship. Hence they cannot claim that the philosophical discussions would lead to the acquisition of any useful spiritual knowledge. Even the indulgence in eating and drinking acts would not serve the spiritual purpose.

Regarding the Mādhyamika Buddhists, they maintain that the realization of *śūnyatva* itself is *mokṣa.* But such a *śūnyatva* exists all the time (*nityasiddha*) and it is not a new state which is to be secured by some causal factors. If it is to be brought about, it cannot be *nitya.* Hence the study of the Sacred texts (Āgamas) of the Mādhyamikas, contemplation over what is learnt, etc., are futile.

The other three schools of Buddhism, viz., Yogācāra, Sautrāntika and Vaibhāṣika admit consciousness in the name of *vijñāna* but at the same time they regard it as *kṣaṇika.* Even this *vijñāna* endures in the form of a series of mental ideas (*jñāna-santati*). It is devoid of attributes (*nirguṇa*) and does not have *bhoktṛtva* or the capacity to experience anything. In the absence of *bhoktṛtva* there would be no scope for an individual to enjoy the fruits of the deeds performed by him. Hence if a goal as prescribed in their Sacred texts is to be attained, it is of no value (*niṣphala*).

The same kind of criticism applies to Advaita Vedānta. Though it admits *ātman* as *nitya* or eternal, it is only of the nature of consciousness (*caitanya-mātra*) and it is also devoid of all attributes (*nirguṇa*). It is neither the subject of knowledge (*jñāta*) nor the *bhoktā* or the subject of experience. Such a kind of *ātman* cannot therefore enjoy the fruits of the deeds performed by an individual. Besides, the *avidyā* which causes the bondage for the *ātman* and also the eradication of it by the knowledge of the true nature of the self are considered as *mithyā* or illusory. Such a view would render the endeavour to be made to attain a desired goal futile (*svābhimata-prayojana-bhaṅga*).

The Jaina school which upholds Anekāntavāda, that is, that the nature of an object or concept is of manifold nature cannot be determined in a specific way. The distinction between *sukha* and *duḥkha* and also *bandha* and *mokṣa* cannot be determined in a specific way. In the absence of settled theories, the attainment of human goals, whether if falls within the purview of our experience (*dṛṣṭa-prayojana*) or is beyond the scope of our experience (*adṛṣṭa-phala*) ceases to have any significance.

This criticism against the Jainas also applies to Bhāskara school of Vedānta which subscribes to the doctrine of

Bhedābheda, that is, Brahman and *jīva* are both different (*bheda*) and also non-different *(abheda)* by overlooking the contradiction involved in the co-existence of *bheda* and *abheda*. Besides, this school which admits *svarūpaikya* between Brahman and *jīva* is open to the criticism of being opposed to the Scriptural texts which speak of *sāmya* or equal status of *jīva* with Brahman in the state of *mukti*.

Regarding the Vaiśeṣika- and the Nirīśvara-mīmāṁsās expounded by Prabhākara, the nature of the goal formulated by them also suffers from defects. They conceive *mokṣa* as a state of existence for the *jīvātman* as totally devoid of all experience, both *sukha* and *duḥkha*, similar to the piece of stone (*pāṣāṇa-kalpa*). This theory is directly opposed to the teaching imparted to Indra by Prajāpati in the *Chāndogya Upaniṣad* about the nature of *mokṣa*, according to which *jīva* in the state of *mokṣa* manifests itself with eight *guṇas*, such as *apahata-pāpamatva*, *satyasaṅkalpa*, *satyakāma*, etc., as distinct from the state of *jīva* (in bondage) and also during *suṣupti* or dreamless state when it does not have any experience.

The school of Mīmāṁsā represented by Kumārila (Seśvara-mīmāṁsā) and the author of *Nyāyabhūṣaṇa*, a commentary on *Vaiśeṣikasūtras* maintains a modified theory of *mokṣa* as the experience of the bliss of one's own self (*svātmānanda-mātra-anubhava*). Even this cannot constitute the higher Spiritual Goal when it is compared to the enjoyment of the infinite bliss of Brahman along with His glory by the *muktātmā* in the state of *mokṣa*, as stated in the Upaniṣads.

Coming to the Sāṅkhya school, they maintain that *kaivalya* or the state of existence of *puruṣa* (the *jīvātman*) totally free from the association with *citta* or mind and all its functions is *mokṣa*. According to the Sāṅkhyas, *puruṣa* is by nature always free and he is neither bound nor liberated.[2] If this is their premise, the attainment of *kaivalya* cannot constitute a *puruṣārtha* or a state to be attained as a Goal (*sādhya*). A section of the Sāṅkhya school maintains a modified view according to which the acquisition of *aṣṭaiśvarya* or eight kinds of higher super-normal powers is *mokṣa*. But this cannot also be regarded as *mokṣa* because it is possible to acquire these powers while the *jīvātman* is in the state of bondage through the yogic practice.

The Pāśupata school believes that the attainment of a status equal to that of Paśupati or Śiva (*paśupati sārupya*) is *mokṣa.* But this theory cannot constitute the Supreme Goal, because Paśupati or Śiva is a Vedic deity like *Caturmukha* Brahmā, Indra, etc., who are brought into existence like other *jīvas* by Brahman. Attainment of an equal status with Paśupati, similar to the attainment of equality with Indra by Nahuṣa, Yayāti, etc., the Purāṇic personalities, cannot constitute the Higher Goal as conceived by the Upaniṣads.

After critically examining the theories of all other schools regarding the Higher Spiritual Goal to be attained, Vedānta Deśika states the correct theory as well established by Viśiṣṭādvaita Vedānta expounded by the *Śārīraka-śāstra* (*Brahmasūtra*) in the following statement:

> *Paramātmādhīna-tattulya tadanubhava mahānanda parama-prayojana.* The highest Spiritual Goal is the attainment of the Supreme bliss of Brahman which is similar to that enjoyed by Brahman (*tattulya* or *samāna-bhoga*) by the liberated *jīvātman* by its being dependent on *Paramātman* (*Paramādhīna*).[3]

That is, the individual self, after it is liberated from bondage, attains the status of equality with *Paramātman* only in respect of the enjoyment of the bliss of *Paramātman* to the same extent as Brahman enjoys His own glory. Even in this state, though the *jīva* is free from bondage and becomes *sarvajña*, it is still dependent on *Paramātman* since *dāsyatva* or dependence on the Lord is his *svābhāvaka-dharma (svarūpa).* Such a concept of *mokṣa* as conceived in the Vīśiṣṭādvaita Vedānta is in full accordance with the Upaniṣadic texts and the *Vedāntasūtras* based on it.[4]

REFERENCES

1. See *Ṛgveda: Yadvai kiñca manuravadat tat bheṣajam.* See also *Ch. Up.*: *Manurvai yat kiñcit avadat tad-bheṣajam.*
2. See *Sāṅkhyakārikā*: *Tasmān-na-badhyate… na mucyate na'pi saṁsarati kāścit.*
3. *Tait. Up.*: *So, śnute sarvān kāmān saha; Brahmaṇa vipaścita.* Also, *Muṇḍ. Up.*: *Nirañjanaḥ paramaṁ sāmyam upaiti.*
4. *VS*, IV.4.2: *Bhogamātra-sāmya-liṅgācca.* Also, *VS*, IV.4.17: *jagad-vyāpāra-varjam.*

22

General Evaluation and Conclusion

In the preceding chapters we have presented the critical observations made by Vedānta Deśika on the fifteen schools of thought. The main points of criticisms on each school are summed up in the following *resumé* outlined by Vedānta Deśika in the concluding chapter of the *Paramata-bhaṅga* named Nigamanādhikāra.

Cārvāka School

This school upholds that *pratyakṣa* or perception alone is the source of knowledge. This is not a correct stand because it is found that inference (*anumāna*) and also verbal testimony (*śabda*) serve as the sources of knowledge. The knowledge derived from the other two *pramāṇas* is not contradicted. The Cārvākas themselves have accepted in a number of cases that the knowledge derived from inference and also on the basis of the statements of reliable persons are true. Vedas or the Revealed Scripture is free from defects and hence it has to be accepted as a source of authority in respect of spiritual matters. It is therefore wrong to deny the existence of *jīvātman* as distinct from body and also the concept of God, which are well established in the Scriptural texts.

Mādhyamika Buddhism

As the Mādhyamika believes that everything is *śūnya* or indeterminable, which almost amounts to non-existence, he hoes not have any valid *pramāṇas* which are needed to establish his own doctrines. He cannot therefore prove that *śūnyatva* is the truth. Consequently, the theories advanced by rival schools would stand valid.

Yogācāra Buddhism

This school maintains that *jñāna* alone, called *vijñāna* in the form of a series of mental ideas, is real, whereas *jñātṛ* or the subject of knowledge and *jñeya* or the external object, do not really exist. The latter are falsely imposed on *jñāna* (*kalpitākāra*). This is opposed to our perceptual experience in the form *idam ahaṁ jānāmi*—"I know this," which involves three factors, viz., the subject denoted by "I," the object denoted by "this" (*idaṁ*) and the process of knowing denoted by "I know" (*jānāmi*). When this is a fact, the denial of the object and the subject would lead to the denial of even *jñāna*, by adopting the Mādhyamika logic of *sarva-śūnyatva*. If, on the other hand, *jñāna* is considered important as it is evident, then he can as well admit the *jñātṛ* or knower and *jñeya* or object.

Sautrāntika Buddhism

This school admits both *jñāna* and *jñeya* or the external object but the latter is to be inferred on the basis of the fact that knowledge has a content (*jñānākāra*). This is not a satisfactory explanation because on the basis of the content of the knowledge, it is not possible to know the object with all its specific qualities.

Vaibhāṣika Buddhism

Though this school accepts both *jñāna* and *jñeya* or the external object, it holds the view that bare being of the object without any qualifications seen at the first moment alone is real whereas what is perceived later along with certain qualities, technically called *vikalpa*, are *mithyā* or unreal since these are superimposed in the subsequent moment by the mind. This view would amount to the denial of the very object which is so evident to our perception. Further, this school along with Yogācāra and Sautrāntika regard that all entities in the universe are momentary in character (*kṣaṇika*). Consequently, we cannot explain the concept of memory (*smṛti*) and *pratyabhijñā* or the recognition of the object seen now as the same as the one seen earlier. Besides, if there is no continuity in the events, the fruits of the deeds done by one at a particular time has to be reaped by another individual at a different time.

Advaita Vedānta School

This school upholds the theory that other than *jñāna* (*ātman*) which alone is real, everything else is illusory(*mithyā*). What is admitted as Reality is one and *nitya* or eternal, unlike the theory of Yogācārā for which *jñāna* is *kṣaṇika* and many (*bahu*) in the form of numerous mental series. But the characteristics of *ekatva* and *nityatva* are also regarded as *mityā* by the Advaitin. For the Advaitin the Vedas which are regarded as an important source of authority (*pramāṇa*), are also the product of *avidyā* and thus it is rendered invalid by its being illusory in character. In the absence of valid *pramāṇas* it is neither possible to prove one's own doctrines nor refute the theories of other schools as invalid. Further, it is maintained that Brahman which is the one Reality and which is pure consciousness devoid of all attributes (*nirviśeṣa*), is eclipsed by *avidyā* whose nature is indescribable as either *sat* or *asat* (*anirvacanīya*). The existence of the *nirviśeṣa* entity and the *mihtyātva* or illusory character of the universe cannot be proved by any *pramāṇas*. Hence this school of Vedānta is not acceptable.

Jaina School

This school does not accept Vedas as a source of authority. Instead, it believes that a person named "Arhan" is *sarvajña* or omniscient and that all that is taught by him is authoritative. But it cannot be conclusively proved that Arhan is *sarvajña* as against a similar claim made for Buddha as *sarvajña*. Further, this school advocates the doctrines such as *sapta-bhaṅgī* which are opposed to our perceptual experience. It also prescribes religious practices as opposed to Vedic teachings. Due to these reasons, it is to be rejected.

Bhedābheda Schools of Vedānta

Bhāskara and Yādavaprakāśa, who are the chief exponents of this school embrace the co-existence of *bheda* and *abheda* like the Jainas, overlooking the contradiction involved in it. Similarly they admit difference and non-difference between *guṇa* and *guṇī* as well as *jāti* and *vyakti*. Brahman is free from all defects and is also *niravaya* or devoid of parts. The admission of *bhedāhbeda* relationship between Brahman and *jīva* would lead to the acceptance of all the defects of the *jīva* in respect of Brahman. Hence this school is refuted.

Śabda-Brahma Vivartavāda

This school expounded by Bhartṛhari, a grammarian, advocates that *śabda* which is technically named *sphoṭa* is itself Brahman and it either illusorily manifests itself as the universe (according to Bhartṛhari) or it directly undergoes modification (*pariṇāma*) as *jagat* (according to Halāyudha). This is rejected on the same ground as that of Brahma Vivartavāda of Advaita and also Brahma Pariṇāmavāda of Bhartṛprapañca. Besides, the theory of *sphoṭa* or the word essence which is claimed to convey the meaning of words and sentences is unproved by any of the *pramāṇas*.

Vaiśeṣika School

This school is also rejected because of the following reasons. In the first place it does not accept that Veda is *apauruṣeya*, that is, it is not ascribed to an author. Āgamas or Revealed Scripture which is generally accepted as a separate *pramāṇa* is included in the inference. In the matter of enumeration of the *tattvas*, it does not admit *prakṛti* or the primordial cosmic matter and its other evolutes as taught in the Upaniṣads. Even with regard to the enumeration of the material entities, it admits the concept of *avayavī* or the aggregate of parts (*avayavas*) as distinct from the combination of parts (*saṅghāta*). More importantly it attempts to establish its theories based on fallacious inferential arguments (*anumāna-ābhāsa*).

Nyāya School

This school adopts most of the theories developed by Vaiśeṣika and hence the criticisms leveled against them would also be applicable to it. But however, Nyāya Darśana is included among the ten *dharma-vidyāsthānas* or the philosophical treatises which are useful for the acquisition of spiritual knowledge. The question therefore arises whether it would be proper to refute it. Vedānta Deśika replies that it is not inappropriate to criticize it since the founders of the Nyāya school have not attempted to interpret or explain their thories in conformity with the Vedānta doctrines.

Mīmāṁsā School

Mīmāṁsā as one *śāstra* or treatise comprising twenty *adhyāyas* which deals with the interpretation of the entire Vedas—both the ritulistic portion and the Upaniṣadic portion, consists of three parts (*kāṇḍas*) similar to the three *adhyāyas* of a treatise each dealing with a particular subject. Of these the first part which is generally acknowledged as Pūrva Mīmāṁsā compiled by sage Jaimini, is further divided into two schools due to the two different interpretations offered on the *Jaiminisūtras* by the later commentators—Kumārila Bhaṭṭa and Prābhākara. The major difference between the two lies in respect of the admission of *Īśvara*. One school which admits *Īśvara* is known as Seśvara Mīmāṁsā and the school which denies *Īśvara* and the existence of celestial deities with bodies for whom *yāga* is performed is known as Nirīśvara Mīmāṁsā. These two schools are also designated as Kabandha Mīmāṁsā after the name of Kabandha, the mythological person whose head was cut off and Rāhu Mīmāṁsā after the name of Rāhu, the mythological demon whose body was taken off. The Kabandha Mīmāṁsā represented by Kumārila Bhaṭṭa accords greater importance to the ritualistic part of Vedas and as such it admits that *karma* or the performance of prescribed deeds is more important than the worship of *Īśvara* for granting rewards for the deeds performed. It is this school of Mīmāṁsā known as Nirīśvara Mīmāṁsā which comes up for criticism and is rejected.

As regards the Seśvara Mīmāṁsā represented by Prabhākara, though it admits *Īśvara*, the ontological doctrines developed by them which are similar to those of Vaiśeṣika, are defective. They admit the theory of *mokṣa* conceived by Vaiśeṣika as a state of existence for the *jīvātman* as devoid of all experience, similar to a piece of stone (*paṣāṇa-kalpa*).

Both these schools admit the Vaiśeṣika theory of *avayava* and *avayavī* which cannot be proved by *pramāṇas*, the concept of *apūrva* or unseen potency caused by the *yāgas* as the bestower of the fruits of the deeds rather than the grace of *Īśvara* as established in the Vedānta and also the denial of the possession of body by the *devatās* as established in the Āgamas. Hence both these schools of Pūrva Mīmāṁsā stand rejected.

SĀṄKHYA SCHOOL

This school, no doubt, admits the authoritativeness of the Vedas unlike the Nirīśvara Mīmāṁsā but it denies the existence of *Īśvara* as a separate *tattva* other than *prakṛti* and *puruṣa*. Further, the *prakṛti* is conceived as an entity comprising three components which are regarded as *dravyas* or substances instead of *guṇas* or qualities. Further, it maintains the theory that the effects (*kārya*) is latent in the causal substance similar to the oil in the oil seeds and what is latent is only made manifest (*abhivyakti*) by the causal factors. This theory is opposed to our perceptual experience.

Regarding the nature of *ātman*, the Sāṅkhyas admit that it is *jñāta* or subject of knowledge, *kartā* or the agent of action, it is subject to bondage and it is also liberated from it but in the same breath, they also say that all these functions do not belong to *ātmā* but belong to *prakṛti*. Thus their teachings involve contradiction. More importantly they deny *Īśvara* as a separate ontological principle. Thus the system which is full of self-contradictions does not deserve to accepted.

YOGA SCHOOL

Though this school enjoys a better status than that of Sāṅkhya by its admission of *Īśvara* as a separate *tattva* other than *prakṛti* and *puruṣa*, it is not sound because this *Īśvara* is regarded as an exalted *puruṣa* (*puruṣa-viśeṣaḥ*) who is only the *nimitta-kāraṇa* or the efficient cause of the universe and not *upādāna-kāraṇa* or the material cause of the universe, as Vedānta says.

With regard to *sādhana* and *mokṣa*, the Yoga school no doubt prescribes the eightfold ethico-religious discipline such as *yama*, *niyama*, etc. Though these constitute a well-formulated discipline, its significance is lost by conceiving the nature of the goal to be attained by the yogic *sādhana* is *kaivalya* or the state of existence of *puruṣa* or *jīvātman* as totally free from the association of *citta* and its functions instead of *Paramātma-sākṣātkāra*.

PĀŚUPATA SCHOOL

This school, like Yoga, admits all the three ontological principles—*prakṛti, puruṣa,* and *Īśvara.* But it does not acknowledge *Īśvara* as *upādānā-kāraṇa* of the universe. He is only *nimitta-kāraṇa* as in the Yoga school. With regard to the enumeration of the *tattvas* it mentions thirty-six instead of twenty-five as generally accepted, by adding unnecessary additional principles. More than anything, the religious observances laid down by the school are opposed to the Vedic teachings. Hence this school falls outside the scope of accepted orthodox schools.

PĀÑCARĀTRA SCHOOL

Though this school is included among the rival schools taken up for critical review, it is not intended for criticism (*bhaṅga*). There are some objections raised by the rival schools questioning its validity (*prāmāṇya*) on the ground that it advocates a few theories such as the origin of *jīva* (*jīva-utpatti*) as against the Upaniṣadic teachings which admit that *jīva* is *nitya.* It is therefore felt necessary to answer these objections and establish the validity of the Pāñcarātra. The religious way of life taught in the *Pāñcarātrasaṁhitās* are in full accord with the way of life advocated by Vedānta. These treatises mainly deal with the subject related to the modes of worship of the *Parama-puruṣa* or Supreme Being referred to in the Upaniṣads, through the means of *upāsanā* or devoted meditation and securing His grace, which alone confers *mokṣa* or liberation from bondage to the devotee. Hence it is to be accepted as most authoritative *Bhagavatśāstra* useful for redemption from bondage.

The above criticisms offered against the fifteen schools of thought are confined to their main philosophical tenets (*tattvas*). Regarding their theories on *upāya* (means of attainment) and *puruṣārtha* (goal), these have been outlined briefly in the chaps. 20 and 21 of the *Paramata-bhaṅga* along with the theories upheld by Viśiṣṭādvaita on these topics. The three fundamental metaphysical doctrines (*tattvas*) of Viśiṣṭādvaita—*cit, acit,* and *Īśvara,* are presented in three in three separate chapters at the beginning of the treatise. Though these are not intended for refutation, the possible objections against the theories of

Viśiṣṭādvaita are answered. Thus *Paramata-bhaṅga* is a distinctive philosophical treatise containing a critical review of all the important systems of Indian philosophy that were prevalent during the time of Vedānta Deśika.

After briefly stating the defects of all the systems of philosophy other than Pāñcarātra that were prevalent at the time of Vedānta Deśika, a question is raised: what about the new schools of thought which may come up in later times and which may advance theories as opposed to Viśiṣṭādvaita Vedānta? Would it then be justified to claim that all possible objections against Viśiṣṭādvaita doctrines are answered?

In reply to this query Vedānta Deśika answers that whatever theories are found defective and hence need to be refuted, this task is already accomplished by the objections levelled against the theories which are similar to what is mentioned (*nirasta-tulya-bhāga-dattottaram*). If there are theories that may be newly formulated somewhat similar to what is presented by Viśiṣṭādvaita, then there would be no need to refute them (*siddhānta-tulya-bhāga na dūṣyaḥ*).

As we have explained in the Introduction, this critical review is not undertaken by Vedānta Deśika for a limited purpose of establishing one's own theories (*svapakṣasthāpana*) through the refutation of the theories of rival schools, but on the other hand, it is intended to provide a correct knowledge about the fundamental teachings of Viśiṣṭādvaita Vedānta as compared to those advanced by the rival schools of thought. As we have pointed out in the preceding chapters, the non-Vedic schools such as Cārvāka, Buddhism and Jainism do not accept the authority of the Vedas. The Vedic schools such as Vaiśeṣika, Nyāya, Sāṅkhya, Yoga, and Nirīśvara-mīmāṁsā, even though they accept the authority of the Vedas, have developed theories which do not conform to the Upaniṣadic teachings and which are also found logically defective. Even among the Vedānta schools such as Śaṅkara's Advaita, Bhedābhedavāda of Bhāskara and Yādavaprakāśa, though they are based on the Upaniṣads and the *Vedāntasūtra*, have advanced doctrines which are found untenable. An aspirant for *mokṣa* is required to acquire a proper and correct *tattva-jñāna* that leads to *mokṣa* and avoid being entrapped in the pitfalls of erroneous theories. It is with this objective that Vedānta Deśika has undertaken to write this special compendium under the title of *Paramata-bhaṅga.*

The question may be raised whether this objective has been accomplished in this work. A dispassionate study of the critical review of the text will reveal that this is satisfactorily achieved. As Vedānta Deśika points out in the first three chapters and also in the concluding chapter, a sound system of philosophy should admit the three fundamental metaphysical principles viz., *cit* or *jīvātman*, *acit* or the primordial cosmic matter and *Īśvara* or the Supreme Being, as stated in the *Śvetāśvatara Upaniṣad.* All the three are to be admitted as real and also different from each other by virtue of their intrinsic nature, as clearly enunciated in the *bheda-śrutis* or the Upaniṣadic texts which speak of difference between them. In the same way, on the basis of the *abheda-śrutis* or the Upaniṣadic texts which speak of non-difference between the three *tattvas,* these are to be admitted as one in the sense that *Īśvara* as organically related to *cit* and *acit* is a *viśiṣṭa-tattva.* When three ontological entities are admitted, a proper relationship between them, that is, between *Īśvara* and *jīva* as well as *Īśvara* and *jagat,* needs to be established. The *Antaryāmī Brāhmaṇa* of the *Bṛhadāraṇyaka Upaniṣad* explicitly states that Brahman is immanent in all sentient and non-sentient entities and that it is the universal Self (*Ātman*) as Inner Controller (*Antaryāmin*) and also that the universe including the *jīvas* are its body in the metaphysical sense. On the authority of this Scriptural text, Viśiṣṭādvaita Vedānta upholds that Brahman as organically related to *cit* and *acit* is one ultimate Reality. Thus on the basis of the body-soul relation, it establishes a satisfactory relationship between Brahman and the two other ontological entities—*Jīvas* and *jagat.* Herein lies the merit of Viśiṣṭādvaita as a philosophical system.

Judged from this standpoint, all other schools of thought including Advaita, Bhedābhedavāda and later school of Vedānta are found defective. The Cārvāka school does not admit *jīva* and also *Īśvara.* Buddhist schools do not admit the eternal *jīvātman.* Nor does it admit *Īśvara* as the Creator and Ruler of the universe. Though the Jainas accept *jīva,* they do not believe in the existence of God other than Arhan as an omniscient person. Coming to the Vedic schools, Sāṅkhyas admit only tow entities—*puruṣa* and *prakṛti.* Though the Yoga school believes in *Īśvara,* He is regarded only as *puruṣa-viśeṣa* and *nimitta-kāraṇa* of the universe. The schools of Nirīśvara-mīmāṁsā, Vaiśeṣika, and Nyāya admit *jīva,* universe and *Īśvara,* but *Īśvara* is not accorded an important place. The Pāśupata accepts Śiva, a Vedic deity, as *Īśvara,* but He is the *nimitta-kāraṇa* of the universe.

Taking the Vedānta schools, though Advaita accepts all the three *tattvas,* Brahman alone is admitted as absolutely real, whereas *jīvas* and the universe are illusory in character. The Bhedābheda schools admit all the three *tattvas* but they do not provide a satisfactory relationship between Brahman and *jīva* as well as Brahman and universe. The later Vedānta schools suffer from the same defect. The schools of Śivādvaita admit Śiva as the Supreme Deity instead of Brahman on the authority of the Śaivāgamas.

Further, the rival schools do not uphold a satisfactory theory of *upāya* and *puruṣārtha.* As stated by Vedānta Deśika in the chapter on *puruṣārtha,* all the schools which are opposed to the Vedic teachings (*Vedabāhyāḥ*) and also those which accept the Vedic authority but misinterpret the Upaniṣadic texts by adopting fallacious logical arguments (*kudṛṣṭayaḥ*), are of no value (*niṣphalāḥ*) because their teachings do not help to attain *mokṣa* which is the Supreme Goal. This view of Vedānta Deśika is well supported by the following statement of Manu:

yo vedabāhyāḥ smṛtayaḥ yāśca kāscana kudṛṣṭayaḥ;
sarvāste niṣphalāḥ pretya hi tāḥ smṛtaḥ.

The teachings of those schools which do not accept the authority of the Vedas and also of those schools which are developed as opposed to the accepted valid *pramāṇas* and also based on fallacious logical arguments, are of no value because they do not serve the purpose of achieving the Supreme Goal (*mokṣa*) by an individual.

This point is explained in the chapters dealing with *upāya* and *puruṣārtha.* As Vedānta is primarily a *mokṣa-śāstra* aimed to show a way to the liberation of the *jīvātman* from bondage, it is relevant to judge the value of other schools of thought in terms of their usefulness to attain *mokṣa.* Hence Vedānta Deśika justifiably affirms that Viśiṣṭādvaita Vedānta expounded by Rāmānuja on the authoritative sources viz., the Upaniṣads, the *Vedāntasūtra* and other allied texts such as Smṛtis with the support of logic, is a sound system of philosophy.

As already stated, the merit of this system is that it admits the three ontological entities—*cit, acit,* and *Īśvara* as mentioned in the Upaniṣads. On the basis of the *bheda-śrutis* or the Upaniṣadic texts which speak of difference between the three *tattvas*, these are regarded as different from each other by virtue of their intrinsic nature. Similarly on the authority of the *abheda-śrutis* or the Upaniṣadic texts speaking of non-difference between the three *tattvas*, these are taken as one in the sense that *Īśvara* as organically related to *cit* and *acit* is one *viśiṣṭa-tattva* in the primary sense (*mukhya-vṛtti*).

An objection may be raised against the above conclusion justifying the soundness of the Viśiṣṭādvaita system of philosophy on the basis of reconciling the *bheda* and *abheda śrutis* by conceiving the relation of *śarīra-ātma-bhāva* or the relation of body to the soul. How can the non-sentient *jagat* and sentiment *jīvas* be regarded as the *śarīra* or body of *Paramātman*? This is a major objection that is generally raised by the critics of Viśiṣṭādvaita and in particular by post-Rāmānuja theistic schools which do not accept the *śarīrātma-bhāva* between the three *tattvas*. Vedānta Deśika himself raises this question in chapter 2 on *cit-tattva*. Is it appropriate to conceive the *jīvātman* who is the owner of the physical body, as the *śarīra* or body of *Paramātman*? In reply, he explains, on the basis of the arguments advanced by Rāmānuja in the *Śrībhāṣya*, that the term *śarīra* is not to be taken in the ordinary sense as the physical body. The Naiyāyikas have defined body as that which is the seat or abode of activity, sense organs and experience in the form of pleasure and pain.[1] This definition of body is considered defective because it is too wide or too narrow. If the body is a seat of activity, even a pot becomes a *śarīra* in so far as it is locus of *ceṣṭā* or some activity. Again the body in the state of swoon does not have any activity but it still continues to be the body. The definition of the body as the abode of sense organs is too narrow as it excludes such material entities which are regarded in the *Antaryāmī Brāhmaṇa* as bodies but do not have sense organs. That body is the basis for the experience of pleasure and pain is faulty because such experience belongs to the soul or the empirical ego (*antaḥkaraṇa*) but not to the physical body. Further, the definition offered by the Naiyāyikas does not apply to the physical elements such as *pṛthivī*, *ap* and other entities described in the *Antaryāmī Brāhmaṇa* as *śarīra* of *Paramātman.* Rāmānuja therefore offers an appropriate definition of *śarīra* which would be applicable to all entities—both sentient and non-sentient. Thus it is defined: *yasya cetanasya yaddravyaṁ sarvātmanā svārthe niyantuṁ dhārayithuṁ ca śakyam tacchesataika-svarūpam ca tat-tasya śarīram.*[2] It means: "In respect of a sentient being, either *Paramātman* or *jīvātman*, whatever entity is wholly and always controlled and supported for its own purpose and which stands to the self in an entirely dependent relation, is called *śarīra.*" The significance of this definition[3] is that the *śarīrātma-bhāva* or the relation of body-soul holds good between two entities (*dravyas*) of which one should be a sentient being, either *jīvātman* or *Paramātman* and both of which should also be inseparably related as long as they endure (*apṛthak-siddhimat*). Taking the example of the physical body of an individual, it is inseparably related to the *jīva.* The body is sustained and controlled by *jīva.* The body exists for the purpose of *jīva.* Thus *jīva* is the *śarīrī* or the owner of the physical body. On the basis of this analogy, the relationship between *jīvātman* and *Paramātman* and so also other entities in the universe are regarded as *śarīra* of *Paramātman* in a metaphysical sense. That is, as that which is wholly and always controlled and sustained by a sentient being. If the term *śarīra* is not understood in the above sense, the twenty-two entities referred to in the *Antaryāmī Brāhmaṇa* of the *Bṛhadāraṇyaka Upaniṣad* as *śarīra* of *Paramātman* who is the universal soul (*śarīrī*) by virtue of His being the *Antaryāmin* or Inner Controller, would not be meaningful. The term *śarīra* used in the *Antaryāmī Brāhmaṇa* cannot be taken in a figurative sense as conceived by Śaṅkara and Madhva. It is employed in the *Bṛhadāraṇyaka Upaniṣad* and also in the *Subāla Upaniṣad* to imply the ontological relationship that exists between *Paramātman* and the universe including *jīvas.*

Brahman as the *śarīrī* signifies three important characteristics of the Ultimate Reality: (1) That it is the ground or source (*ādhāra*) of the entire universe; (2) that it is the controller (*niyantā*) of all; (3) that it is the Lord (*śeṣī*) of all. All these characteristics are well established in the Upaniṣads. Brahman as the primary cause of the universe establishes the fact that it is the ground or *ādhāra* of the inverse of *cit* and *acit.* Thus the *Chāndogya Upaniṣad* affirms that all beings have their root in the *sat* (Brahman) and that they are grounded in the *sat* (*sanmulāḥ saumya imāḥ sarvāḥ prajāḥ sadāyatanāḥ satpratiṣṭhāḥ*).[4] The *Antaryāmī Brāhmaṇa* declares that Brahman is the controller of the entire universe including the *jīvas.*[5] Brahman as the creator of the universe and the universe created by Him out of His *saṅkalpa* as a sport (*līlā*) reveals the fact that the universe including the *jīvas* are intended to subserve the purpose of the Supreme Lord similar to the pleasure-garden created by an individual for the benefit of its owner. Thus the definition of *śarīra* offered by Rāmānuja is well-supported by the Upaniṣadic teachings.

On the basis of the theory of *śarīrātma-bhāva* or the body-soul relation, the Viśiṣṭādvaita Vedānta maintains that the entire universe of *cit* and *acit* stands in a relation of a body to the soul. All sentient and non-sentient beings constitute the *śarīra* or body of Brahman in the technical sense, viz., the former are wholly dependent on the latter for their existence (*sattā*); they are completely controlled by Brahman and they subserve the purpose of the Supreme Being. Brahman is called the *Ātman* or *śarīrin* because it is the ground (*ādhāra*) for the universe, it is the controller (*niyantā*) of the universe and it uses it for its own purpose (*śeṣī*). The three concepts used to explain comprehensively the ontological relationship that exists between Brahman and the universe of *cit* and *acit* are: (1) *ādhāra-ādheya* (sustainer and sustained), (2) *niyantā-niyāmya* (controller and controlled), and (3) *śeṣī-śeṣa* (the self-subsistent and dependent). On the basis of this organic relationship that exists between *jīva* and Brahman, Vedānta Deśika defines *cit* or *jīvātman* as that which is necessarily *ādheya, vidheya,* and *śeṣa.*[6] These three characteristics constitute the very *svarūpa* of not only *cit* but also *acit.*

Another significant philosophical implication of this relation is that it satisfactorily reconciles the apparent conflict between the *bheda-śrutis* and the *abheda-śrutis.* That is, it accounts for *bheda* or difference that exists between the three ontological entities viz., Brahman, *cit* and *acit* by virtue of their intrinsic nature as taught in the Upaniṣads. It also explains *abheda* or non-difference between them in the sense of oneness or organic unity (*viśiṣṭa*) between Brahman as well as *cit* and *acit.* In other words, Brahman as organically related to *cit* and *acit* is one *viśiṣṭa-tattva.* If such an explanation is not admitted, then it would not be possible to reconcile both the *abheda* and *bheda* relation between Brahman and the other two ontological entities in the primary sense. Śaṅkara accords greater importance to the *abheda-śrutis* and regards the *bheda-śrutis* as less important. Madhva, on the contrary, accords greater importance to the *bheda-śrutis* and lesser importance to the *abheda-śrutis* which are taken in a figurative sense. This is not appropriate because all the Upaniṣadic texts have to be admitted as equally valid and authoritative. The stand taken by Rāmānuja therefore accords equal importance to both *abheda-* and *bheda-śrutis.* This stand taken by Rāmānuja has the support of the *Vedānta-sūtras* dealing with the nature of *jīva*'s relation to Brahman and also the relation between Brahman and the universe. Bādarāyaṇa employs the term *aṁśa* to explain the *jīva*'s relation to Brahman. The term *aṁśa* interpreted in the sense of an integral part of the whole or the essential attribute as inherently related to the substance, provides the satisfactory explanation for both difference and non-difference. Epistemologically a substance and attribute are different by virtue of their nature, like the red rose and its colour redness, but the substance as inherently or inseparably related to the attribute is one complex entity, similar to the rose as inseparably related to its redness. The colour does not subsist by itself except as inherent in the substance. In the same way the pure substance without its attributes, is inconceivable. As Vedānta Deśika points out, all entities in the universe, both material as well as spiritual such as *jīva* and *Paramātman*, are *viśiṣṭa* in character, that is, qualified with some attributes. A pure substance without any qualities is non-existent, like the sky-flower. The difference between substance and attribute is unquestionable, as explained in the first chapter of *Paramata-bhaṅga* and in detail in the *Tattva-muktā-kalāpa.*[7]

According to Rāmānuja, Brahman is organically related to *cit* and *acit* at all times, both during the state of dissolution and even after creation of the universe. During the state of dissolution it is associated with *cit* and *acit* in their subtle form (*sūkṣmāvasthā*) and in the state after creation, the same Brahman becomes associated with *cit* and *acit* in their gross or manifest state (*sthūlāvasthā*).

An objection may be raised whether such a *viśiṣṭa* entity can be regarded as the Ultimate Reality. The *Chāndogya Upaniṣad* states: "*sadeva idaṁ agra āsīt ekameva advitīyam.*" The same fact is also stated in the *Bṛhadāraṇyaka* and *Aitareya* Upaniṣads dealing with the causation of the universe.[8] If these texts are taken as they are, they emphasise that the Ultimate Reality is one only without a second. That is, the Ultimate Reality is one undifferentiated Being (*nirviśeṣa* entity) devoid of all attributes. This is the view maintained by Advaita Vedānta. Vedānta Deśika refutes this theory. Oneness of Reality in the sense of *svarūpaikya* or *tādātmya*, as Advaitin maintains is untenable. As explained in chap. 1, all entities, both material and spiritual such as Brahman and *jīvātman* is a quality one (*viśiṣṭa*). That is, that which is characterized by attributes. A pure being devoid of any quality is a metaphysical abstraction similar to the sky-flower and it is beyond logical and mental comprehension.

Further, as stated earlier, if the validity of both *bheda-śrutis* and *abheda-śrutis* is to be upheld in the primary sense (*mukhyārtha*), it is possible to do so only by admitting it in the sense of *viśiṣṭaikya*, that is, Brahman as organically or inseparably related to *cit* and *acit* is one. As stated by Vedānta Deśika, though there is absolute difference between *Īśvara* and the other two ontological entities and also between the individual souls and matter, the Ultimate Reality is considered as one because as an organic entity it is one (*prakāra-prakāriṇoḥ prakārāṇāṁ ca mitho atyanta bhede api viśiṣṭaikyādi-vivakṣaya ekatva vyapadeśaḥ*[9]). This is the only way of reconciling the apparent conflict between the *bheda-śrutis* and *abheda-śrutis*. This fact is well brought out in our analysis of the Bhedābheda schools of Vedānta as well as other post-Rāmānuja theistic schools and, in particular, Dvaita.

Vedānta Deśika is therefore fully justified in coming to the following conclusion after the critical review of all other schools of thought, viz., that Viśiṣṭādvaita Vedānta as expounded by Rāmānuja on the authority of the Upaniṣads, *Vedāntasūtra* and Smṛti texts supported with logic is the soundest system of philosophy. A *mumukṣu* or one who aspires for *mokṣa* should adopt the right way of spiritual life as established by the Sacred texts properly interpreted in accordance with sound logical arguments and also by making use of allied treatises such as Smṛti texts which elucidate the Vedic teachings. One should also be guided by the path shown by great sages and *ācāryas* such as Manu, Parāśara, Śuka, Śauṇaka, Nāthamuni, Yāmuna, and Śrī Rāmānuja. Those who attempt to establish philosophical truths only on the basis of *tarka* or logical arguments are bound to go wrong since *tarka* alone without the support of Scriptural texts cannot conclusively establish a theory since it is possible by the adoption of same logical arguments to disprove a theory. In the opinion of Vedānta Deśika, it is safer and appropriate to follow the way shown by the great sages for overcoming bondage and attaining the Supreme Spiritual Goal.

REFERENCES

1. See *Nyāyasūtra*, I.1.1: *Ce' ṣitendriyārthāśrayaḥ śarīram.*
2. See *RB*, II.1.9.
3. See *FVV*, pp. 50–51, for fuller details of significance.
4. *Ch. Up.*, VI.8.4.
5. See *Bṛ. Up.*, V.7.7.
6. See *supra*, chap. 1 on *Cit-tattva.*
7. See *TMK*, I.1–8. Also, *FVV*, chap. 1, pp. 26–31.
8. *Bṛ. Up.*, I.4.10: *Brahma vā idamagra āsīt. Ait. Up.*, I.1.1: *Ātmā vā idam ekameva agra āsīt, nanyat kiñcana miṣat.*
9. See *NS*, p.1.

Glossary

abhāva	non-existence; a logical category according to Nyāya-Vaiśeṣika.
abheda	non-difference; identity of *jīva* and Brahman according to Advaita.
abheda-śrutis	Scriptural texts speaking of non-difference between two ontological entities such as Brahman and *jīva*.
abhivyakti	manifestation of what is latent in a causal substance.
abhimāna	attachment.
acetana	that which is devoid of the capacity to know, such as *dharma-bhūta-jñāna, nitya-vibhūti*, as contrasted to *jīva*, according to Viśiṣṭādvaita.
acintya	indescribable or inconceivable.
acit	non-sentient matter, the primordial cosmic matter.
adharma	deeds prohibited by the sacred texts; evil; principle of rest according to Jainas.
adheya	that which is wholly and always supported and controlled by a Higher Being, as in the case of *jīva* and cosmic matter.
adhikāra	a chapter dealing with a specific subject.
adhikaraṇa	topical section comprising one or more *Vedāntasūtras*, dealing with a specific subject.
adhyavasāya	determination.
adravya	non-substance; an attribute which does not serve as substrate of another quality.
Āgamas	sacred texts.
āgantuka	accidental.

ahamartha	entity denoted by the notion of "I;" *jīvātman* according to Viśiṣṭādvaita.
ahaṅkāra	an evolute of *prakṛti*; the ego caused by delusion.
ahikuṇḍala	serpent and its coil.
ajaḍa	what is spiritual, such as God, *jīva*, etc.
ajñāna	ignorance or absence of knowledge; cosmic ignorance which causes world illusion, according to Advaita.
akarmavaśya	no subject to *karma*.
ākiñcanya	utter incapacity of a person to do an act enjoined in the scripture.
akṣara	*jīva*; also Brahman *prakṛti* associated with the aggregate of *jīvas* (*jīva samaṣṭi*).
anādi	having no beginning or origin.
ānanda-tāratamya	gradations in the experience of bliss of *Paramātman* by *muktas*.
aṇḍaja	other realms.
Anekāntavāda	the theory of the Jainas that all things in the universe are of indeterminable nature; the doctrines of relative pluralism.
antaḥ-karaṇa	internal sense-organ.
antarikṣa	sky.
Antaryāmin	Brahman as inner controller by being immanent in all *jīvas*.
aṇu	that which is monadic in nature.
anubhūti	knowledge or consciousness; the transcendental knowledge according to *SB*.
anumāna	inference as a means of knowledge.
anumantā	one who approves the action of another individual.
anupraveśa	entry of Brahman along with *jīvas* into the bodies.
anyonya-abhāva	mutual non-existence.
aparokṣa-jñāna	knowledge of immediate nature; direct intuition of Reality, according to Advaita
apasiddhānta	wrong theory.
apṛthak-siddha	that which is inseparably related.
apūrva	the potency generated by the performance of rituals according to Pūrvamīmāṁsā.

asatkāryavāda	the theory of causality which upholds that the effect does not exist in the cause, according to Nyāya-Vaiśeṣika.
āśrama	stages of life.
āstika	orthodox; one who accepts Vedas as authority.
atīndriya	that which is beyond the scope of sense-perception; super-sensuous.
aupādhika	what is caused by *upādhi* or limiting adjunct.
avasthā	an accident modification of a substance.
avasthiti	abiding of one thing in another.
avayava	parts of a whole.
avayavī	the whole consisting of parts; the aggregate of *avayavas* according to Nyāya-Vaiśeṣika.
avedya	that which is unknowable.
avidyā	ignorance; the cosmic principle which causes the appearance of Brahman as the universe according to Advaita.
avyakta	*prakṛti* in its unmanifest form.
avyākṛta	that which exists as unmanifest.
ayuta-siddha	invariable connection between two entities such as *guṇa* and *guṇī*.
baddha	the *jīva* associated with bondage.
bandha	bondage.
bhaṅga	refutation; critical review.
bhedābheda	The relation of difference and non-difference between two entities.
bheda-śrutis	Scriptural texts speaking of difference between two ontological entities such as *jīva* and Brahman.
bhogya	the object of experiences; *prakṛti* and its products according to Viśiṣṭādvaita.
bhoktā	the one who experiences pleasure and pain.
bhūta	physical element.
caitanya	consciousness.
cetana	the entity which is sentient in character such as *jīva*.

cit	sentient being; the individual self.
Darśana	school of thought; a well-developed system of philosophy.
dharma	righteousness; principle of action according to Jainas.
dharma-bhūta-jñāna	knowledge as the essential attribute of the self; attributive knowledge as distinct from *svarūpa-jñāna.*
dharmī	substance; the substrate in which *dharma* inheres according to Viśiṣṭādvaita.
dik	directions such as east, west, etc.
dravya	substance; that which serves as the substrate of qualities according to Viśiṣṭādvaita.
dvyaṇuka	combination of two primary atoms.
gandha	odour.
hita	the ways and means to be pursued to achieve the Spiritual goal.
Īśvara	The Supreme Being; Brahman; God of religion.
jaḍa	that which is material, such as *prakṛti*, pot, etc.; inert; inanimate object.
jāti	generic character; unique characteristic of an object, according to Viśiṣṭādvaita.
jīvanmukti	liberation of a *jīva* while embodied.
jñātṛtva	capacity to know; knowership.
jñānendriyas	cognitive sense organs.
jñeya	object of knowledge.
kaivalya	the state of existence of the individual self dissociated with its mind and functions, according to Sāṅkhyas; blissful state of existence of a *jīva* free from bondage.
kalpa	epoch.
kāma	sensual pleasures; desire.
kāraṇa-vākya	Scriptural statements dealing with causation of the universe.
karma	prescribed ritualistic deeds; action in the form of movement of an object according to Nyāya-Vaiśeṣika; results of past deeds.
karmendriyas	cognative sense-organs.

kartā	the agent of action; *jīva.*
kartṛtva	capacity to do an act.
kṣaṇa	the absolute instant, according to Buddhists; the conglomeration of various causal factors which are operative in producing an effect according to Viśiṣṭādvaita.
kṣaṇika	momentary.
mahat	the first evolute of *prakṛti.*
Maṇipravāḷa	Tamil language interspersed with Sanskrit words.
mata	a well-developed system of philosophy; religious sect.
māyā	cosmic principle which gives rise to the world illusion according to Advaita; the primordial cosmic matter; that which is an instrument of wonderful creation according to Viśiṣṭādvaita.
mithyā	illusory; that which is neither real nor unreal but different from both, according to Advaita.
mokṣa	liberation from bondage.
mukta	the *jīva* liberated from bondage.
muktātmā	the liberated *jīva.*
mukti	state of liberation of *jīva* from bondage.
mūlaprakṛti	primordial cosmic matter.
mumukṣu	one who is desirous of attaining *mokṣa.*
nairghaṇya	cruelty.
naraka	hell.
nāśa	destruction.
nāstika	heterodox; one does not accept Vedas as authority.
nimitta-kāraṇa	instrumental or efficient cause.
nirguṇa	devoid of attributes; undifferentiated; devoid of defilements (*heyaguṇa*) according to *RB.*
nirvikalpaka	indeterminate; devoid of all qualities.
nirvikāra	devoid of modification or any change.
nirviśeṣa	devoid of all differentiation.
nitya-mukta	*jīva* which is eternally free from bondage.

pañca-bhūtas	five gross elements.
pañcikaraṇa	admixture of five elements in certain proportion.
parāk	what manifests itself for others such as *dharma-bhūta-jñāna.*
paramākāśa	transcendental world.
paramāṇus	partless, imperceptible and infinitesimal reals, according to Nyāya-Vaiśeṣika; atoms; smallest particles according to Viśiṣṭādvaita.
paramapada	the Supreme Abode; the abode of Viṣṇu.
pāramārthika	real; transcendental real according to Advaita.
paratantra	dependent on something else for its existence.
pariccheda	limitation.
parimāṇa	dimension.
pariṇāma	modification; evolution of an entity into a different state.
paryāya	modifications; modes according to Jainas.
pradhvaṁsa-abhāva	posterior non-existence of an object.
prāgabhāva	prior non-existence of an object.
pralaya	dissolution of the universe.
pramāṇas	means of valid knowledge, such as perception, inference and verbal testimony.
prāṇa	vital breath.
prapañca	universe.
prapatti	the doctrine of self-surrender to God as a direct means to *mokṣa.*
praśāsitāra	One who commands all beings.
pratijñā	the statement to be proved; the declaration.
pratyak	what is self-revealed such as *jīva.*
pratyakṣa	perception as a means of knowledge.
pratyabhijñā	knowledge by the recognition of what is seen earlier.
pravṛtti	capacity to function.
pṛthaktva	separateness.
pudgala	the means given by the Jainas to the cosmic matter which undergoes modification.
puruṣārtha	the goal of human endeavour; the Supreme Spiritual goal such as *mokṣa.*

rajas	one of the three qualities of *prakṛti*, which stands for whatever is active.
śabda-brahma	Cosmic sound essence as Brahman conceived by the grammarians.
sādharmya	having common features.
saguṇa	that which is qualified with attributes.
sahopalambha	that which is cognized as together, invariable association.
śakti	potency; the power inherent in an entity according to Viśiṣṭādvaita.
samādhi	the state of trance; the final stage of eightfold yoga discipline.
samārādhana	worship of *Paramātman*.
samaṣṭi	aggregation or collection of several parts.
samaṣṭi-sṛṣṭi	creation of the aggregate universe.
samavāya	the relation of inherence.
saṁsarga	to become united with another entity.
saṁskāra	latent impressions of past experience.
samyāvasthā	state of equilibrium.
saṁyoga	relation of conjunction.
saṅghāta	aggregate.
saptabhaṅgi	sevenfold description of an object, according to Jainas.
śaraṇāgati	see *prapatti*.
śarīra	body; that which is wholly and always supported and controlled and which serves its purpose.
śarīrī	one who is the owner of the body; the Supreme Being who sustains and controls the universe including *jīvas*, according to Viśiṣṭādvaita.
sarvagata	omnipresent.
sarvajña	omniscient.
Śāstra	Sacred texts accepted as authoritative source in spiritual matters.
satkāryavāda	the theory of causality which upholds that effect is pre-existent in a potential form in the causal substances, according to

	Sāṅkhya; the theory that an affect is the modified state of the causal substance according to Viśiṣṭādvaita.
sattā	existence of an object.
sat-tarka	sound rational arguments.
sattva	one of the three qualities (*guṇas*) of *prakṛti*, which stands for whatever is fine and light.
satyasaṅkalpa	one whose will is not obstructed.
savikalpaka	determinate; differentiated.
śeṣa	that which exists for the purpose of the Supreme Being.
sphoṭa	essence of sound which produces knowledge of things; it also denotes the *śabda-brahma* as conceived by the grammarians as the ultimate Reality.
sthāvara	inanimate object.
sthiti	continuation of an object produced.
sthūla	gross.
śuddha-sattva	spiritual substance; transcendental realm according to Viśiṣṭādvaita.
sūkṣma	subtle.
śūnyavāda	the theory of Mādhyamika Buddhism that everything in the universe is void and non-existent; nihilism.
suṣupti	the state of dreamless sleep.
svabhāva	the nature of an object; the characteristics of an object, according to *RB.*
svābhāvika	that which is natural.
svalakṣaṇa	bare unrelated particular presented in the initial stage of perception, according to Buddhism.
svatantra	independent.
tamas	*prakṛti* in its subtle form combined with *jīvas* in their subtle form, according to Viśiṣṭādvaita; one of the three qualities of *prakṛti*, which causes ignorance.
tanmātras	the subtle elements.
tarka	logical arguments.
tattva	metaphysical categories.

tattva-jñāna	spiritual knowledge of metaphysical Reality.
tejas	fire.
trivitkaraṇa	admixture of three elements.
tryaṇuka	combination of three atoms.
tuccha	non-existent.
upādāna-kāraṇa	material cause.
upādhi	limiting adjunct.
upāya	the means or the spiritual discipline adopted to attain a higher goal.
utkrānti	exit of the *jīva* from the body after death.
utpatti	production.
vaidharmya	having distinctive features.
vaiṣamya	partiality.
vaiṣamyāvasthā	state of disturbance.
vibhu	all-pervasive.
vidheya	That which is wholly and always controlled by a Higher Being, such as *jīva.*
vidhi	injunction.
vidyāsthāna	branches of learning which serve as supplemental treatises for acquiring knowledge, such as the six Vedāṅgas—Kalpa, Śikṣā, Vyākaraṇa, Jyotiṣa, Nirukta, and Chandas.
vijñāna	knowledge; series of mental ideas according to Buddhism.
vikṛti	the evolutes which evolve from *prakṛti* and which also serve as the cause of other evolutes.
vināśa	destruction.
viśeṣa	individuality as a special quality that subsists in eternal objects according to Vaiśeṣikas.
viśeṣaṇa	quality; attribute.
viśeṣya	substance or substrate in which quality inheres.
viśiṣṭa	that which is qualified with attribute; a characterized entity.
viśiṣṭaikya	oneness or organic unity of a substance as inseparably related to its attributes.
vivarta	illusory appearance of an entity as different from what it actually is.

vyāpti	pervasion; invariable concomitance between two objects.
vyaṣṭi-sṛṣṭi	creation of the variegated universe.
vyāvahārika	empirical; that which is accepted as real for practical purposes.
yadṛcchā	chance.

Bibliography

Primary Sources

Paramata-bhaṅga of Vedānta Deśika with the commentary *Desikāśaya Prakāśa,* in Sanskrit by Villivalam Vatsya Narayanacharya, 2 vols., Madras, 1979 and 1982; with the commentary *Anapāya-prabhā,* in Tamil by Uttamur Veeraraghavacharya, Madras, 1978; with the commentary *Maṇipravāla* by Ayya Krishna Tatarya, vol. 1, ed. Srimad Anandavan Asramam, Srirangam, 2005.

Śrībhāṣya of Rāmānuja with *Śrutaprakāśikā* commentary of Sudarśana Sūri, ed. Uttamur Veeraraghavacharya, 2 vols. Madras, 1967.

Adhikaraṇa-sārāvalī of Vedānta Deśika with the commentaries of Kumara Varadacharya and Srivan Satakopa Ramanuja Yati, ed. Ahobala Mutt, Madras, 1940.

Mīmāṁsā-pādukā of Vedānta Deśika, ed. P.B. Annangaracharya, Conjeevaram, 1940.

Nyāya-siddhāñjana of Vedānta Deśika with commentaries of Rangaramanuja and Kanchi Krishna Tatarya, ed. Uttamur Veeraraghavacharya, Madras, 1976.

Nyāya-pariśuddhi of Vedānta Deśika, ed. P.B. Annangaracharya, Conjeevaram, 1940.

Śatadūṣaṇī of Vedānta Deśika, ed. Srivatsankacharya, Madras, 1973.

Ṣaḍdarśana Samuccaya of Haribhadra with the commentary of Maṇibhadra, Chaukhamba Sanskrit Series, Banaras, 1905.

Sāṅkhyakārikā of Īśvarakṛṣṇa.

Sāṅkhyatattvakaumudī of Vācaspati Miśra.

Sarvadarśanasaṅgraha of Mādhavācārya, ed. Vasudeva Shastri Abhyankar, Poona, Bhandarkar Oriental Research Institute, 1924.

Śeśvara Mīmāṁsā of Vedānta Deśika, ed. P.B. Annangaracharya, Conjeevaram, 1940.

Tattva-mūktākalāpa with *Sarvārtha-siddhi* commentary of Vedānta Deśika, ed. Uttamur Veeraraghavacharya.

Vedārthasaṅgraha of Rāmānuja with *Tātparya-dīpikā* commentary of Sudarśana Sūri, ed. T.T. Devasthanam, Tirupati, 1954.

SECONDARY SOURCES

Chari, P.N. Srinivas, *The Philosophy of Viśiṣṭādvaita,* Madras: Adyar Library and Research Centre, 1978.

—, *The Philosophy of Bhedābheda,* repr., Madras: Adyar Library Research Centre, 1972.

Chari, S.M. Srinivasa, *Advaita and Viśiṣṭādvaita*—A Study Based on Vedānta Deśika's *Śatadūṣaṇī,* Delhi: Motilal Banarsidass, 1976.

—, *Fundamentals of Viśiṣṭādvaita*—A Study Based on Vedānta Deśika's *Tattva-muktākalāpa,* Delhi: Motilal Banarsidass, 1998.

Chattopadhyaya, Deviprasad, *Carvaka/ Lokayata: An Anthology of Source Materials,* New Delhi: Munshiram Manoharlal Publishers, 1994.

Cowell, E.B., trans., *Udayana's Kusumāñjali.*

— and A.E.Gough, trans., *Sarvadarśanasaṅgraha* of Mādhavācārya, repr., Delhi: Motilal Banarsidass, 2000.

Dasa, Satyanarayana, "Caitanya and Bengal School of Vaiṣṇavism," in *Theistic Vedanta,* New Delhi: Centre for Studies in Indian Civilization, 2003.

Dasgupta, S.N., *A History of Indian Philosophy,* 5 vols., Delhi: Motilal Banarsidass, 1975.

Deva, Ramesh M., "Navya-Viśiṣṭādvaita," in *Theistic Vedanta,* New Delhi: Centre for Studies in Indian Civilization, 2003.

Ghate, V.S., *The Vedānta—A Study of Brahmasūtras with the Bhāṣya of Śaṁkara, Rāmānuja, Nimbārka, Madhva, and Vallabha,* third edn., Poona, 1981.

Hiriyanna, M., *Outlines of Indian Philosophy,* repr., Delhi: Motilal Banarsidass.

Jaini, J., *Outlines of Jainism*, Cambridge University Press.
Keith, A.B., *Buddhistic Philosophy*, Cambridge University Press.
—, *Indian Logic and Atomism.*
Mahadevappa, N.G., "Vīra Śaivism," in *Theistic Vedanta*, New Delhi: Centre for Studies in Indian Civilization, 2003.
Mishra, Kamalakar, "Kashmir Śaiva Advaitism," in *Theistic Vedanta*, New Delhi: Centre for Studies in Indian Civilization, 2003.
Murty, Sat Chidananda, trans., *Ṣaḍdarśana Samuccaya* (with notes), Delhi: 1986.
Radhakrishnan, S., *Indian Philosophy*, 2 vols.
Sharma, B.N.K., *Philosophy of Madhvāchārya*, repr., Delhi: Motilal Banarsidass, 1991.
Shastri, Sunanda Y., "Philosophy of Vallabhācārya," in *Theistic Vedanta*, New Delhi: Centre for Studies in Indian Civilization, 2003.
Shastri, Yajneshwar S., "Svābhāvika-Bhedābheda of Nimbārka," in *Theistic Vedanta*, New Delhi: Centre for Studies in Indian Civilization, 2003.
Sinha, Jadunath, *Indian Philosophy*, 3 vols., Delhi: Motilal Banarsidass.
Sinha, Nandalal, *The Sāṁkhya Philosophy containing Sāṁkhya Pravacana Sūtra*, New Delhi: Munshiram Manoharlal Publishers, 2003.
Vidyabhusana, S.C., trans., *The Nyaya-sutra of Gotama*, New Delhi: Munshiram Manoharlal Publishers, 2003.

Index